Praise for

Peace Meals

"With careful observation, [Badkhen] sees beyond the heartbreaking stories of the families and soldiers, refugees and warlords, she meets. Her eloquent, honest words tell an in-depth history of recent war, and also make known courageous and resourceful people whose actions, or lack thereof, are forced by circumstance."

—*Christian Science Monitor*

"Illuminates the strange, dark history of the past couple of decades—the wars in Afghanistan and Iraq, and drought-stricken East Africa. Most chapters chronicle her connections with particular individuals . . . each character providing insight into local customs and quirks, but more significantly, illustrates and humanizes regional complexities. Badkhen regularly encounters real danger, but meets it with compassion and graveyard humor . . . the resulting range of events both large and small is both honest and real."

—*Publishers Weekly*

"The philosophical connection is interesting . . . absorbing observations . . . An intriguing premise."

—*Kirkus Reviews*

"Anna is that rare war correspondent with natural writing gifts, an empathetic heart, and a sharp eye for the telling detail . . . Her prose nestles inside your head—in near cinematic overtones, and not always comfortably. Your sensibilities, prejudices, and prior opinions are reshuffled."

—Bill Katovsky, author of
Embedded: The Media at War in Iraq

"Badkhen is the ideal hostess: offering rich, stimulating fare, and leaving her guests wanting more. The weave of food and political realism is constantly thought-provoking, and Badkhen's point that even in the worst of conditions a meal unites us comes across tenderly and convincingly."

—Richard Wrangham, author of
Catching Fire: How Cooking Made Us Human, and
professor of biological anthropology at Harvard

"Readers can't help but pull away feeling that they too have driven along Rweished-Baghdad highway, or grabbed a roadside syrupy jelebi in a Pashtun village with strangers who have instantly won their trust . . . Out of all the eclectic flavours of the nations and cultures [Badkhen] has graced throughout her career, *Peace Meals'* most enduring aftertaste is of humanity and dignity in the most inhumane times. That, in the end, leaves readers with plenty food for thought."

—*Jordan Times*

"[A] gritty memoir of Afghanistan and Iraq that focuses not on frontline reportage but on behind-the-scenes kindnesses of local families, many of whom shared their hearths, and their bread, with the foreign journalist. In *Peace Meals* [Badkhen] uses those simple meals as a window, a graceful way to bear witness to the devastation she was covering. But don't think that her book is about food. It's about humanity."

—*Entertainment Weekly*

PEACE MEALS

*Candy-Wrapped Kalashnikovs
and Other War Stories*

Anna Badkhen

FREE PRESS
New York London Toronto Sydney New Delhi

Free Press
A Division of Simon & Schuster, Inc.
1230 Avenue of the Americas
New York, NY 10020

First Free Press trade paperback edition October 2011

FREE PRESS and colophon are trademarks of Simon & Schuster, Inc.

For information about special discounts for bulk purchases, please contact
Simon & Schuster Special Sales at 1-866-506-1949 or
business@simonandschuster.com.

The Simon & Schuster Speakers Bureau can bring authors to your
live event. For more information or to book an event, contact the
Simon & Schuster Speakers Bureau at 1-866-248-3049 or
visit our website at www.simonspeakers.com.

Manufactured in the United States of America

1   3   5   7   9   10   8   6   4   2

Library of Congress Cataloging-in-Publication Data

ISBN 978-1-4391-6648-2
ISBN 978-1-4391-6650-5 (pbk)
ISBN 978-1-4391-6663-5 (ebook)

Permissions

Grateful acknowledgement is made to the following for permission
to reprint previously published material:

Random House: Excerpt from *Broccoli and Other Tales of Food and Love* by Lara
Vapnyar, copyright © 2008 by Lara Vapnyar. Reprinted by permission. *Page 133–4.*
Alfred A. Knopf: Excerpt from *Imperium* by Ryszard Kapuściński, copyright © 1994
by Klara Glowczewska. Reprinted by permission. *Page 261.*
Koninklijke Brill NV: Excerpt from *Annals of the Caliph's Kitchens*
by Ibn Sayyar al Warraq, copyright © 2007 by Koninklijke Brill NV.
Reprinted by permission. *Page 245.*
Meir Shalev: Excerpt from *Four Meals* by Meir Shalev, copyright © 1994
by Meir Shalev. Reprinted by permission. *Page xi.*

Photographs:
Courtesy of David Filipov: *Page 79.*
Courtesy of Thorne Anderson: *Page 230.*
Courtesy of Mimi Chakarova: *Page 261.*
Courtesy of Kabir Dhanji: *Page 263.*

To my family, for tolerating my wanderings and my cooking

Contents

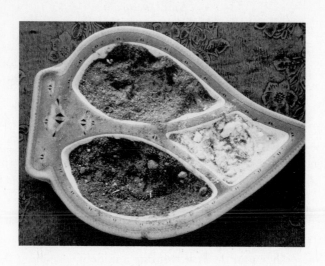

Introduction

All the gifts are nothing. Money gets used up.
Clothes you rip up. Toys get broken up. But a good meal,
that stays in your memory. From there it doesn't get lost
like other gifts. The body it leaves fast, but the
memory slow.

—Meir Shalev, *Four Meals*

A boy spots a piece of shrapnel shaped like a dinosaur tooth on top of a tank berm. He kicks it off the stone wall of the battlement with the tip of his toe, and listens intently and with satisfaction to the sound of metal scraping against rock as the cast-iron nugget falls into the frontline valley of emerald wheat.

A guerrilla fighter hoists his rifle onto his shoulder, shuts his eyes, and sways to a popular tune that crackles through the static on a friend's transistor radio.

A girl in a hand-me-down dress several sizes too large picks a flower from the spray of scarlet wild poppies stretching skyward on unsteady stems from a crater hollowed out by an air-to-surface missile. She adds the blossom to her braid.

A woman carefully selects the ripest vegetables and the freshest meat for an elaborate meal. A firefight rages outside, and the woman's family will generously share their dinner with me, an outsider, in the relative safety of their home.

These straightforward acts of humanity in lands of terror, conflict, and seemingly intractable grief reveal the most important lesson I have learned as a war correspondent: there is more to war than the macabre—the white-orange muzzle flashes during a midnight ambush; the men high on adrenaline scanning the desert through the scopes of their machine guns as their forefingers caress the triggers; the scythes of razor-sharp shrapnel whirling through the air like lawn-mower blades spun loose; the tortured and the dead. There are also the myriad brazen, congenial, persistent ways in which life in the most forlorn and violent places on earth shamelessly reasserts itself.

Of those, sharing a meal is one of the most elemental.

This book is more than a collection of memories about war and food: it is a dinner party, to which I am inviting you, a stranger, just as I myself have been invited to so many meals. Like any dinner party, it is an amalgam of recipes, relationships, and shared stories. Friends come into your house, pour the drinks, put food on their plates, sit. One tells a funny joke, and everybody laughs. Another tells about a recent loss, and everyone falls silent for a few beats. Suddenly, a guest picks up a guitar and starts strumming. For a moment at least, the room lightens up. The conversation resumes its flow, from frivolous to tragic to exhilarating. When friends sit down for an intimate meal, you cannot expect to never feel elated or sad.

What you do expect, with any luck, is good food, and good company—and this book has plenty of each. How much you get out of those depends on you. Given that we are both here, sitting down, I like our chances.

PEACE MEALS

One

Dolma with Ahmad

The wife and daughters of Ahmad Shawkat squatted around a large aluminum basin that wobbled atop the uneven concrete tiles of a sun-drenched courtyard in northern Iraq. The black, embroidered *abaya** gown cascaded off the older woman's shoulders, glistening like a sheet of oil. Grape leaves, peeled onions, seeded zucchini, peppers, and eggplants soaked in a pot of water nearby, next to a blue plastic bowl filled with a mixture of minced lamb, rice, and spices. With their heads bowed low to shield their eyes from the white Arabian sun, the women stuffed the

---

*Abaya—a loose, long coat some Muslim women wear. It covers the whole body except for hands, neck, and head. An *abaya* is often black, and is usually worn with a head scarf that covers the hair, *hijab,* or most of the face, *niqab*.

vegetables with deft movements and tucked these little bits of dolma into the basin, row after neat row, like a mosaic of food. Mostly, they worked in silence. The only noise came from the blinding sky, where American bombers thundered invisibly high, circling over their targets. It was late March 2003. The war to depose Saddam Hussein was in its second week.

Occasionally, Roa'a, at age twenty the chief inheritor of her father's quick wit, would whisper something to her mother and sisters and the four would giggle softly at the joke. But the smile did not linger on the face of Ahmad's wife, Afrah. From time to time, she looked up from the food and squinted at the small, stooping frame of her husband. To make sure that her man was still there, near her.

"My queen," Ahmad called out to his wife, tenderly. As if his affectionate words could dismiss the constant fear with which Afrah had grown to live in their twenty-nine years together: that any day they may come for him, take him away, torture him, kill him. That he may not survive this war. That she may never see him again.

Ahmad Shawkat, a writer and a journalist, had spent so much time in prison, shuttling between solitary cells and torture chambers, that his oldest son, Sindbad, had trained himself to be a tailor so he could support his mother and seven siblings during his father's frequent arrests. The writer's run-ins with the Iraqi government had begun in the late 1960s, when the police in Mosul, Ahmad's ancient hometown, would detain him and forcibly cut his hair, which he had liked to wear long, like the Beatles. Then, in 1980, Iraq launched an eight-year war against Iran; the war would devastate both nations and leave more than a million people killed or maimed. Four years into the fighting, Ahmad criticized the military campaign in an article he somehow had managed to smuggle out of the country and publish in a Saudi Arabian magazine. The Mukhabarat, Iraq's security police, took him away for a four-month descent into the hell of Saddam's dungeons. Prison guards burned his back with hot irons. They taped electric wires to his genitals and flicked the switch: On. On. On again.

"This experience was very crude," Ahmad recalled in the careful, precise English that seemed too elegant to convey the torture. "They had an electric chair that was like a cage. It makes you smaller, like a little ball, and turns you into a bird. I fainted."

My friend's frail, middle-aged body was relaxed, his large brown eyes looked calmly at his guests. The women were preparing the dolma for our lunch, but I was no longer hungry. Ahmad must have noticed. Graciously, he waved away his memories.

"After that," he said, "prison was easy."

In the early 1990s, Ahmad was imprisoned twice for holding underground poetry readings that had a tendency to turn into political discussions as the night went on. In 1997, the Mukhabarat arrested him again, this time for sneaking thinly veiled criticism of the government into his second collection of short stories. The agents collected the entire thousand-copy-print run from the bazaar in Mosul, piled the books on the ground, and ordered Ahmad to torch them.

Imagine the memories that fire must have rekindled in the ancient Nineveh soil: on these very shores of the biblical Tigris River, in the seventh century before our era, the conquering armies of Babylonians, Medes, and Scythians burned down the vast library of the neo-Assyrian king Ashurbanipal—the first systematically arranged library in the ancient Middle East, a collection of tens of thousands of texts pressed into cuneiform tablets. Some of the clay tablets melted, some fell apart like frass, but many survived—and so today we can read the ancient Sumerian *Epic of Gilgamesh*, one of the earliest known written texts.

Paper, on the other hand, simply burns. In less than an hour, Ahmad's work of many years was gone. The pages and the cardboard bindings became a small mound of black powder, a blemish in the heart of Mosul's pearl-white marble walls; then the mound, too, crumbled, and the wind swept the ashes under vegetable stalls.

Then the Mukhabarat threw the writer into a rat-infested solitary cell for nine months.

"Even now, I cannot believe that he is out of prison," Afrah told me. She had finished stuffing the vegetables for dolma and was leaning against the wooden door frame of their rental house, listening to her husband's stories. I could not tell to which of Ahmad's six stints in prison she was referring.

———

Reporters go to war to tell stories about the human and humanitarian tragedies that otherwise would go largely unnoticed by the rest of the world: concealed by the governments that commit them, eclipsed by the battles that generate them, blurred into irrelevance by the simple fact of their remoteness, or their lack of cable-news appeal. Most of us tell stories about life in places that are inaccessible to our readers. Ahmad told stories about the war his own government secretly but deliberately perpetrated against his own people, and this made his job, and his life, appreciably more dangerous. But he recognized the risks. He was willing to take them. Leaving for war is easy when you have a purpose.

But comforting those who stay behind—that is hard. Our determination to bear witness to some of the world's most unspeakable cruelties, and to put them into words, will never negate our loved ones' worries.

I thought of Ahmad's difficult story, and of that afternoon we spent at his rental house in Irbil, the ancient capital of Kurdistan—the women cooking under the white spring sun; the high-pitched clatter of aluminum bowls in the kitchen; the glow of pride and love in Ahmad's eyes; the wrinkles of worry on Afrah's face—as I knelt, some years later, on a red wooden chair at the dining table in my parents' summerhouse in Russia. My mom and my sister, Sonya, were standing next to me. We were making dolma for dinner and catching up on the year we had spent apart: my son Fyodor's achievements in school, dad's work, Sonya's university, mom's students, my life in suburban Massachusetts, so far away from the imperial palaces of St. Petersburg, the city of my birth. Our fingers touched as we reached into a large bowl to scoop up some minced lamb and rice stuffing spiced with cumin, sumac, and cinnamon. Three fragrant stacks of pickled grape leaves oozed brine the color of fresh lime onto our cutting boards. I picked a leaf from the stack in front of me, spread it on my board, centered a pinch of stuffing near the base of the leaf, flapped the sides over the meat, rolled the leaf upward into a short, thick tube, placed it gently on the bottom of a giant enameled pot, and repeated the whole process all over again. My mother and sister did the same. I had taught them to make this Middle Eastern dish after I had met Ahmad, and our hands moved swiftly as we told jokes and asked questions, all the while scooping, folding, rolling into each leaf Sonya's quips, mom's stories, our love.

Then mom asked about my upcoming trip to Baghdad.

Over the years my mother has learned to hide her worries about my travels to war zones, at least during our phone conversations and email chats. But I am still afraid to look at her when we talk in person about the dangerous places I visit for my work, embarrassed and ashamed to see the worry that my trips cause her. Afraid to see that look on her face. Afrah's look.

Guilt. Is this what Ahmad felt when he looked at his wife the day she was preparing our lunch?

I told my mother about my travel plans—keeping my eyes low, avoiding her face—and recalled watching Ahmad's peace overtures to Afrah: the crow's-feet around his eyes brimming with warmth, his shoulders tilting toward her. I recalled the way she had responded, her eyes running up and down her husband's slight figure, probing, as though feeling to see that it was really him, not a figment of her imagination. And all the while, her fingers had been moving, kneading, scooping, rolling—the same way my mother's fingers did as her stomach grabbed at my response. Later, other diners would try to guess the undefined spice that lingered on the tongue like a farewell, but I would know it instantly from that lunch in Irbil: the warm tang of a woman's melancholy. I also remembered watching Afrah's fingers. It was the first time I had seen anyone make dolma.

Afrah had spent her lifetime afraid that Saddam's secret police would come for her husband and steal him away from her forever. Now the invading American troops were about to overthrow Saddam's regime, but Ahmad was in harm's way again: as a translator for my husband, *Boston Globe* reporter David Filipov; my colleague, Michael Goldfarb, a radio journalist for WBUR; and me, on assignment for the *San Francisco Chronicle,* he was making daily trips to the front lines, where the Kurdish antigovernment fighters calling themselves *peshmerga**, or "those facing death," and armed with handheld grenade launchers and assault rifles, were readying to fight—and be killed by—Iraqi army tanks and field guns.

David and I had crossed into northern Iraq from Iran on March 19, 2003, several hours before President George W. Bush ordered a missile strike at the Baghdad bunker where he believed Saddam Hussein was hiding. On our long drive from the border to Irbil, we passed throngs of families moving in the opposite direction: they were fleeing to the brilliant virescent cliffs of the Hasarost Mountains northeast of the city, where, they believed, they would be safer in case Iraqi soldiers encamped on the west bank of the Great Zab River were to launch a chemical strike against Irbil. Like millions of Americans, these people, too, believed that Saddam had in his possession—and was going to use—weapons of mass destruction. For most of the next three weeks, the war we observed was largely anticlimactic, evocative less of "Shock and Awe" than of World War I: sixty thousand Kurdish fighters in trenches burrowed in neglected fields of winter wheat faced off against one hundred and twenty thousand soldiers of the well-dug-in Iraqi infantry, and waited to be gassed.

Occasionally, the Iraqi forces lobbed mortars and rockets at the Kurds. The shells churned the spring soil, interrupting the serenades of finches that tried to woo their mates in the rolling hills furrowed with foxholes and sparkling blood red with wild poppies. The Kurds, a hardened bunch who sometimes brought their children to the front line, to teach them to like war the way the adults themselves liked it, worked in tandem with about two thousand American special forces and paratroopers—the extent of the allied presence in Northern Iraq at the time. The special forces used the incoming fire to spot Iraqi positions for the F/A-18 Hornets and B-52s, which then dropped bombs on or near Iraqi

---

*Peshmerga—a term ethnic Kurds use for Kurdish fighters (both men and women). When the United States invaded Iraq in 2003, *peshmerga* rebels in northern Iraq faced off against Iraqi forces.

encampments and mortar pits. The Kurdish guns, for now, were mostly silent.

For Ahmad, traveling with us to the northern front line of the war against Saddam Hussein was a way to watch his country's history unfold firsthand. For us, his company presented a chance to learn about Iraq. Crouching in trenches filled with trash, bullet casings, and human excrement; cowering in someone's yard when Iraqi shells bit into the packed earth outside and spewed jagged shards of shrapnel into the air; and shuddering on a potholed road in the back of the mud-spattered Japanese four-wheel drive we had hired, we listened to Ahmad's well-reasoned observations about war, culture, religion, and society, and admired his astounding composure under fire.

"You see," Ahmad told us in his deliberate, cultured accent the time we were racing across a tottering bridge that spanned the Great Zab River, "the Iraqi army is quite incompetent because they are mistreated."

The turbid water to our right spouted upward in opaque funnels where 122-millimeter shells from the Iraqi army's Soviet-made D30 howitzer slammed into the surface and detonated underwater with muffled explosions, missing our bridge by no more than twenty yards. Sami, our driver, frowned and floored it. David called out, from some misplaced reflex of self-preservation: "Watch out!" I swore, gripped the fake leather of the backseat, and held my breath, ready for our car to plummet into the river.

Ahmad, who was sitting in front, next to Sami, serenely crossed his legs at the knee, turned to face us, and went on to explain, in the voice of someone expostulating on the relative qualities of limited-edition cognacs, that Iraqi recruits were mostly rural teenagers who essentially had been press-ganged into the military, and who now were barely fed and were constantly hazed by their officers.

I recalled Ahmad's words a few days later in the frontline Kurdish village of Bashira when I interviewed four Iraqi infantry soldiers who had defected to the *peshmerga* positions the night before, when their fortifications had once again turned into purgatory. American attack helicopters had swept in quietly from downwind, under the cover of a moonless night, and poured lead into their trenches. The wounded screamed amid body parts and clumps of clay. Blood soaked their clothes: whether it was theirs or someone else's was impossible to tell. The soldiers described living in constant terror: of the American warplanes that rained death almost nightly upon their encampment; of their own officers, who treated them like cannon fodder; of the special execution squads of the Fedayeen Saddam* paramilitary force, which had set up checkpoints just outside the positions of each Iraqi military unit in order to shoot deserters trying to sneak away from the front.

"We had three pieces of bread every day and in the morning we also had soup," one of the soldiers described his frontline life. He wore no socks inside army boots so old the thick black leather had cracked and his bare feet were showing through; two of his comrades were wearing soft shoes with tassels. "For lunch there was sometimes rice and meat, but often there was no dinner.

"But it was the bombing," he continued, "that destroyed the morale in our ranks." He and his friends described the American air strikes as acts of some terrible, merciless god: "It was so bright that night became day." "It felt like we were in hell." Two of the soldiers were sixteen years old, the other two in their late teens.

In return for sharing his insights Ahmad asked me questions about life that no man in the Middle East had asked me before or since. Did I think couples should have sex before they get married to see if they are compatible in bed? If men are allowed to have more than one wife, should women be allowed to have more than one husband? Was the institution of marriage even important? What did I think about abortion?

These conversations always took place while I was preoccupied with some news story I was chasing, or was frenetically typing to file by deadline. Now, at Ahmad's house in Irbil, I had the time at last to listen to the writer and his family describe their life—a leisure newspaper reporters in war zones rarely afford themselves. Two hours after I had watched the

---

*Fedayeen Saddam—literally, "Saddam's Martyrs," during the rule of Saddam Hussein, a feared Iraqi paramilitary organization that numbered between eighteen and forty thousand men. The Fedayeen operated almost entirely outside the law, and included a special unit known as the Death Squadron, whose members (they usually wore black uniforms and ski masks) performed political executions of suspected dissidents and their family members, often in the homes of the victims.

Shawkat women roll the lamb and rice into thumb-size cylinders in the courtyard, Roa'a and Afrah served the food on a plastic tablecloth they had spread on the living room floor. Freshly cooked dolma towered in a giant basin over a sea of tomato sauce lava. We sat cross-legged on mattresses, our backs to the wall.

"Like Arabs," Ahmad, a Kurd, half-joked, apologetically, explaining that his furniture had stayed in his Mosul house.

It was a patronizing remark that Afrah, an Arab, pretended not to notice. Her life on the edge with Ahmad had been full of silent frictions and quick jabs.

Money was always a problem: because the Iraqi government, which controlled most of the country's economy, had essentially deemed Ahmad an enemy of the state, he had trouble getting work.

Religion was another point of contention. Ahmad, a trained scientist, was decidedly secular. ("I am without," was how he explained it to me. "I am without, too," I replied, and we laughed and shook hands: in a country where religion soon was to become a matter of life and death, meeting someone who did not abide by it merited an impromptu handshake.) But Afrah, who had been raised in a Shiite family, had grown more and more religious with each of Ahmad's arrests. Then Sindbad, whose sewing business consisted mainly of producing embroidered *abayas,* joined an Islamic society, and Roa'a, Ahmad's favorite daughter, one day began to wear long skirts in public, instead of jeans, and to cover her hair with a modest head scarf. Ahmad liked to say that he believed faith should be a personal choice. But he talked about his family's newfound and intensifying religious devotion in a manner that was at once somewhat condescending and a bit nervous. I could sense the tension in the household.

"We must fight in two directions: against Baghdad" (Saddam was still in power) "and against those people who are Islamist radicals," Ahmad said to me once, stopping short of directly criticizing his loved ones' beliefs.

Perhaps if Ahmad or Afrah had zoomed in on such disappointments, the memory of one slight would have pulled out the next, and the next— some petty, some not—and their entire marriage would have come unraveled like a ball of yarn. He had risked his life and their freedom too many times; she was too conservative. But for them, letting go of each other would have been equivalent to handing one to the regime: after all, the purpose of Saddam's dungeons was not so much to hurt the body of the victim as to crush the soul. Letting go of each other would have been surrender. It occurred to me that what had kept this couple together was what has kept together so many couples I had met in extremity—couples who were falling in love as firefights whipped their streets, getting married as warplanes decimated their cities, having babies despite the terrifying uncertainty with which conflicts and privation shrouded their future. What had kept them together was more than love: it was defiance.

After he was released from solitary confinement in 1998, Ahmad fled to the Kurdish-controlled northern Iraq. Iraqi Kurdistan was protected from Saddam's reach by a no-fly zone set up after the first Gulf War and monitored for breaches by the American and British air forces. By the time Ahmad arrived, the Kurdish region was essentially a quasi-autonomous state, with its own language, its own school and university system, and its own set of laws. Ahmad, a Mosul Kurd with an Arabic last name, aroused suspicion. In the city of Suleimaniyah, the heart of the Kurdish unfulfilled nationalist movement, local officials accused him of being a Mukhabarat spy. He spent two months in a Kurdish jail, until the International Committee of the Red Cross demanded his release.

In the meantime, the Mukhabarat in Mosul arrested his family and put everyone in jail—even the children. Afrah was nine months' pregnant with the couple's youngest daughter, Zaynab.

Over dolma, I listened to stories about Ahmad's arrests; about Sindbad the Tailor (Ahmad had named his firstborn after Mosul's famous seafaring son; that their professions ended up rhyming in English was, of course, a coincidence); about how Zaynab had been born in a Mosul jail while Ahmad was in Suleimaniyah; and about how, because of her birth, the Mukhabarat released Ahmad's family ten days after they had been arrested, and ordered them into exile in Kurdistan.

"Go look for your father," the secret police agents told Afrah and her children after they had loaded them into a military truck, driven them to the border with Kurdistan, and dumped them in a fallow wheat field, by the side of the road. Three months later, Ahmad found his wife and children at a hostel in Irbil.

The last article Ahmad had written while Saddam was still in power came out in July 2002. A Syrian newspaper published it. The headline left little about Ahmad's political beliefs to readers' imagination: he had titled the article "We Have to Get Rid of Saddam's Regime Before We Get Rid of His Weapons of Mass Destruction." Three days after it came out, Ahmad decided to travel to Jordan. For that he needed to leave Kurdistan and cross the swath of Iraq controlled by Saddam. It's hard to say what he was hoping for: A miracle? An adventure? The Mukhabarat was waiting for him. He was arrested and imprisoned for four months, until November, when Hussein amnestied all prisoners. Some thought the dictator did it in an effort to appease Western critics of his repressive regime, draining the potential American invasion of international support even further; others figured he was just trying to amass as many armed men as he could before the United States attacked.

Either way, that was the last of Ahmad's brushes with Saddam's law. Iraqi forces were retreating, and the Americans were pushing up from Kuwait. The steam from the dolma filled the room with a zesty aroma. For the first time since the war had begun, we relaxed.

The B-52 Stratofortress long-range bomber that circled the clear sky above the Shawkats' house in Irbil that sunny afternoon glided so high we could not see it, but during my time in Afghanistan in 2001 and 2002 I had learned to recognize the rumble of the subsonic plane, and anticipate what came next: a succession of explosions so powerful the tomato sauce rippled in the basin with the dolma. The Americans were dropping five-hundred-pound bombs on Mosul, fifty miles to the west, the way they had been doing almost every day since the war had begun. Each of these bombs, which are sometimes called "dumb bombs" because they are simply released from the airplane, without any modern computer technology to guide them, carries about two hundred pounds of explosives, has a blast radius of some forty feet, and, when it hits the ground, leaves a crater fifteen feet deep. Coalition forces targeted Mosul because it was believed that a senior cadre of Saddam's top security and intelligence personnel had sought refuge there. Ahmad's two married daughters, Rasaq and Sana, were living in Mosul. My friend did not know whether they were still alive. The phones in Rasaq's and Sana's houses, like the landlines of everybody else in Mosul, had stopped working when the war began. Cellular phones, which are harder to track and monitor than landline telephones, were banned in Saddam's Iraq. Afrah and Ahmad did not speak about their oldest daughters, but I knew that each bomb that fell on Mosul tore a fifteen-foot crater through their hearts.

Ahmad preferred to speak of the invasion as an opportunity, a door opening toward a different, better Iraq. But neither he nor his dissident friends were rushing to help the American and allied forces push that door open. One of these friends, a former Iraqi army colonel, recalled the last time he had seen images of Baghdad in flames and American tanks rolling up the Iraqi desert: twelve years earlier, when another American president, George H. W. Bush, had been fighting Saddam's troops and had encouraged the Iraqi opposition to seize the moment and rise up against the oppressive rule. The colonel had heeded the call then— but the American-led forces had suddenly declared a cease-fire, abruptly withdrawing their support for the popular uprising. The Iraqi government cracked down on the rebels, hard. Tens of thousands were killed. The colonel spent the next year in a solitary prison cell; the Mukhabarat forced his wife to divorce him, confiscated his house in Mosul, and, after he was released from prison, exiled him to Kurdistan.

"We have lost confidence in American help," the man told me, flicking through satellite television channels in Ahmad's living room. All channels showed the same picture. On the screen, like twelve years earlier, black smoke billowed once again from torched oil wells near the southern port city of Basra.

But every day, as the American air assault pushed the front line farther and farther north toward Baghdad, and al Jazeera and CNN reported from battlefields closer and closer to the capital, Ahmad became more inspired. On March 31, when we sat down for dolma at his house, Ahmad was talking about his plans for Iraq after the war.

When this war is over, Ahmad said, many scars would have to heal before his country became whole again. He saw a role for himself in post-Hussein Iraq: he would publish his opinions, helping steer his country toward a respectful, democratic society in which everyone had the right to speak his or her mind.

"I will be a point of light," he said, taking a line from Forty-one's inaugural address. We ate and listened to the bombing: each bite an explosion of spicy heat in our mouths. Plates rattled with every blast. Roa'a came in with coffee, steeping the room in the scent of cardamom.

Nine days later, American marines helped pull down the statue of Saddam Hussein in Baghdad's Firdos Square. In Irbil, hordes of young Kurdish men drove through city streets, firing celebratory rounds in the air and waving the bright yellow flags of the Kurdish Democratic Party (and also, rather incongruously, one flag depicting a bare-armed Sylvester Stallone as Rocky on a background of the Stars and Stripes). The Mukhabarat functionaries who had persecuted Ahmad lost their jobs; some of them were arrested, a few assassinated in a spate of reprisal killings, others went into hiding. Ahmad visited Mosul and learned that his older daughters, Rasaq and Sana, had survived the bombings. Across the country, other Iraqis were checking on their loved ones, too: relatives excavated acres of barren land to unearth the remains of some of the estimated three million people the Baath Party* had executed since it had come to power in 1968. For months, fields all over the country were filled with hundreds of wailing men, women, and children who mingled among skeletal remains, rusted crutches, and scraps of rotting clothing, searching for their parents, siblings, children, spouses. Hot desert wind blew tufts of human hair against their bare ankles.

---

* Baath Party—an Arab socialist party formed in Damascus, Syria, in the 1940s (the first official party congress took place in 1947). In Iraq, the Baath Party came to power through coups in 1963 and 1968. From 1968 it remained the ruling party until the American invasion in 2003, and played a role similar to the Communist Party in the Soviet Union. If you were Iraqi, and you wanted any sort of government job—even teaching math at a public school— you pretty much had to join the Baath Party, since otherwise you would have been suspected of being disloyal.

With freedom, almost immediately, came mayhem. In the north, foreshadowing the ethnic and sectarian violence that would debilitate Iraq for years, the country's ethnic Kurds began to redraw the map of Iraqi Kurdistan, with a vengeance. With the help of armed *peshmerga* fighters they started to expel Arabic families from towns and villages where Kurds had lived decades ago, before Hussein had forcibly replaced them with Arabs from the south of the country in his drive to ethnically cleanse northern Iraq. Hussein had called the campaign al Anfal, or "the Spoils," after a chapter in the Koran on the rules of military conduct that permit Muslim armies to destroy and take the wealth of "unbelievers." Al Anfal had claimed more than a hundred thousand lives in mass executions, nighttime arrests, and anonymous burials (many graves of the killed Kurds were marked in Arabic, as part of an effort to erase all traces of the Kurdish culture). Three million Kurds were evicted from their homes. The highlight of the campaign was the 1988 attack on the Kurdish town of Halabja. Iraqi bombers dropped mustard gas and nerve gas on the town, killing about five thousand people, mostly civilians, in two days.

"All these years we have been waiting," a *peshmerga* fighter named Jamal Star Ahmed, a tall man with a bushy black beard who kept a wide, flat knife tucked into his cummerbund and six hand grenades hung from his belt, had told me during one of my visits to his frontline trench a week and a half before the fall of Baghdad. "We hope to return to our home soon."

I had thought it to be an expression of longing. It turned out to have been a warning. Now the Kurds were claiming what they said had been taken away from them. The Arabs, who had no place else to go, were resisting. In Mosul, which is kerfed almost in half by the Tigris River, Arabs mounted red, white, and black Iraqi flags on street corners and rooftops on the west bank; on the east bank, Kurds flew their yellow colors from storefronts and Russian-made jeeps. Crossing the river became akin to crossing a border between two warring states.

Everywhere, looters ransacked museums and torched office buildings. Firefights raged in alleyways and on wide boulevards. The Mukhabarat jail, in which Ahmad had been tortured, was set ablaze. One day, dinars plastered the square in front of the Iraqi national bank like confetti. Men and boys were dashing about, zigzagging in traffic, raking up the banknotes and stuffing them into their shirts. Their sudden riches did not seem to make them happy. Their faces wore grimaces of anger.

"Freedom's untidy," Secretary of Defense Donald Rumsfeld famously said then, dismissing the street violence and looting that were erupting all over Iraq. Just a phase, he said. "Stuff happens."

Ahmad disagreed.

"Our real war is just starting," he warned, "and it may be more difficult than the military one."

Ahmad had dreamed of returning to Mosul as soon as it became free of Saddam's rule, but the city was too dangerous to move to with his family. He did rent an office in Mosul, and launched a weekly magazine he called *Bilattijah*, which, in Arabic, means "without direction." The name contained two references at once—to Ahmad's vision that with Saddam out of power, it was too early to tell which direction Iraq as a nation was going to take; and to the fact that, at last, no one was dictating to Ahmad what he could or could not write.

Neither lasted long. As summer turned to fall, clerics moved to fill the power vacuum in the country, inspiring calls for Iraq to become an Islamic state. Ahmad wrote editorials criticizing religious extremism, the lack of a U.S. plan for a post-Saddam Iraq, and the Baath Party supporters still clinging to power. He started receiving death threats.

"He had integrity," Roa'a later would tell Reporters Without Borders. "Of course, his freedom of thought did not please everyone."

The Shawkats, like many Middle Eastern families, stuffed everything: onions, zucchini, peppers. When I make dolma I skip most of the vegetables and wrap the rice and lamb mixture in grape leaves—in the States you can usually get them, canned, in the Greek section of a local supermarket. Stuffing dolma is a lengthy, repetitive process, a good time to socialize if someone is doing it with you, or to reminisce if you are doing it alone. The monotony of slicing, kneading, and wrapping is a healing process, a therapy, reliving the heartache of war-ravaged destinations and relieving it. In a quiet Massachusetts suburb, at a friend's apartment in New Jersey, or in my parents' kitchen in Russia, I can share these memories with my family and friends in a way that everyone can appreciate and enjoy: by cooking.

Here is a memory I save for last, after I have rolled up the final grape leaf and am moving about the kitchen pouring tomato sauce and water into the dolma pot. I turn my back to everyone else in the room, and this way the memory stays private and doesn't burden my mother and sister, who are preparing the dish with me. This way dolma—the perfect communal dish, my favorite party food, a meal I make in such quantities that there are always leftovers to pick at for at least a couple of days after the guests are gone—forever remains my personal tribute to Ahmad Shawkat.

Six months after our dolma lunch in Irbil, I got an email from Michael Goldfarb. Michael had spent much more time with Ahmad than I ever had, and the two men had become so close that in one interview Michael had described Ahmad as almost a brother; two years later, Michael's book, *Ahmad's War, Ahmad's Peace,* paid a warm tribute to this friendship. The email was brief. On October 28, 2003, Ahmad went up to the roof of his magazine office in Mosul to make a phone call from his satellite handset. Two men followed him there and shot him dead. He was fifty-two.

My sorrow, when it comes to Ahmad, is not that I could not be there when he died. I could not have saved him. He had spent his whole life putting his life on the line for the Iraq he believed in. In the real Iraq, that amounted to a death sentence. My regret about Ahmad is the same regret I feel about most of the people with whom I have become close in war zones: that our friendship was so brief.

Together, we had survived such terrible, turbulent times. One would think that when you live through the horrors of war with someone, you would at least remain good friends. As one American battalion commander in Iraq said to me once about the men alongside whom he had fought, "People who go through this, they're a small fraternity."

But I am a war correspondent. I come to report a story, and while I work, I entrust my life to complete strangers. For a spell, we become friends, we become family. We share the food we eat and, often, the floor we sleep on. We are ready to die for one another. But when the story is over, I move on to the next assignment, knowing that I may never see or hear from these people again. Many of my war zone friends carry on with their lives in places with no Internet, no reliable telephone network, and barely any electricity, and there is no way for us to communicate after I leave. Although they have played crucial roles in my life, I will never again play any role in theirs. And because they live amid the world's worst conflicts, often the worst happens.

Sometimes we manage to keep in touch sporadically. The American boys who for weeks in 2005 in Iraq shared with me their army-issue meals, their menthol cigarettes, their water, and their heartbreak in an armored humvee* with a faulty air conditioner—once, on my thirtieth birthday, it choked all of us with sour Freon fumes—write me occasionally. Shatha, who worked for me as a translator in Baghdad in the spring, summer, and fall of 2003, emails once every few weeks; her friend and another former interpreter of mine, Thanaa, writes a few times a year. I don't know what became of Wahid, who translated for me in Afghanistan in 2001 and 2002: when we knew each other, Afghanistan had no email, no cell phones, and no mail service. Najibullah, the exquisitely unhinged gunman who in 2001 fogged my van with heady hashish smoke in the forbidding gorges of the Hindu Kush—where are you now? Even if email had existed back then, it would not have helped us stay connected. You were illiterate.

Before he died, Ahmad and I did not keep in touch. Once, after

---

*Humvee—the preferred way of calling HMMWV: high mobility multipurpose wheeled vehicle, a military jeep. In the beginning of the war in Iraq, American troops rode around in canvas-topped humvees, often with the tops down. By 2005, most humvees in Iraq were armored. By 2008, even the armored kind were considered too vulnerable to use in the country.

Ahmad was killed, I got a note from Roa's, but when I responded, she never wrote back.

My sorrow, when it comes to Ahmad, is not that I could not be there when he died. It is that I did not have a chance to know him better when he was alive. What I do have left of our brief friendship is this recipe for dolma.

Dolma
Stuffed Grape Leaves
Serves about 8

*W*hen dolma is ready, the rice inside the grape leaves puffs up, making the leaves taut like the skin on a drum. Each bite reveals layers of taste: the velvety sourness of the tomato sauce on the outside of the leaves; the briny, rough shell of the leaves themselves; and then, inside, the garlicky, sweet, lingering heat of ground lamb, rice, and spices. Dolma may take up to 2 hours to simmer before it is done, but once prepared, it takes only a couple of minutes to heat up in the microwave. It is a perfect dish to bring to potlucks. (For vegetarian dolma, substitute 2 additional cups of rice and some extra fresh herbs for the lamb.)

For the dolma:
Long-grain rice, preferably basmati, about 2½ cups
    (the same volume as the lamb)
2 pounds minced lamb
2 cloves garlic, crushed
1 large onion, finely diced
1 bunch parsley or cilantro or both
Pinch each of salt, black pepper, ground cumin,
    ground allspice, ground cardamom, dried thyme,
    and ground coriander
1 tablespoon ground sumac (sumac is a crimson spice
    you can get in most Middle Eastern groceries.
    If you can't find it, use the juice of 1 lemon.)
Two 15.2-ounce jars grape leaves in brine
Oil, for the bottom of the cooking pot
One 28-ounce can peeled, diced tomatoes

For the sauce:
1½ cups plain kefir or nonfat yogurt
1 tablespoon olive oil
1 teaspoon salt
1 tablespoon minced fresh mint (or dill)

1. Rinse the rice and mix with the lamb, garlic, onion, herbs, and spices.

2. Drain the grape leaves. Take a leaf and spread it on your work surface so that the stem end is closest to you. Discard the stem. Place a small dollop (the size of a 5.56-caliber bullet from a Kalashnikov rifle, or approximately half a pinkie) of the rice mixture onto the leaf, near the stem end. Fold the sides of the leaf over the filling, then roll the leaf up, tucking the ends in fairly tightly but not too tightly, because the rice will expand during cooking.

3. Place the stuffed leaf, seam side down, on the lightly oiled bottom of a large pot. Repeat the process with the remaining leaves and filling, arranging the dolma snugly in the pot. Shape any leftover filling into small meatballs and place those on top of the dolma. Pour the diced tomatoes on top of the dolma and add 1 to 1½ cups water; most of the dolma should be submerged.

4. Cover and simmer over low or medium heat for about 1½ hours, or until the rice is completely done. (Sacrifice one to check.)

5. In the meantime, whisk together all the ingredients for the sauce. Serve the dolma hot, with the sauce on the side.

Two

Dreaming of Lettuce

My introduction to war went like this: at three o'clock one moonless autumn morning, I crossed the Pyandzh River into Afghanistan on a dirty, rusty platform that ferried people and things (and sometimes tanks) across the water with the help of a thunderously loud rope-tow contraption.

David and I were traveling together. We were loaded with sleeping bags, laptops, some clothes, a satellite phone, and a first-aid kit that included syringes and disinfected gauze. It was completely dark—either because Northern Alliance* fighters were trying to keep our crossing a secret from the Taliban or, most plausibly, because there was no electricity in that part of the country, ever. The rope tow, like many things that moved in Afghanistan, sputtered along on dirty, watered-down diesel.

Invisible gunmen ushered us up a steep bank and helped us drag our duffel bags into a tiny stone booth illuminated by a sole, hissing gas lamp. There, three bearded, armed men in flat *paqul* hats of boiled wool leafed roughly through our passports and scribbled something in Dari, the Persian dialect spoken in northern Afghanistan, next to the visa stamps. The visa stamps were messy and uneven, like imprints of something a middle school student had cut out of cork in art class. We had obtained the visas in Tajikistan's capital, Dushanbe. They were issued by the opposition, not the Taliban government, which at the time was still in power in most of the country. They were, therefore, valid only in the northeastern sliver of Afghanistan controlled by the Northern Alliance. Technically, we were in the country illegally.

Our combined knowledge of Afghanistan was limited to half-forgotten high school history lessons, scarce recent news reports, and whatever we had read in a borrowed *Lonely Planet Guide to Central Asia*.

The Afghanistan chapter in that 576-page book was nine pages long. Wars—first the revolution; then the decade-long insurgency against the Soviet Union, funded largely by the CIA (and facilitated significantly by Osama bin Laden); then internal fighting among local warlords, followed by the hostilities between the Taliban government and the anti-Soviet rebels who, now that there were no more Soviets to fight, opposed the strict Islamic regime—had rendered the country pretty much off-limits to casual travelers and researchers. The Taliban's general distrust of most foreign visitors, particularly Westerners, also didn't help. A significant chunk of the nine-page chapter in the guidebook was dedicated to travel warnings and information about political unrest and abundant land mines.

The "When to Go" box advised, bluntly: "Don't go."

---

*Northern Alliance—a loose coalition of ethnic militias, Communists, monarchists, and tribal fighters in northern Afghanistan against the Taliban government. By 2001, the Northern Alliance was comprised of about fifteen thousand badly trained regulars and an unknown number of guerrillas.

It was October 17, 2001, and I was a freelance reporter based in Moscow, Russia. After the September 11, 2001, attacks on the United States, President Bush demanded that the Taliban hand over the terrorist mastermind Osama bin Laden and other top leaders of his al Qaeda network, or else. The Taliban refused, and on October 7, 2001, the United States commenced the bombing of Afghanistan. On the ground, American military planners were relying on a motley coalition of about fifteen thousand ragtag fighters who traded precious stones and opium for rocket launchers, helicopters, tanks, and ammunition from Russia; mistrusted each other; and were united by a single common goal: to oust the Taliban. The *San Francisco Chronicle* asked me to cover the ground war. I went.

When David and I got off the ferry, we knew we were in the friendly, if uncouth, hands of the Northern Alliance—but we did not know how far their territory stretched to the south or west, or where, exactly, the front line lay. The front line tended to move every few months, and thus was not marked on any map—particularly not on the map I had purchased in a Moscow bookstore before the trip. This one had been drawn by some bygone topographers during the Soviet occupation a decade and a half earlier, and showed only a fraction of the country's towns, and none of its villages. (While maps produced in the United States tended to place North America smack in the middle of the world, Soviet maps tended to leave things out, and often distorted distances on purpose, lest the charts fall into enemy hands.)

In a mix of English, Russian, Dari, and sign language, the Afghan guerrilla border guards instructed us to climb into a Russian-made jeep and explained that it would take us to our hotel for two hundred dollars. Although we had no idea where exactly that hotel was, or how far, the price appeared a bit much. But the jeep was the only car around, so bargaining seemed inappropriate. Plus, we knew not a single word of Dari. We got into the backseat, behind the driver and a teenage boy weighed down with a Kalashnikov* rifle as big as the boy himself, and took off into the night.

---

*Kalashnikov—in this book, I refer to the developing world's weapon of choice as "Kalashnikov" instead of the more popular "AK-47" because at least some of the Soviet-designed assault rifles one encounters in places like Afghanistan are AK-74s. An AK-74 is an updated

We drove through the desert. There was no road. There was no suspension. There were also no rocks, no trees, no stars—absolutely no landmarks, as far as I could see, by which to tell direction in the black flatness. I whispered to David that I hoped we didn't drive into a minefield. David, who had been reporting from war zones for years, whispered back that he hoped we didn't drive into an ambush.

Just then, the driver slammed on the brakes, grabbed the Kalashnikov from the teenage gunman, jumped out of the car, and ran off, out of the small circle of light cast by the car's headlights, firing shots into the hostile, dark unknown.

I thought of the children. I guess that's what mothers do when they sense trouble. Fyodor, my four-year-old son, was staying with my parents in St. Petersburg, Russia. Alex, my five-year-old stepson, was in Massachusetts, with David's mother. Good, I thought: the children are safe. In the rank cabin of the jeep, abandoned by the driver who had our only gun, I squeezed David's hand, too afraid to hear whether the driver's shots were being returned.

As suddenly as he had left the car, the driver reappeared in the headlights, unscathed. No Taliban fighters surrounded him. Instead, in an outstretched hand, he was carrying a dead gray fox. He hurled the animal into the backseat, between us, climbed into the jeep, and, without a word, floored the accelerator.

For twenty minutes, we drove in absolute silence as the fox next to us grew cold. Then, the seemingly infinite desert in the headlights abruptly became a stucco wall: we had arrived at the guesthouse for foreign reporters run by the Northern Alliance, clearly in the middle of nowhere. (The town, Khojabahauddin, was not on any map we ever owned, Soviet or otherwise, and thus got routinely misspelled many creative ways in reporters' datelines; David once drew his own map, photographed it, and emailed the digital image to Boston so that his editors knew where

---

version of the weapon that replaces 7.62-millimeter bullets with smaller, 5.45-millimeter ones, and therefore can be fired more accurately. Like its predecessor, an AK-74 has only eight moving parts, which makes it easier to take apart, clean, and put back together than most LEGO toys. Since I am no weapons expert I cannot always tell them apart, especially when it is dark, or when someone is pointing one at me.

we were.) We grabbed our duffel bags, paid the hunter-driver and the underage gunman, and they drove off. And the fox?

"Tomorrow's dinner," David said, foreshadowing our protein-rich, vitamin-poor diet for the next few weeks.

I had been in a war zone for less than two hours, and already food had begun to shape the course of my war corresponding.

This bizarre episode, our welcome to Afghanistan, taught me three things about war.

One: that situations you think are dangerous often turn out to be trivial—like that time on the front line when three Northern Alliance commanders in plastic flip-flops instructed me to hide from Taliban bullets behind the crumbling clay wall of a dilapidated farmhouse, and then, half an hour later, invited me for a leisurely cup of very sweet tea and a cigarette in front of the very same wall (the Taliban, I gathered, were also on their lunchtime break).

Similarly, two: that whenever you think you are safe you are, in fact, in precipitous danger, like that time when the bodyguards I had hired to protect me from highway bandits tried to rob me at gunpoint one sunny December afternoon.

And three: war is for meat-eating men with guns. Get your lettuce someplace else.

Actually, number three isn't strictly true. Since that first trip to Afghanistan, I have eaten wonderful vegetables in conflict zones: Iraq's succulent scarlet tomatoes that taste like sunshine; Georgia's colorful *pkhali,* a fragrant paste made from vegetables ground with walnuts and garlic. In Indian Kashmir, garlicky dishes made with eggplant and potatoes drummed upon my tastebuds like tabla players at a wedding. Stuffy cafés in the crowded camps of the Gaza Strip served delectable *fattoush* salad and *baba ghanouj,* the creamy eggplant dip. Afghanistan, too, as it turned out after we had finally made it out of Khojabahauddin and got to our first real market town, had all sorts of vegetables.

I should reword number three as follows: in a war zone, no one can guarantee that your next meal will be something you want. No one can guarantee that your next meal will be there when you are hungry. No one can guarantee that you will live to have a next meal at all. So you eat what you find: salad, meat, yesterday's rice, stale bread. Having hungered, and eaten, in a dozen conflict zones, I now understand why that Afghan driver near the border was ready to forget all about his human cargo when his dinner so fortuitously happened to run across the road.

Food delivers nourishment, and it also delivers comfort. When David and I met, in Moscow, he often ate at the Starlite Diner, a stylized eatery a few blocks from the Kremlin screaming with brightly colored, kitschy Americana: its chocolate milk shakes and overpriced French fries reminded him of the food he used to eat with his dad, when they would step ashore after a day of sailing past the drumlins of Boston Harbor. In Somalia, Spanish, Canadian, and British medics working for Médecins Sans Frontières* hired a local chef who could make lasagna: their reward at the end of a long and heart-scraping day trying to save malnourished babies from dying of tuberculosis in an anarchic war zone. They would take their Italian meals at a long, communal table, with a tossed green salad on the side. Todd Wood, the commander of an American infantry battalion in Tikrit, Saddam Hussein's tribal hometown, dined almost exclusively on corn dogs, burgers, and Jell-O at his army base mess hall, hungry for something—anything—that reminded him of home.

Wherever I went, at the end of the day I often ate with the people I wrote about. Over these meals, I would talk to my hosts and fellow diners about their lives and tell them about mine. The food we shared helped me open the door into the lives of strangers, and our simple conversations that accompanied this most ordinary act of eating brought us closer together: friends despite cultural and linguistic barriers, hosts despite the lack of conditions for hospitality. People I would never forget despite the

---

*Médecins Sans Frontières—known in the United States as "Doctors Without Borders," a Paris-based international organization that provides health care and humanitarian aid in war-torn and particularly destitute parts of the world. Winner of the 1999 Nobel Peace Prize.

lack of any way to contact most of them ever again. People like Ahmad Shawkat.

Or like Mahbuhbullah, the farmer and businessman whose two-story house of clay, straw, and donkey dung in the small northern Afghan town of Dasht-e-Qal'eh for a while became my home.

Like many Afghan men, Mahbuhbullah had one name, two wives, and many lively children who had inherited their father's quick smile. He had a handful of shaggy chicken in different shades of brown, a couple of dairy cows, and the highest measure of wealth in the impoverished northern Afghanistan: his own hand-drawn well. Each morning before dawn one of Mahbuhbullah's preteen daughters would lower an empty bucket on a rope into that well, then crank the metal handle of a wooden spool until the bucket came back up brimming with cold water. With that water, Mahbuhbullah's wives nurtured his vegetable patch. As it turned out, the harvest of turnips and pumpkins that grew in that patch would be directly responsible for the *San Francisco Chronicle*'s war coverage in the first weeks of the U.S.-led campaign to remove the Taliban from power.

Each afternoon, Mahbuhbullah's sons would bring out an old daybed frame of dark wood polished by weather and rain, large as a stage, and set it next to the well. The farmer's friends would arrive and sit cross-legged on that bed, smoking cigarettes and listening to the war on BBC Persian, broadcasting on an old transistor radio. The actual fighting took place within earshot of Mahbuhbullah's compound: every few hours, a B-52 would dump the contents of its bomb bay above the frontline that snaked through abandoned fields of rice and winter wheat a few miles away. But I think my host and his friends preferred to hear about the war on the radio because that made the violence seem more distant.

Mahbuhbullah's life had not always been this languid and orderly. In the 1980s, during the Soviet occupation of Afghanistan, Mahbuhbullah had been a low-level army commander. He had served under the Communist regime of President Mohammad Najibullah.

Before the Kremlin had appointed him to rule the country, President

Najibullah had headed Afghanistan's KGB-style secret police, KhAD, notorious for torturing and killing suspected and real dissidents it detained. For that, he was not well liked. After the Soviet Union pulled out of Afghanistan in 1989, it was clear that Najibullah's unpopular rule would crumble and his officers would face retribution from the incensed citizens. But hard Afghan fighters make poor losers. In the honor code of many a tough Afghan warrior, being on the losing side is a sign of weakness, not befitting a man. So Mahbuhbullah switched sides and joined the antigovernment militia of General Abdul Rashid Dostum.*

Dostum himself was one of Afghanistan's most notorious turncoats. At one point, the general, too, had fought in President Najibullah's army. His enemies had been the U.S.-backed, anti-Soviet fighters, who called themselves mujahedin** or "holy warriors," and who had included among their ranks bin Laden—at the time, a young Saudi man with powerful connections.

When it became apparent that Najibullah's days in power were numbered, Dostum, an ethnic Uzbek, joined forces with Ahmad Shah Massoud***, a mujahedin warlord and an ethnic Tajik—and the future leader of the Northern Alliance. In 1992, with the help of foot soldiers like Mahbuhbullah, the mujahedin took control of Kabul.

After that, tribal and ethnic rivalries between different mujahedin factions disintegrated into four years of fratricidal fighting for control of the capital. Weakened by the battles that leveled entire sections of Kabul, the warlords were easily overrun by the better organized and ideologi-

---

*Abdul Rashid Dostum—an Afghan warlord, an ethnic Uzbek, famous for switching political alliances and for running a ruthless militia. Many human rights organizations believe that members of his militia, Junbish-e-Milli, have committed numerous war crimes.

**Mujahedin—a name for Afghan fighters who fought against the Soviet troops and Afghanistan's pro-Soviet government; later, the name for Afghan fighters who resisted the Taliban government.

***Ahmad Shah Massoud—an Afghan war legend. He was one of the leaders of the Afghan guerrillas (mujahedin) who fought against the Soviet Union and the Kremlin-appointed government in Kabul. Later, he became an anti-Taliban rebel leader. Massoud was killed on September 9, 2001, by two suicide bombers posing as journalists. In his iconic portrait, which in central and northern Afghanistan is everywhere, Massoud looks a lot like Bob Marley, except instead of a joint he carries a Kalashnikov.

cally driven Taliban gunmen, who in 1996 swept to power and installed a strict rule based on a very conservative interpretation of Sunni Islam. Seeing no honor or holiness in becoming dead, and continuing their tradition of wartime flexibility, mujahedin commanders—Dostum among them—fled the capital. They would from now on direct their fight against the Taliban.

(As for the deposed Najibullah, the Taliban tracked down the former president, who had been hiding at a United Nations compound, castrated him, dragged him behind a jeep, shot him, and then strung his dead body on a noose from a post in the center of the nation's capital. Perhaps those warlords who switched sides and fled the battlefield before their side lost were on to something, after all.)

Before all that grotesque violence took place, however, the serene Mahbuhbullah realized that military exploits were not for him. In 1992, he left Dostum's gang to pursue a slightly more lucrative avocation. By the time I met him, this burly man with a bushy beard and a bear hug had become a successful booze smuggler and tomb raider.

———

Mahbuhbullah made half his money running vodka from the post-Soviet Tajikistan into northern Afghanistan. His clients were a small group of unemployed former engineers and officers who had studied in Moscow and Volgograd during the Soviet occupation and had developed a fondness for the drink that was forbidden in their own Islamic state. I never found out who sold Mahbuhbullah the vodka, or what he paid for it—or, for that matter, how much he sold it for; he preferred to keep his business dealings private. Although his undertaking was clearly unsavory from the point of view of the Koran, Mahbuhbullah faithfully observed the five-times-a-day prayer, and fasting on Ramadan*—whether to atone for his sins, or out of habit.

His business had taught him a peculiar, albeit limited, Russian vocabulary, which he proudly tried out on me from time to time. A blissful

———

*Ramadan—the ninth month of the Islamic calendar. Muslims are expected to dedicate the holy month to fasting, spirituality, and good deeds.

smile would gleam on his friendly moon of a face that floated atop his heavy torso like an acaulescent flower as he hesitated over the diphthongs and said to me: *"Yob' tvoyu mat'."* I would smile back, unable to bring myself to tell my host that what he was saying meant not "welcome" but "fuck your mother."

The rest of Mahbuhbullah's income came from digging up and fencing 2,300-year-old artifacts from the abandoned ruins of Alexandria Oxiana, a town that Alexander the Great—*that* Alexander the Great, one of the many leaders who, over the centuries, had briefly and fatefully invaded this unruly land—had built, not far from where Mahbuhbullah now lived, for Roxanne, the emperor's Afghan trophy wife (literally: he married her after defeating her dad). Afghans had rechristened the town, poetically, Ai Khanum, or "Lady Moon."

Flamingos and garden gnomes being unavailable in northern Afghanistan at the time, Mahbuhbullah had arranged fragments of Corinthian columns in his compound as yard sculptures. A giant, marble lion's head served as a doorstop for his gate of sheet metal, which he had painted green to ward off evil spirits. Zamzama, Mahbuhbullah's boisterous five-year-old daughter who liked to ride around her dad's vegetable patch on my hip, wore around her neck a thread of ancient turquoise beads that once may have belonged to Roxanne herself.

In a way, our looter was saving the ancient treasures from certain destruction. War inspires art but cares little for it. Nomadic invaders had sacked and burned Ai Khanum—with its citadel, temples, palace, and gymnasium—in the second century before our era; more than twenty-one hundred years later, Afghanistan still showed little regard for historic artifacts. The Taliban government had pronounced all non-Islamic art to be idolatry, and had famously demolished, in the rusty mountain face of Bamyan, two of the world's tallest standing statues of Buddha. In Ai Khanum, shepherds let their herds scamper up and down what remained of the crumbling walls of the ancient city, partially excavated by European archaeologists in the 1960s. Anti-Taliban fighters used column remnants for target practice.

But Afghanistan's most lucrative export was opium, not artifacts. Mahbuhbullah's antique business was not exactly thriving. He needed other sources of income to feed his dairy cows, maintain his well, and tend his vegetable patch.

Then, on September 11, 2001, terrorists attacked the United States. Less than a month later, American long-range bombers began to rain "dumb bombs" upon Taliban positions near Mahbuhbullah's house, and foreign journalists loaded with American dollars poured into his part of Afghanistan. An adroit businessman, Mahbuhbullah was happy to supplement his income by renting out his guest room for forty bucks a night. The room typically slept four: David; Wahid the translator; the driver, Ghulam Sahib; and me.

Mahbuhbullah's large farmhouse was just two miles from Mount Qal'eh-Kata, an arid knoll on the front line where the Taliban and the Northern Alliance showered each other every day with 7.62-millimeter rounds fired from Soviet-made machine guns and sniper rifles. Whenever American bombers would pummel the Taliban positions on Qal'eh-Kata, Mahbuhbullah's house would shake. His younger children, Zamzama and two-year-old Zayeed, would scream in panic: their fear of jets had begun after a Taliban plane bombed their own town a year earlier, killing four hundred people. His older kids would root for the American planes the way, in peacetime, they would have rooted for their favorite soccer team. They would scuttle up the stucco walls of his compound and cheer, tracing the course of the planes with their fingers and chanting: *"Tayora, tayora!"*—"A plane, a plane!"

David and I became Mahbuhbullah's first customers. The setup was convenient for us, two reporters on assignment to write about the American-led war. From the flat roof of the house, we could see explosions rip through the cloudless western sky. We had the front-row view of the front line.

I was twenty-six. I had been born into the perfunctory managed economy of the Soviet Union, and became an adult in post–Soviet Russia, where obtaining fresh, quality food required bulling through a crowd of disgruntled, battle-hardened shoppers who would rather trample you than allow you into their midst. I started working as a reporter at the age of twenty, writing about crime and human rights for the *St. Peters-burg Times* of Russia, a biweekly newspaper in my hometown. Although the paper was published in English, in the mid-nineties it was the only local muckraker, respected and feared by the city's politicians and busi-nessmen. We worked for a pittance—in my salad days at the *Times,* my monthly paycheck peaked at six hundred dollars—and for glory. Secu-rity police had tapped my home phone. I worked insane hours to bring down the crooks, and celebrated each thinly veiled threat from govern-ment officials as though it were a badge of honor.

Fyodor was born when I was twenty-one. Until 2000, I was raising him and supporting a talented but unemployed artist boyfriend. We lived on red beans, pickled herring, and homemade bread (the boyfriend supplemented his diet with abundant booze). I bulled my way through the hallways of the local police headquarters and legislators' offices, and I bulled my way through life with a baby on my hip and a cigarette in my teeth, like a modern-day Amazon.

By 2001, I had broken up with the boyfriend, and Fyodor and I were living in Moscow, alone. I was working at the *Moscow Times;* the Eng-lish-language daily paid me enough to go out for sushi from time to time. I met David, who was the *Boston Globe*'s correspondent in Russia, and we moved in together. I left the *Times* and started freelancing for American newspapers and magazines; David and I traveled together to the periph-ery of combat in the Caucasus, where the collapse of the Soviet Union a decade earlier still reverberated in separatist and ethnic conflicts. I sold a few stories to the *San Francisco Chronicle*. The paper's request, after Pres-ident Bush announced the beginning of his "war on terror," that I report for them from Afghanistan—and the dizzying offer of a retainer of fifty thousand dollars a year—was validation of that work.

The *Globe* was sending David, too. He boarded the ferry across the Pyandzh three weeks after the memorial service for his father, a passen-ger on American Airlines flight 11, the plane terrorists had steered into the north tower of the World Trade Center. A lot of reporters we would meet in Afghanistan would ask David whether reporting and writing about the war against the regime that had given shelter to the terror-ists who had killed his father made his work harder, or easier. To me, it looked as though David was taking solace in his work. In any case, being together at the time, even in a war zone, was some comfort.

Our children went to stay with their grandparents. In our rental apartment in Moscow, I packed my sleeping bag, laptop, malaria pills, some clothes, and a lot of notebooks. At a doctor's suggestion, a few syringes went into the duffel bags, too—I suppose, in my unending quest for self-sufficiency, I was going to learn to use them on the fly, if need be. I was ready to muscle my way through this new assignment the same stubborn way I had always muscled my way through everything else.

Then I got there.

None of my previous travels to the outskirts of conflict—a city of clammy tents on the border of Chechnya, a town Afghan refugees had built out of straw in a dried-up marsh in southern Tajikistan—had prepared me for the arbitrary horror of minefields, the lethal crop that generations of fighters had planted in Afghanistan's fields and orchards, replacing past harvests of rice, wheat, and almonds. Or for the heart-rending absurdity of the war that had forced almost all fighting-age men to face off against each other—father against son, brother against brother—on mountaintops that glittered underfoot with spent shell casings. Or for the abject poverty that had made bitter orach plants, cooked in water that had tested positive for typhoid, dysentery, and malaria, seem desirable.

In Azerbaijan, I had seen refugees sweep snakes and frogs out of their dugout shelters every morning. In Afghanistan, I saw a woman pick undigested maize kernels out of dry cow manure: she would boil them for lunch. Suddenly, I was riding a horse bareback across a muddy river to the front line (there was no bridge, and no saddle), charging my laptop by attaching it to a car battery with homemade crocodile clips (there was no electricity), and learning to tell the difference between the thuds and the cracks of incoming and outgoing artillery fire.

Afghanistan immediately became the country of superlatives. It had the tallest mountains I had ever seen: 15,000-foot peaks, stern and eternal, convulsed like the frowns of ancient gods, dropping into narrow, dim gorges that seemed to sponge up daylight. It had the finest dust I had ever seen, as well: it penetrated absolutely everything no matter how well

I wrapped it. Dust was taking over Afghanistan; it spilled onto roads, entombed vineyards and orchards, and destroyed machinery. The main reason for this desertification lay not in the droughts that wrack the region every few years but in the war that had been boiling here, with varying levels of intensity, forever. So many farmers were dead or fighting on the front line that Afghanistan no longer grew enough crops to keep its soil in place. What's more, left without access to oil or electricity, Afghans chopped down trees and vineyards—or, to be more accurate, they twisted them out of the ground in their entirety, roots and all—to use for cooking fuel, and to sell for firewood (the roots, which retained more moisture than any other part of the tree, were heavier and, therefore, sold for more). No longer restrained by roots and left without any organic matter, such as rotting leaves or straw or corn husks to nourish it, the clay soil turned to dust within months in the dry Afghan sun. Winds did the job of spreading it around. It clouded into the car through cracks in the glove compartment. It weighed down your eyelashes. Several news photographers I met in Afghanistan had their cameras destroyed by the dust within days. The screen of my laptop periodically broke out into bright pink lines.

The country was also home to the most exquisite lamb kebab: four thumbnail-size pieces of the freshest meat grilled over hot coals with three tiny nuggets of fat skewered between them, just big enough to make sure the lamb doesn't dry out (but more on the kebab in the next chapter). And when, sometime during that trip, I had OD'd on exquisite kebab, I had the best dream I have ever had.

The dream was about lettuce.

I know: lettuce doesn't sound like much. But when I had the dream about shoving handfuls of juicy, silky, crunchy iceberg lettuce in my mouth, I was sleeping, once again, on a floor made of a mixture of dirt and straw, in a room I shared with three men and a Kalashnikov assault rifle.

The floor was shaking, again, because B-52s were dropping, again, loads of thousand-pound bombs on distant Taliban positions. Around me lay the desiccated moonscape of northern Afghanistan: infinite plateaus of yellow, clumpy dust festooned with thousands of land mines, studded with burned-down villages and refugee camps fashioned from burlap sacks and sticks; mountains hollowed out with bomb craters and tunneled with dried-up irrigation ditches in which gunmen hiding from each other worried their prayer beads and clutched their machine guns.

I had been living on a diet of bread, lamb kebab, and malaria pills. The only thing that my teeth had crunched for two weeks had been the aforementioned dust. Barren Afghan soil seemed incapable of producing anything green. Lettuce was more than a coveted, unattainable luxury— it was a symbol of normalcy: of grabbing a BLT at the Starlite Diner on Mayakovsky Square in Moscow; of stuffing Caesar salad leftovers into my mouth as I zipped the kids into snow pants for a day of sledding; of shopping for groceries at an overpriced supermarket on Novy Arbat— all of the deliciously mundane activities I had left behind when I came to Afghanistan. This was my first time in a war zone; I may as well have traveled to Mars. Lettuce was a big deal.

Years later, when Fyodor would pick around the lettuce in his salad, secretly hoping to will it off his plate, I would glare and explain, for the thousandth time, the benefits of fiber. But to myself I would say: How wonderful that the boy is bored by lettuce. Let him dream of something more fun.

What happens when a search for stories coincides with a search for food? After weeks of driving, sometimes almost vertically, through minefields on perilous mountain roads, and nights of eating nothing but lamb kebab, Wahid, our tireless fixer (former wrestler, former refugee, former political prisoner, and now part translator, part personal assistant, part social anthropologist, who guided us through his country's ethnic maze and confusing allegiances), instructed our driver, Ghulam Sakhib, to turn into a winding, unpaved street (they were all unpaved) barely wide enough for our jeep. The street dead-ended at the gate of Mahbuh-bullah's walled compound.

And when, on my first night at Mahbuhbullah's house, one of his older sons spread a plastic *dastarkhan* tablecloth on the carpeted floor in front of me and placed, on top of it, two pewter plates, my world changed. Pale slices of raw rutabaga glittered in the flickering orange light of the hissing gas lamp, and next to them, cubes of stewed, cinnamon-specked pumpkin oozed cheap cooking oil like molten gold. I knew right away that these vegetables, more than the Taliban's unexpected retreat, more even than the imminent fall in Kabul of the regime that had harbored bin Laden, would dictate the course of my reporting trip from then on.

There I sat, in the dimly lit guest room of a tomb raider and vodka smuggler, sidetracked by a turnip.

In Mahbuhbullah's house made of clay, mud, and straw, I learned lesson four of war reporting. You get an assignment, and you prepare as well as you can. You pack body armor and mosquito repellent. You hide wads of cash in money belts and shoes. You buy phrase books and memorize the names and political alliances of local warlords.

None of it matters much when you arrive.

You are in a completely new world, and you control nothing. The generator breaks down because the gas you have been buying from children peddling it out of yellowed plastic jugs is diluted with too much water or mucked up with too much dust. The car can't make it over ridiculously narrow and icy mountain paths because the local warlord, whose political alliance or ethnic roots are utterly irrelevant at this point, had just bought the last set of tire chains in town. Your painstakingly memorized "Thank you for providing me with food and shelter" in the local language helps you make no inroads at a roadblock manned by a bunch of nervous, jumpy teenagers armed with rocket-propelled grenade launchers, who materialize in front of you, blocking the pair of parallel ruts in the dirt where just the day before there were no checkpoints. The malaria pills promise only a seventy percent chance of protection against the disease (and, indeed, on one of your trips the other thirty percent catches up to you and you pass out face-down after getting sick over the slippers of a very irritated rebel commander); you take them anyway, and they give you neon, LSD-tinged dreams. Your body is screaming for anything with vitamin C. So you compromise.

I had a choice. I could embark on a weeklong alpine expedition to the outskirts of the embattled Kabul. This option held the promise of trudging through the snowy, gray spine of the Hindu Kush on (or alongside) donkeys laden with our sleeping bags, somewhat effective malaria pills, syringes, and gauze; eating many fine kebab dinners; and covering the biggest story in the world: the fall of the Taliban regime.

Or, I could stay at Mahbuhbullah's house to tell stories of captured Taliban fighters, of starving refugees forgotten by the world, of illiterate children whose only toys were artillery shells, and of an unfortunate rice farmer whose wretched field was all that separated Taliban troops from the guerrilla fighters of the Northern Alliance. Overhead, a B-52 circled before dropping another payload of thousand-pound bombs on Taliban positions in neat rows of twelve. Mahbuhbullah was courteously holding a light to my cigarette, smiling, and gently offering, in Russian, to do unspeakable things to my mother. And on the table—strike that: on the scarlet *dastarkhan* spread over the earthen floor—fresh turnips and spiced pumpkin glistened on pewter plates.

I stayed.

Kaddo Bowrani

Afghan Pumpkin with Yogurt Sauce

Serves 8

Café Titanic (yes, it, like many other local businesses, was named after the blockbuster film, immensely popular in Afghanistan, a completely landlocked country), a hopping establishment in Mazar-e-Sharif, added ground beef to this dish. Helmand Restaurant in Cambridge, Massachusetts, serves this pumpkin as part of a vegetable platter. Many *kaddo* recipes call for baking the pumpkin in an oven for hours at 300°F, but try telling that to Mahbuhbullah's wives. What oven? Nargiz, Mahbuhbullah's second wife, fried her pumpkin in an aluminum wok over an open flame in the backyard. In solidarity, and also because hers tasted really good, I use the stovetop.

> 1 or 2 pumpkins, about 3 pounds total
> 2 tablespoons vegetable oil
> 1 teaspoon ground cinnamon
> ¼ cup sugar (it does seem like a lot, but it won't
> come out too sweet, I promise)

For the sauce:
1 cup plain Greek yogurt or unflavored kefir
1 clove garlic, crushed
Salt and black pepper, to taste
Pinch of chopped fresh mint

1. Peel the pumpkin with a vegetable peeler and cut it in half. Remove the seeds and strings. Cut into about 2-inch chunks.

2. Heat the oil over high heat in a skillet or cast-iron Dutch oven and add the cinnamon. When the cinnamon becomes very fragrant (but before it starts to burn), add the pumpkin and brown for about 5 minutes, until golden brown (do not let it scorch). Add ½ cup water, sugar, cover, and cook for 10 minutes. Uncover and cook until the water has evaporated and the pumpkin is cooked through. If necessary, add more water.

3. While the pumpkin is cooking, whisk together all the ingredients for the sauce and chill. Serve the pumpkin hot. Your guests can pour the cold sauce onto their own plates. Think warm thoughts.

Mullah's Turnip Salad

Serves 8

*I*n Afghanistan, sliced turnips and radishes are often served with hot meat or rice dishes—and that's how Mahbuhbullah's wives served them. Mullah, the cook who worked at the rental house in Kabul where I lived after the Taliban had fallen, often prepared this slightly glorified version of the simple side dish.

2 large turnips
3 medium crunchy apples, cored (Golden Delicious work well)
2 small lemons, diced
¼ cup sunflower or sesame seed oil
Salt to taste
1 tablespoon sesame seeds, for sprinkling

Thoroughly wash the turnips and peel them. Julienne the turnips and apples into matchstick-thin pieces. Toss with the lemons, oil, and salt. Sprinkle with the sesame seeds. Serve immediately.

Three

The Kebab Diaries

The guests arrive on Saturday and I can't sleep. I watch shadows of slow, large snowflakes crawl down white bedroom curtains and think of what I will cook for dinner.

We will fill our plates and talk about work and kids and movies we have seen. Maybe someone will ask about the exotic and dangerous places I have traveled to: a gun market in Fallujah, a mined road in Afghanistan, a Somali market street where warlords parade in rusted Russian armored personnel carriers. But, unbeknownst to my guests, my most intimate memories from these trips will be arranged in colorful heaps on their plates: the crunchy puff pastries stuffed with the thyme seeds I picked up in Gaza when I was writing about the second Palestinian intifada; the garlicky beet salad a Chechen widow served me in a refugee camp drowning in mud. The homemade hummus, ivory colored and topped with olives, the kind I used to have with Bassam, my late Jordanian friend and driver who once braved a killer sandstorm in a bandit-ridden Iraqi desert because he trusted no one else to drive me out of Baghdad. Ahmad's dolma. Mahbuhbullah's pumpkin. My two worlds—my friends, and my work—will converge on the dining table.

In the blighted places where I work, food is the closest thing to normalcy. You hold your breath tiptoeing across a minefield, and you hold your breath again at the deathbed of a child. You take notes as people kill in fear and die in agony. You write, your stomach muscles grabbing and your throat tight over the injustice of the world. You weep as you write. You file.

And then, if you're lucky, you eat.

Over food, you talk to your hosts and fellow diners about their lives and tell them about yours, and after all the horrors of that day, such simple conversations make everyday life worth living. Sometimes dinner is bread and a fried egg eaten with a spoon from a plastic tablecloth spread on the earthen floor of a farmer's hut, or a packet of trail mix from a U.S. army-issue ready-to-eat meal packet in the back of an armored humvee. Sometimes it is a lavish, four-course meal at the house of the local warlord. Sometimes it is a plate of rice and boiled meat in a funeral tent.

In Afghanistan, more often than not, it was lamb kebab.

———————

The restaurant was like many others that interrupt the pale monotony of northern Afghanistan's half-marked roads: a house of mud and straw propped up on exposed, crooked wooden beams, with no name, no tables, and no chairs. Along the dining room walls ran a wide, wooden seating area that resembled a stage; upon it, the diners sat cross-legged, with their shoes off. Elevating the floor was the easiest way to keep the food from being mixed with too much dust. Plastic *dastarkhans* lay spread on wooden planks before the diners. Unlike the scarlet beauties hand-embroidered with magical flowers and birds that wealthier Afghans save for meals served to important guests, the *dastarkhans* in these roadside diners were essentially linoleum runners that usually came in thick rolls. One end of the runner was always rolled up over yards and yards of extra plastic, like wrapping paper; the free end was reused until it became too tattered or grimy to be considered presentable, even by Afghan roadside diner standards. At such a time, the owner of the *dastarkhan* snipped off the tattered end and tossed it away, into the vast desert. This was not littering. Nomads or paupers always recycled the plastic as shelter material.

To accommodate Berget and his friends—these, at the moment, included several Northern Alliance militiamen, Wahid the translator, Ghulam Sakhib the driver, David, and me—the restaurant owner had rolled out several feet of *dastarkhan* before us. The fighters rested their battered Kalashnikov rifles, muzzle up, within their reach, against uneven mud-brick walls. They ate unhurriedly, deliberately tearing off small pieces of thin, flat *nan* bread and wrapping them around tiny pieces of marinated lamb meat and fat cooked over hot coals on sharp metal skewers. They pulled the meat off the skewers with elegant, long fingers that looked more like they belonged to violinists than to gunmen.

We had met Berget earlier that day, in the middle of a vast, harvested rice field that separated two armies: the embattled troops of the ruling Taliban and the bedraggled soldiers of the Northern Alliance. It was the same field where I first had been told to hide from Taliban snipers behind a wall, and then invited to the other side of the wall for a hot cuppa.

It was the same scorched, dry field Berget had crossed three days earlier, when he had abandoned his post on the Taliban side and joined the Northern Alliance.

Berget, at twenty-six a skinny, pale man with a straggly beard, had joined the Taliban of his own volition, in 1995. Rival warlords had been battling over control of the country, razing entire villages and raping their way through Kabul block by city block, laying waste even further to a land that had not yet recovered from the decade-long Soviet occupation. People like Berget—who, even after his defection, recalled fondly the way Taliban troops had confiscated all weapons from Kabul's residents and stopped, at least temporarily, the pillaging—had seen the militia as a unifying force that could restore order. (Berget had been less enthralled by the new regime's moral police and strict rules that banned all movies and music.) The reason for his defection, Berget explained, was that many Taliban commanders were Pakistanis or Arabs. If there is one thing all Afghans have agreed on since time immemorial, it is that foreigners have no business running their country.

"I thought that if the fighting ever ends and the opposition wins, how would I look my brothers in the eye if I were fighting on the same side as foreigners?" Berget said. Maybe there was a lesson or two there for American troops who were trying to quash the Taliban's network. Nine years after that dinner with Berget, the White House—now under President Barack Obama—was still trying to defeat the Afghan insurgency, which, rather than die down, had grown stronger with time.

Now, the young Tajik was a Northern Alliance fighter. He was eating kebab, bragging about Taliban losses at the hands of American air strikes and rebel mortar fire as though they had been all his doing ("Since the beginning of the U.S. strikes, most of the Taliban have been killed, and a lot of their ammunition and radar installations have been destroyed"), and telling jokes (Taliban leader Mullah Mohammed Omar* at a Friday prayer: "Do not listen to music, because it is a sin. Do not shave your beards, because it is a sin. Above all, do not watch movies, because it is the gravest sin of all sins, and it will make your souls sink to the bottom of the ocean, like Leonardo DiCaprio in the blockbuster *Titanic*"). Berget's new comrades, weathered, sinewy fighters whose gray and brown plastic flip-flops sat in a neat row at the foot of the eating stage, listened and laughed with him as though he had not trained his gun on them—and they, on him—just days before. From time to time, the men sitting to Berget's left and right would drape their slender hands around his shoulders, in the universal gesture of brotherly love.

Berget's swift transition from enemy to ally was not at all extraordinary. As our smuggler-host Mahbuhbullah had taught me, switching sides was common among Afghan fighters, be it a foot soldier who would rather defect than be captured or killed, or a renowned warlord like his former Uzbek commander, Dostum. Acquaintance, family relations, and simple survival were often more important than political affiliation. The local rebel commander, incidentally, turned out to have been a friend of Berget's family.

"I fought"—this had been against the Soviet troops—"alongside his father and brothers," the commander had recalled when I had sat with him and Berget in the middle of the harvested rice field, before our meal. "He," the commander had pointed at the defector with his bearded chin, "used to bring us lunch to the front lines."

And now we were all sharing a meal of kebab. All's well that ends with a few skewers of lamb over a plastic *dastarkhan*.

Especially that cursed, hungry year.

---

*Mullah Mohammed Omar—the one-eyed leader of the Afghan Taliban, which he is believed to have first organized in 1994. After the United States attacked the Taliban in 2001, Mullah Omar reportedly fled to Pakistan and continued to head the militia from exile.

It was late fall, and the first winter frost had hit prematurely the previous week, destroying whatever crops had managed to push through the dehydrated desert floor. Ice had encrusted the massive tangle of the Hindu Kush. Snow had silenced the mountain passes. In the spring, the snowmelt would run off the crumpled peaks, nourishing the thirsty valleys below. But right now, snow was bad news, possibly a killer of millions. It had blocked the Northern Alliance supply routes to the militiamen fighting on the southern frontier: the rickety old Soviet eighteen-wheelers that the guerrillas were using to transport ammunition and artillery to the front lines could not make it through the ice and snow. Relief agencies no longer had a way of getting food and clothing to Kabul's northern outskirts: because of the air war, all helicopters and planes that were not part of the U.S.-led military campaign had been grounded. Some anti-Taliban commanders worried that American air strikes, which were supposed to give the mujahedin an edge over the ruling militia, were not going to produce enough momentum to defeat the Taliban before it became too cold to fight. If the standoff were to continue into the winter the skies would remain off-limits to relief agencies, and no humanitarian aid would be delivered to millions of Afghans suffering from famine after the fourth consecutive year of drought. While we were turning up our noses at too much kebab, the United Nations was reporting that more than five million people—one quarter of Afghanistan's population—were on the verge of starvation. The military campaign that was supposed to deliver Afghanistan from an inhumane regime was delivering a new humanitarian catastrophy. We left Mahbuhbullah's house and his vegetable patch, shared a meal with Berget, and headed south, toward Kabul.

At the end of each day, Ghulam Sakhib, Wahid, David, and I would find an eatery where unshod patrons sat on a wooden table-stage. We would take off our own mud-caked boots and climb onto the podium as well, swatting away flies and making a true spectacle of ourselves: two Afghan men, a foreigner with long hair, and an unveiled woman with a crew cut who smoked cigarettes and ate with the men. Almost always, I was the only woman in these *chaikhanas*. Almost always, we were the only unarmed diners. Every time we dined out, we were the entertainment: everyone would stare at the foreigners as they ate.

The restaurant owner would approach to take our order. Inevitably, we would order "kebab, *garm*"—hot, one of the most important words in Dari for foreign travelers who believe that heat kills bacteria—and a few minutes later, the man would reappear with a pewter tray laden with bouquets of thin skewers spearing juicy meat.

Around the world, grilled meat on a skewer is the ultimate bonding dish, the object of envy and the subject of mockery, the source of bitter disputes between friends and rivals, and the meal of celebrations. In Somalia, it was made with goat. At the al Hamra Hotel and Suites in Baghdad, chicken tikka was a reliably overcooked (and barely edible) staple. At the palace of one Iraqi sheikh in Saddam Hussein's tribal village of Auja, kebab was made with lamb (not as good as the meat we had had in Afghanistan, sorry). The photojournalist Kim Komenich and I were in Auja in 2005 to report on an American army doctor making house calls as part of the U.S. military's "hearts and minds" strategy for winning over hostile Sunni tribes. The doctor, a full colonel, was a woman, which was why everybody assumed that it was Kim—with his imposing 280-pound frame and a neatly trimmed gray beard, both clear signs of superiority—who was the guest of honor. While the rest of us were handed plates with moist, perfectly spiced red meat, Kim, with much ceremony and to everyone's amusement, was served a pair of grilled lamb testicles.

In Afghanistan, sometimes the owner or the other diners would join us, telling stories of loss: of family members killed in the quarter century of fighting; of wealth and youth robbed by wars and droughts; of fertile gardens left behind when the Taliban invaded their villages, forcing all men to either join the militia's ranks or run away. Kitchen help—boys barely in their teens, tomorrow's warriors, who had known no heroes or role models other than rebel field commanders—would listen politely, waiting for the older men to ask the question that was the most important to everyone, the question we had no answer for: how soon would the war end, how soon would the men of Afghanistan be able to put down their guns and return to their fields?

At first, the dusty, cracked trails upon which we traveled were only vaguely distinguishable from the fields they cut through, fields that had borne nothing but ash-colored sand and small outcroppings of rocks after five successive years of drought. Sometimes a fox would trot across a field. Prairie dogs stood at attention. A rare buzzard swooped down.

The roads were so wrecked by decades of aerial strikes, the shifting of tectonic plates, the avalanches, floods, and age, and the front line along which they curved was so jagged, that it took several days to travel a hundred miles. I imagined the armies of Alexander the Great trudge through the same dun topography, and the Achaemenid forces before them, at the same speed. The people we met on the way—farmers in clothes that, over years in the fields, had become the same color as the soil; indigent refugees with the piercing eyes of the dying; hard rebel soldiers who had been fighting since they were children, usually without pay, surviving on handouts from their commanders and sympathetic local shopkeepers— generously and matter-of-factly recited the war crimes they had witnessed, suffered, or committed. Each new village we passed told of new heartbreaks. At dinner, tiny nuggets of skewered lamb carried the stories of shepherds plotting their courses across minefields, of butchers driven out of their villages by fighting, of restaurant owners who could barely feed their own children, of down-and-out gunmen kicking back without shoes after a long day of war. The farther we drove, the more people we met, the more the pained landscape along the road looked like a kaleidoscope of woe.

In Lolaguzar, a xeric camp where the wind sculpted sandcastles out of dust inside the refugees' haphazard lean-tos and dugouts, a young woman named Zulfiya told me about fleeing her home the day the Taliban had press-ganged her husband into the army. Zulfiya had four children. With her husband gone, and with no male family members around to protect her, she had feared that Taliban fighters would rape her, so she had grabbed her children and walked for six days to Lolaguzar. She had clutched her infant son, Yakobullah, to her chest the whole way. When she was leaving her house, Zulfiya had only had the time to dress her five-year-old daughter, Shikuriya; her three small sons had gone naked. Now they wore misshapen rugs someone had given them. Half a mile away, past the skeleton of an unmanned armored personnel carrier and an old Soviet tank that guarded the entrance to the camp, the Pyandzh River, the only source of drinking water, bored muddily through the desert, spreading malaria in the summer, tuberculosis in the winter, and dysentery at all times of the year. Zulfiya's new home was a ripped piece of canvas thrown on the dusty ground beneath a dirty sheet of blue plastic propped up on sticks. I recognized the texture and the flower pattern on the plastic: it was a discarded restaurant *dastarkhan*.

A couple of days of travel later—it could have been ten miles on those damned roads, or one hundred—I met a shopkeeper named Mohammad Sobr. We drove up as he was shuttering his ramshackle store for a long, hungry winter. When there is nothing left to cook, no one will need the Iranian cooking oil he peddled from his sloping clay shelves, he explained—and his village, Ortinjilar, was rapidly running out of food. Crops had failed to sprout for the fourth year in a row, and Mohammad Sobr, the village's sole shopkeeper, sold only soap, matches, cigarettes, candles, and oil, but no food. I asked how far the nearest market town was.

"Seventeen hours by foot," Mohammad Sobr replied. In his village of two thousand people, no one had a car.

No restaurants were selling kebab in Ortinjilar. Before we continued down the road, Mohammad Sobr offered me a gnarled fistful of long, green raisins.

On a treeless mountaintop above the town of Kishim, we came upon a lonely, Soviet-made T-54 tank. The Soviet troops had abandoned the tank after withdrawing in 1989, and now a five-man Northern Alliance crew aimed the beat-up hundred-millimeter cannon of this dented beast of a bygone war at the foothills on the other side of a desolate valley. The Taliban controlled those foothills. The tank, a howitzer that protected it, and—in position a couple of miles away—another antiquated rebel tank paired with a rocket launcher were confronting a Taliban force of at least seven thousand soldiers and eight tanks. The T-54 on the hill was an emblem of the outnumbered and outgunned anti-Taliban resistance: the Northern Alliance army was a hodgepodge of about fifteen thousand ragged militiamen, most of them barefoot; the Taliban numbered, according to some reports, forty thousand men. At an abandoned, unheated two-story house that served as the militia's headquarters in Kishim, a trio of radio operators sat cross-legged on brightly colored mattresses, swilling sweet tea, promising to each other that American air strikes were weakening the Taliban government, and waiting for the order from Mohammed Fahim, the rebel defense minister (and the owner of the house) to broadcast the command to launch a wide-scale offensive against government troops. But the men at the tank, so clearly outmatched by government troops, shared with me their pessimism about their prospects as a fighting force.

"We are defending, not attacking," their commander said, bitterly.

He shivered in his thin, corduroy *shalwar kameez* suit. Winter was closing in on the fighters, the shopkeepers, the refugees under wind-torn sheets of recycled *dastarkhans*.

———

To help out that fall, American C-17 cargo planes dropped hundreds of thousands of packages on the Afghan soil. The packages were yellow and marked, in English, with the words "Food Gift from the People of the United States of America." They contained ready-to-eat rice, lentils, beans, beef stew, and—much to the delight of David, who was homesick for familiar comfort food in the land of kebab—peanut butter, jelly, and generic versions of Pop-Tarts and Fig Newtons: all in all, twenty-two hundred carefully calculated calories of sustenance, the balanced, albeit boring, daily diet of an adult male who doesn't exert too much energy and likes American junk food.

Within weeks, Northern Alliance warlords—these important Washington allies, foot soldiers of the U.S.-led campaign to dethrone the Taliban—began sending their men to the drop areas to snatch the goods before the local peasants could get at them.

Some arrived in tanks. (I, too, once went shopping for bread in a Bradley fighting vehicle, but that was different, I swear. You'll see.) The militias would sort through the humanitarian aid, which also included olive green winter parkas and wool hats for the harsh winter in the mountains; keep for themselves what they needed; distribute most of the leftovers among civilians whose loyalty they believed to be important; and sell the rest. Rather than reaching the neediest, most of the rations quickly found their way to Afghanistan's village markets, where local movers and shakers peddled them, mostly to Western journalists (which is how David got to delight in the Fig Newtons and the Pop-Tarts). A humanitarian food ration cost ten cents a bag; a parka, ten dollars each. While many Afghans appreciated the rice and the stew, most had no taste for peanut butter. David saw a woman feed peanut butter from one of those rations to her donkey.

When more than one militia arrived at a drop site, the gunmen would fight and the winners would take the humanitarian loot. In Dasht-e-Qal'eh, the local prosecutor, security commander, and prison warden kept behind bars a young man named Faizullah, on allegations that he had wounded a man during one such battle for American aid. Faizullah was facing death by hanging.

He denied all charges. There appeared to be no witnesses. When I asked the security commander and the warden how they knew Faizullah was guilty, they immediately pointed at his garb: the telltale, brand-new olive green parka and black knit hat. Faizullah pointed right back: both the prosecutor and the security commander were wearing the very same parkas.

"We bought ours at the bazaar," they assured me.

Then again, who in Afghanistan was not needy that horrible fall? The prison warden and the security commander, too, could hardly afford to eat meat once a month. Their children, too, were malnourished and went barefoot in the biting cold. Their wives, too, scraped every last grain of rice out of every bag they bought in the market. Their fields and vegetable patches, too, had borne nothing.

Simultaneously with dropping the Pop-Tarts and parkas of discord, American warplanes were delivering different payloads of bright yellow packages to the Afghan soil: thousands of BLU-97/B submunitions.

These metal, seven-inch-long canisters, commonly known as bomblets, were antitank and antipersonnel weapons, and came in efficiently packaged clusters of 202. Delivered by a B-52, the canisters would rain down from the sky onto an area of roughly five thousand square yards and disgorge the bomblets while in flight. The bomblets were set to explode on impact. But many failed to blow up right away and became, in effect, antipersonnel mines lying in wait for their victims, ready to detonate and destroy at a single touch.

Dozens of such unexploded bomblets littered the potholed clay tracks and arid courtyards of the village of Mengchuqur, which Taliban forces had used as a garrison from 1998 until a U.S. aerial attack had chased them out in November 2001.

Later that month, Mengchuqur's 2,400 residents returned to the looted, scorched rubble of their homes from self-imposed exile in the mountains of eastern Afghanistan and northwestern Pakistan. They had ridden on rooftops of busses, on trailers piled high with cotton, on donkey-drawn carts; they had walked for days. They were hungry. They had seen the yellow packages of food aid in some of the villages they had passed through on their way home. No one had warned them about the yellow cluster bomblets.

On his first day home after three years in exile, a young man named Islamuddin went to check out what had remained of his sister's house. Two feet away from the wall of his compound, a low, three-room house with a small, square yard of trampled-down clay, Islamuddin spotted something bright and yellow on the dry clay soil.

He must have thought it was one of those food rations, one of his neighbors later said.

"Some people here eat only once every two days," explained the neighbor, lifting the leathery palms of his farmer's hands to the sky in resignation and acceptance.

Islamuddin bent down to pick up the yellow canister. The bomblet exploded in his hands. He died instantly.

A few days later, another villager, a father of six preteen children, showed me the six bomblets he had found in his backyard. He had partially covered them with clumps of dry soil. Down the street, another man used a large cooking pot to cover the unexploded canister dug into the dirt outside his house; to make sure his five children stayed away, the man spent most of his time squatting next to the bomblet, guarding it. As for the pot, he explained to me, his family had nothing to cook in it anyway: nothing had grown in the wheat and rice fields of Mengchuqur since the villagers had fled from the Taliban three years earlier. The neatly packaged food gifts from the people of the United States of America, meanwhile, remained an unattainable luxury: although the villagers could hear the C-17s pass overhead at night, the cargo planes for some reason did not drop their payloads on the village. The nearest landing spot for the humanitarian rations was an hour's drive away, and in Mengchuqur like in Ortinjilar, no one had a car.

Seven years after the bombing of Mengchuqur, Afghanistan became one of ninety-eight countries to sign the international Convention on Cluster Munitions, which bans the signatories from manufacturing, selling, stockpiling, or using cluster bombs. As I write this, the United States has not signed the treaty; one advanced cluster bomb, the Sensor Fuzed Weapon, which is designed to spray forty bomblets of molten copper across thirty acres, is manufactured in Massachusetts, not far from where I came to live from Moscow in 2004.

I returned to Mengchuqur almost a year after my first visit, in the fall of 2002. A de-mining team had come to clear the village and the fields around it that summer, nine months after the villagers had come home. By then, the yellow bomblets had killed ten other people.

Of course, Afghanistan offered a variety of other means to die. The most common man-made killer ticked just beneath the topsoil.

There are many ways to classify minefields. U.S. Army Field Manual FM 5-102 distinguishes five types of minefields: protective (planted around a specific site); tactical (planted as part of an obstacle plan); point (this one uses all types of mines—antipersonnel, antitank—to hinder enemy movement); interdiction (placed within or just on the outskirts of enemy territory); and phony (pretend mines, metal objects that look like mines half buried in the dirt, for when you don't have real ones or don't have the time to lay them); the manual further divides protective minefields into two kinds: hasty and deliberate.

In Afghanistan in 2001, few people, if any, concerned themselves with such an elaborate classification. From the point of view of public knowledge, Afghan minefields came in two kinds. One kind was marked by international de-mining organizations, such as Halo Trust*—rocks painted red to identify the mines that could still blow up, rocks painted white to identify the mines that have been defused; sometimes there were also triangular metal flags depicting a skull and crossbones with the word MINES! written on it, in English and Dari. The other kind of minefield was unmarked. This kind, obviously, was the more dangerous to the people who lived near them and to travelers like me.

From the point of view of style, each of these types of minefields, in turn, had subclasses of their own: the minefields left by the Kremlin's troops during the decade-long Soviet occupation of the country, and the minefields left by mujahedin fighters who fought against the Soviets and then against each other and the Taliban.

The Soviets laid mines around their military outposts and other sensitive security objects, or along whatever the front line was at the time. (FM 5-102 would identify the minefields as "protective" and "interdiction.") They would arrange their explosives in neat grids and map their locations so that they could dismantle them when the front line moved. Some de-mining organizations working in Afghanistan had managed to obtain some of the maps; I was told that even those minefields for which no maps were available were relatively easy to defuse once the general location of the explosives was established, because the patterns of the grids the Soviets had used to plant their mines were almost always the same.

The Afghans, on the other hand, preferred the deadly ad hoc art of nuisance mining. Here is how it works: plant a mine or two somewhere on a giant plane before you retreat, let it be known that the place is mined, and voilà, you've got yourself a minefield. The entire area is now off-limits. Enemy units will not dare to occupy your abandoned positions

---

*Halo Trust—a British charity that helps disable land mines in former (and sometimes current) war zones. In 2000, the Russian government kicked Halo Trust out of the country, accusing the world's biggest mine-clearing charity of training Chechen rebels in explosive techniques.

because the explosives could be anywhere. This was a local take on FM 5-102's phony minefields, except the mines weren't phony at all.

Of course, you want to know where your minefields are in case you ever regain control of the land. But instead of mapping the mines, Afghan fighters—most of whom were illiterate and could not have read maps anyway—used the buddy method: the sapper who lays the mine tells his buddy. Now the two of them are the only people in the world who know where death has been sown. And if both of them get killed, which happened more often than not, then the people living in the area are plain out of luck.

"You have to treat each suspected object as a mine, and each suspected area as a minefield," Susan Helseth, who worked at the UN Children's Fund in Kabul to help educate Afghans about the risk of mines, told me in 2004. That year, the United Nations estimated that Afghanistan was ticking with about ten million land mines and an unknown number of unexploded ordnance that killed or maimed an average of one hundred people a month. Limbless, scarred land-mine victims begging for food or money were a common sight in marketplaces.

You learned to pick your path carefully, making sure that you placed your feet only where you saw marks of someone else's recent footsteps. You learned to keep in mind that powerful spring freshets of mountain snowmelt could flood minefields, pushing the mines downstream, so even if the villagers told you there were no mines in their area, neither they nor you could really know for sure. If there was a paved road, you tried to stay on it at all times. You learned to urinate directly behind the rear tires of your car: you could be certain that that soil had been driven over. For months after my first three trips to Afghanistan in 2001 and 2002, I felt very nervous about walking on grass. I would break a sweat just thinking of throwing a Frisbee in the park.

I don't know how many minefields we drove through in Afghanistan. People told me, afterward, of three. But our Russian-made UAZ-469 military jeep always made it out under the masterful hands of our taciturn driver. If there was a minefield in our path, Ghulam Sakhib would somehow intuit his way around or through it. If a cavernous gorge suddenly bisected the road, Ghulam Sakhib would quietly steer our jeep down on a nauseating spiral, then muscle it back up. We would cheer and applaud, making him blush and bow theatrically behind the wheel.

With every stretch of our trip, Afghanistan's treacherous landscape transformed. Dusty planes turned to precipitous gorges, and I mentally resigned myself to certain death a dozen times a day—like the time we were suddenly driving off-road up a mountain at an impossibly steep angle, or the time we were navigating a shallow, pebble-strewn river-bed guarded by Taliban tanks on each side. After all, the name of the five-hundred-mile range we were crossing, Hindu Kush, means "Slayer of Indians." Who were we to think that we would be any luckier than the millions of foreigners—ancient Persians, Indians, Greeks, British soldiers, Soviet army conscripts—who had perished in these mountains that prop up the sky fifteen, twenty thousand feet above sea level?

Occasionally we would pass other cars and trucks. Some bore English inscriptions on their sides: KING OF THE ROADS, GOD CHILD, LION OF AFGHANISTAN, and HILUX PICKUM, the meaning of which will forever remain a mystery. One day, on a road with clay surface the consistency of melted marshmallows, the wheels of Ghulam Sakhib's jeep locked for a few seconds and he accidentally ran over a lone chicken, thus earning the nickname of *Morgh Kush*: Chicken Killer.

We thought the nickname was amusing; Ghulam Sakhib said nothing. He, in general, rarely said anything. The blood of taciturn Uzbek horsemen—those who usher their horses through rapids and firefights by clicking their tongues mysteriously and whistling, never by force or word—ran in his veins. In my mind, he was the true King of the Roads. No matter the landscape, three things remained unchanged: our daily diet of lamb kebab, Ghulam Sakhib's silence, and his superior driving skills. The Russian jeep had no shock absorbers to speak of, and even a trip of several miles lasted excruciating hours on these roads, but one of the main tricks in war reporting is getting there. And Ghulam Sakhib always got us there, and always in time for some freshly skewered meat.

Only once, in the rebel capital of Faizabad, did Ghulam Sakhib fail to get us someplace on time. We were about to cross a ten-thousand-foot ridge, and the two slippery grooves that steeply climbed the granite mountainside were almost certainly covered in snow. Under the pretext of buying an astronomically expensive set of snow chains for his tires, our driver asked us for six hundred dollars one morning and disappeared from the guesthouse where we were staying. The morning went by, then the afternoon. We had planned to travel across the mountain pass to the next frontier that day. But as the sun began to sink behind the Hindu Kush it became clear that we were going to spend another night in Faizabad: the mountain road had no guardrails or markings, the shoulders were most likely mined, and traveling on it by night was too dangerous.

A few times we asked Wahid to find Ghulam Sakhib and inquire as to how much longer we had to wait, but each time Wahid would return to tell us, with a mysterious smile on his face, that the snow chains were still not ready. I was beginning to wonder whether a local blacksmith was wringing iron out of the mountains and forging the chain links from scratch.

Finally, at sunset, Ghulam Sakhib strolled through the gate. Usually reticent, he was now too triumphant to keep his secret, and within minutes we knew the reason for the delay: he had used most of the money to secure a marriage to a local beauty who would become his second wife; his negotiations over the bride's price with her father had continued into the evening. We were, of course, invited to the wedding, which would take place after the war was over.

To his credit, Ghulam Sakhib also got the chains.

I don't think I wrote any stories from Faizabad on that trip—the stop turned out to have been entirely for Ghulam Sakhib's marital purposes—but we did go out to a nice, nameless *chaikhana* to celebrate our intrepid driver's engagement.

The place's signature dish? Mouthwatering lamb kebab.

❧

Afghan Lamb Kebab

Serves 8

*I*n Afghanistan, fat-bottomed sheep wander the pastures every-where, oblivious of the land mines, so there is never any question about the freshness of the meat on your skewer. The lamb you'll buy in the United States is most likely imported from Australia, therefore you should allow it to marinate overnight to make it more tender. If you can, use a char-coal or wood grill.

3 tablespoons fresh lemon juice
4 cloves garlic, crushed
Salt and white pepper, to taste
2 pounds boneless lamb (leg will work) and about
    8 ounces lamb fat, cut into thumbnail-size cubes
Ground sumac (sumac is a crimson spice you can get
    in most Middle Eastern groceries)
Lemon wedges, for serving
4 loaves fresh lavash or other flatbread

1. Combine the lemon juice, garlic, salt, and pepper in a large bowl. Add the lamb and lamb fat. Mix well, cover, and marinate in the refrigerator for several hours or overnight.

2. Skewer the lamb, threading 4 pieces of meat and 2 or 3 pieces of fat onto each skewer. Alternate the meat and the fat so that the fat nuggets are skewered between pieces of meat. (You don't have to eat the fat, although Berget and his crew did; its main purpose is to keep the meat moist while you're grilling it.) Grill, turning frequently, over smoldering coals for about 15 minutes, until the lamb is brown and cooked through (when you pierce the meat with a fork or a sharp knife, juices should run clear). Sprinkle with ground sumac and serve with lemon wedges, flatbread, and hot black tea, preferably very sweet.

Four

Candy-Wrapped Kalashnikovs

High on Valium and potent Afghan hashish, Najibullah balanced his Kalashnikov rifle on his left shoulder and reached for the *jelebi*: a pyramid of honey-colored, deep-fried rings of hot, syrupy dough stacked on a street vendor's dusty aluminum folding table by the side of a potholed dirt road. He hooked one *jelebi* with his long index finger, raised it above his head, lifted his bearded face, and, crooning a Bollywood jingle in a tentative falsetto, began to nibble at the sugary doughnut like some tropical bird, swaying slightly to the rhythm of a song that he alone could follow.

Our clunky Toyota minivan was parked near a bustling outdoor bazaar in the wooded foothills of the Spin Ghar range in eastern Afghanistan, where Osama bin Laden was believed to have been hiding in a honeycomb of caves, tunnels, and bunkers outside the town of Tora Bora. The mountain complex had been a favorite hiding place for generations of Afghan fighters—warriors who had fought against the British, then the Soviets, then against each other, and now against U.S.-led forces. It had been so elaborately upgraded over the years that by 2001 it was said to have its own ventilation system and a power supply provided by hydroelectric generators.

Whatever had been in these massive caves on the border with Pakistan was being destroyed at that very moment. It was December 2001, and the Battle of Tora Bora was under way—a massive, joint aerial and ground attack by American forces trying to smoke out the terrorist mastermind and a thousand al Qaeda and Taliban fighters believed to be hiding with him. I had come to Spin Ghar to write about this battle.

Guided by U.S. special forces commandos and backed by scruffy Afghan guerrillas, the Americans were pummeling the caves with a dazzling array of ordnance delivered by B-52 bombers, F-14 and F/A-18 Hornet fighter jets, and AC-130 gunships: "daisy-cutters" (fifteen-thousand-pound bombs that, when they explode, create a blast wave that kills everyone within roughly three acres, leaving in their wake enormous charred craters and very little else); bombs equipped with sensors known as JDAMs (for "joint direct attack munition") to guide them to their targets; cluster bombs packed with dozens of bomblets that could wreck roadways and runways and cripple infantry (and, as I had learned in Mengchuqur, civilians unfortunate enough to happen upon them later); and TV-guided air-to-surface missiles that weighed three thousand pounds. I could feel the impact through the soles of my feet miles away whenever the heavier payloads struck the caves. The echo of occasional gunfire ricocheted off the steep slopes, making the firefights seem both dangerously close and elusive.

A week earlier, Najibullah had been holed up in an abandoned mountain barn near one of those caves, fighting al Qaeda and Taliban gunmen. Snow had coated the mountains outside, and Najibullah had been freezing in his light summer clothes. Now he was kicking back after a lifetime of war: the Eastern Shura, a loose coalition led by tribal elders who opposed the Taliban and therefore had allied themselves with the United States, had finally prevailed in this corner of Afghanistan—although it was impossible to say that the area had been purged of the Taliban, just as it would have been wrong to say that the Eastern Shura had established complete control. The mountainous border between Afghanistan and Pakistan, where many Taliban fighters had found refuge, was not really guarded by anyone on either side. Some members of the militia were still holding out around Tora Bora, taking potshots at American special forces operatives and Western journalists who crawled about sections of the mountainside. Some had blended in with the local population: in line with a long-standing Afghan tradition, which allows the victor to choose, at will, between violently punishing the defeated foe and granting him complete forgiveness (this code of war also permits the victor to double back on his choice unpredictably at any given moment), the Eastern Shura had allowed most local Taliban fighters to walk free (theoretically, they were supposed to surrender their weapons). The locals, mostly ethnic Pashtuns, had largely supported the Taliban regime, and Najibullah believed that many al Qaeda members, too, had gone into hiding and were being sheltered by villagers in hamlets like the one where we were buying sweets—a cluster of mud-brick and straw huts clinging to the glaucous mountainside. Perhaps, Najibullah mused, bin Laden was also hiding in one of these villages, disguised as a shepherd with a coarse camel wool blanket draped over his head, shoulders, and back.

"There they go! There they go!" Najibullah had yelled earlier that day, pointing excitedly out the car window at two men in dark turbans walking down a village street. "See how they try to hide their eyes? They are former Taliban fighters!"

He rolled down the window, leaned out, and, shaking his gun—the same beat-up Kalashnikov he had carried since he was twelve—shouted at a passing villager:

"Where are you hiding the Taliban, huh?"

The villager ignored him. Our driver, Yarmohammad, decided that it was best, for the sake of our safety, not to stop.

But then Najibullah spotted the *jelebi* vendor and ordered Yarmohammad to pull over. Najibullah had been smoking hashish all morning, and now he had the munchies. We had to respect that. After all, this man—with his addiction to tranquilizers, his unpredictable mood swings, his little juniper hash pipe, and his disconcerting tendency to lean out of our car window and fire his gun across the valley just for fun—was our bodyguard.

———

I made Najibullah's acquaintance in December 2001, toward the end of my second trip to Afghanistan. The journey had begun right after the Taliban regime fell and its army surrendered Kabul and most major Afghan cities and towns, in November. David and I had once again floated into the country across the Pyandzh River from Tajikistan, on the diesel ferry. The day we arrived two gunmen had shot and killed a Swedish television cameraman, Ulf Strömberg, in Taloqan, a city in northern Afghanistan a few hours' drive from our first stop on this trip, the hospitable compound of Mahbuhbullah the Tomb Raider. Mahbuhbullah had heard about the killing on his handheld AM radio and told us as soon as we drove up to his house.

Strömberg was the eighth journalist to be murdered in the country in four weeks. Earlier that month, two French radio correspondents and a writer for a German magazine had been ambushed and killed after a rocket-propelled grenade blast threw them off an armored vehicle driven by the men of an anti-Taliban rebel commander in northern Afghanistan. A week before Strömberg's killing, four Western journalists driving in a convoy on the stretch of the ancient Grand Trunk Road* between Jalalabad and Kabul—where bandits had waylaid their prey for centuries—had been forced out of their vehicles, marched off to the side of the road, and executed. The journalists' drivers, who had managed to escape, relayed the assailants' defiant words: "You thought the Taliban was dead? The Taliban is still here!"

That was true. Wherever we went during our second trip to Afghanistan, we saw members of the deposed militia wandering around in their black turbans. Maybe they still listened to their leader, Mullah Omar, on the shortwave radios every man in Afghanistan seemed to carry in the folds of his robes. Maybe they had heard the one-eyed mullah's promise of a fifty-thousand-dollar bounty for every Western journalist they killed.

David and I huddled on Mahbuhbullah's earthen porch, poring over the newswire reports about Strömberg's death that we had downloaded onto our laptops. We had not known him. But it was easy to imagine that Strömberg had been just like us: an unarmed reporter trying to find a compelling way to bring the news from this faraway, tragic land to the audience back home.

Reporters who cover wars put a huge amount of faith in the idea that

---

*Grand Trunk Road—one of South Asia's oldest routes, which stretches from Bengal in India, through Peshawar in Pakistan, to Kabul.

none of the people we write about would ever find a reason to aim their guns at us. As obdurate as this notion may seem to anyone who has not traveled to a war zone, or anyone who has fought in one—especially given that reporters do get kidnapped and killed in wars—our almost delusionally uncritical faith in the kindness of strangers is the only thing that emboldens unarmed geeks with thousands of dollars in our money belts and, usually, few combat skills to venture into places where civilians are being killed, whether by accident or intent, by the dozen daily.

This is also the main reason we react with such shock when one of our number is targeted and killed in such a place.

The news reports said that at two in the morning, two masked men armed with Kalashnikov assault rifles had scaled the stucco walls of the compound where Strömberg and three of his colleagues were staying. I glanced up at the walls of Mahbuhbullah's compound to see whether an intruder could climb them. A bunch of our host's kids were hanging out on top; they waved at me when they caught me looking at them.

We read on. The gunmen had taken money, computers, and satellite phones. Afghanistan was a cash-only economy, and between the two of us, David and I were carrying more than fifteen thousand dollars to pay for the services of our drivers and translators, as well as lodging, food, and other contingencies. Our satellite phone, a brand-new Thrane & Thrane, state of the art at the time, gleamed on the rooftop of Mahbuhbullah's house: we were using it to download the reports about the Taloqan killing, at the frustrating rate of fifty-six hundred bytes per minute. The gadget's bright turquoise LAN cable dangled from the phone to our laptops on the porch below. To make sure no one tripped over it in the dark, we had adorned the cable with little flags fashioned from reflective silver duct tape. That cable was probably the single brightest thing in this town that had no electricity.

Even if we brought down the Thrane & Thrane, this was our second time staying at Mahbuhbullah's house, and other reporters had lived here between our visits. By now everybody in Dasht-e-Qal'eh knew that Mahbuhbullah was hosting foreigners. Strömberg, too, had been staying in a compound well known for housing foreign reporters.

In response to Strömberg's killing, several media outlets decided to pull their reporters out of northern Afghanistan. David and I were not leaving, but we felt that we needed to respond in some manner, so we made four rules. One: we would never get out of our car in crowded public places. Two: we would avoid places where Westerners often stayed. Three: we would not travel from Kabul to Jalalabad on the Grand Trunk Road, which we privately renamed, not too creatively, the Death Road. And four: we would do something neither I nor David—who had covered the war in Chechnya for seven years before coming to Afghanistan—had ever done before. We would hire armed guards.

We ended up breaking all four rules, of course. We even spent several unsettling hours in Taloqan—not just without a bodyguard, but also without a translator or a driver. But that November afternoon in Dasht-e-Qal'eh, when we were pondering how to report from a land where journalists were being killed simply for being there, Mahbuhbullah, ever the discerning host, detected our unease. In the evening, after a dinner of rice, flatbread, and stewed pumpkin, he paraded several of his sons in front of us. The oldest was sixteen. The boys, Mahbuhbullah explained, would take turns standing guard in front of our room at night. We didn't need to pay them; their services were part of our hospitality package. Mahbuhbullah showed us the weapon his kids would use: a Kalashnikov assault rifle with a well-worn wooden butt stock.

Around one in the morning, when I went outside to smoke a cigarette, I saw our guard sleeping on the porch. It was Abdullah, the industrious twelve-year-old who would always serve us the meals prepared by Mahbuhbullah's invisible wives and clean up afterward. Mahbuhbullah's children were better dressed and better fed than most kids in this infertile swath of northern Afghanistan. But even so, the malnutrition and disease that were so rampant in the country—in 2001, one out of four Afghan children died before reaching the age of five—had taken their toll on Abdullah. The skinny boy was about as tall as an average American third-grader.

He was my favorite of all Mahbuhbullah's kids, with a spray of freckles on his turned-up nose, huge eyes, and a face that was quick to blossom into the most beautiful, kind smile. Now his face looked relaxed in the greenish moonlight. He was crouched up with his back against the wall and the assault rifle in his hands. He looked cold. I went back inside, fetched a flowery acrylic blanket, and wrapped it around him, trying not to disturb his gun.

The next morning, as usual, Abdullah came into our room, rolled out a plastic *dastarkhan* on the threadbare carpet that somewhat contained the dust on the earthen floor, and arranged on it our breakfast: last night's leftover bread; fresh, hot eggs deep-fried in canola oil; a little bowl of salt; a small saucer of honey; and a large thermos of steaming, sweet tea. Then, with much ceremony, he approached each of us with a beat-up, plastic ewer, pouring water over a large pewter bowl so that we could wash our hands before the meal. As he squatted next to me, he asked me something in Dari, flashing his heartwarming, earnest smile. I asked Engineer Fazul, the translator we had hired at the border, to interpret.

"He asks," the translator said, "if you think he was a good guard."

How could I thank a twelve-year-old boy for risking his life for mine? I felt compelled to give Abdullah something, but how does one even compensate for such a sacrifice? Anything I could have done or said would have been disproportionately, ridiculously trivial. I thought of our kids, of their safe lives in big, modern cities. Alex was five at the time; Fyodor was four. I thought of what they liked. I went to my duffel bag, and fished out a Snickers bar.

Abdullah was the youngest gunman to ever guard my life. So what if he was doing it in his dreams? Of all the boys and men who have served as my protectors in Afghanistan, Somalia, Iraq—some earnestly, some halfheartedly—Mahbuhbullah's son was the most sincere in his efforts, even if his dad's Kalashnikov was nearly as tall as he was, even if guarding me meant he had to stay up way past his bedtime, and his work went unpaid apart from a chocolaty treat.

This chapter is an overdue ode to my Afghan bodyguards, and to the sweets they ate.

———

We left Dasht-e-Qal'eh in the company of Mahmoud, a white-bearded friend of Mahbuhbullah's, and his Kalashnikov. They were going to travel with us for the next few days. That evening, we broke two of our freshly minted security rules when our driver pulled over in front of a three-story hotel looming over a bullet-scarred square in downtown Imam Sahib, a provincial backwater (and a key layover point for opium smugglers) on the Pyandzh River, captured by the Northern Alliance only days earlier. The dusty streets were teeming with former Taliban fighters. The Taliban fighters had been mostly disarmed. They felt disenfranchised. They clung together in small, angry-looking groups.

The hotel was the only three-story building in a single-story town. We were to become its only guests. We were instant celebrities! A crowd immediately encircled our car. Kids elbowed their way through to peek at the foreigners inside. Several men in black Taliban turbans skulked a few paces away.

So much for traveling incognito. I was trying to explain to the security guard that it was a really bad place for us to get out of the car when the trunk popped open and a handful of accommodating young men started taking out our bags and hauling them to the hotel. The driver gallantly swung open my door. Mahmoud winked at me from the shotgun seat. I swore, and began to follow the bags through the crowd.

Suddenly the people around me grew considerably more agitated. "Ahmad Zahir," people murmured. Someone shouted: "Ahmad Zahir, is that you?"

That meant David had gotten out of the car, too.

My future husband bore an uncanny resemblance to Afghanistan's most popular singer. The saccharine crooning of Ahmad Zahir—lovingly known in his homeland as Bulbul-e-Afghan (the Nightingale of the Afghans)—had conquered the hearts of his people long before the Taliban banned music. He was killed in an automobile accident in 1979 (some fans called the circumstances of his death mysterious, and speculated that a woman—or was it politics? perhaps both?—was to blame), but many Afghans simply refused to believe that the Nightingale was gone. Traveling with David through Afghanistan was a little bit like traveling to Graceland with the ghost of Elvis.

In the Northern Alliance trenches outside Dasht-e-Qal'eh, David's celebrity look-alike status had earned him the affection of a group of rebels who liked to ply him with Iranian sugar-coated almonds and say slightly disconcerting things like, "You are so sweet, have some more candy to make you even sweeter." I suspect that David's looks had granted us unfair access to many a Northern Alliance frontline encampment.

But showing up in Imam Sahib with Bulbul-e-Afghan two weeks after the fall of the Taliban was a different story.

Have I mentioned that the Taliban had banned music?

I was trying to estimate how long Mahmoud, with his single gun, would be able to hold off a raid on our hotel by a posse of Islamic fundamentalists when I learned that hiring a security guard did not necessarily mean he was going to protect me. Mahmoud walked into my hotel room (free continental breakfast; panoramic view of war rubble; bring-your-own-satellite-phone Internet access; two twin-size mattresses on the floor; a greasy, fume-spewing kerosene stove made of unevenly soldered iron in lieu of a fireplace; handheld plastic ewers and buckets of freshly boiled water in lieu of a shower; a shared, squat-over toilet down the hall; and very affordable lamb kebab room service during the day), leaned his Kalashnikov against the concrete wall, and announced that he was going shopping.

"Shoot anyone who tries to come in," he advised, and headed to the bazaar, leaving me alone with my new semiautomatic assault rifle. After a couple of hours, most of which I spent puzzling over how to take the safety off the damn thing without accidentally shooting myself in the head, Mahmoud returned bearing a tray of delicious green raisins and freshly baked bread. Supper!

We picked up Nik Mohammed, our next bodyguard, in the shadow of Mazar-e-Sharif's fabled Blue Mosque, the fifteenth-century shrine and a reputed final resting place of Prophet Mohammed's cousin and son-in-law, Hazrat Ali. One legend says that Ali, who was assassinated in the year 661 by a poisoned sword while praying a hundred miles south of Baghdad, was originally buried in Iraq, but then his supporters, worried that his body would be desecrated, unearthed his remains and sent them east on the back of a trusted she-camel. After journeying thirteen hundred miles across deserts and mountains of modern-day Iraq and Iran, the camel allegedly fell, exhausted, in this northern Afghan city, and Ali was reburied here. (Iraqi Muslims dispute this tale of exhumation, and insist that Ali's remains still rest in the holy city of Najaf.) Some also believe that the shrine is built atop the tomb of Zarathustra. Ten thousand white pigeons flock to the shrine's tiles, which bloom with intricate flowers in cobalt, ocher, and turquoise; the locals say the site is so holy that, should a gray pigeon join the flock, it will become completely white in forty days. The shrine gave the city its name: "*mazar-e-sharif*" means "tomb of the saint" in Persian.

We didn't so much hire Nik as a local commander informed us that he would not allow us to leave his city without this bodyguard he had personally chosen for us. The commander also explained that we would have to pay him, up front, the five hundred dollars for the bodyguard's services. Then he introduced us to the scrawny, balding man wearing oversize military fatigues and lugging a rifle that looked like no one had fired it since Afghanistan was a British protectorate.

Nik was silent through the introductions; he did not look excited about the prospect of accompanying us any more than we were thrilled at having this brooding, feeble-looking man as our security guard. Looks can be deceiving, I told myself as I shelled out the cash and handed it to Nik's boss. For all I knew, Nik could have been the second coming of Ahmad Shah Massoud, the slain anti-Taliban commander whose fabled courage in fighting first the Soviets, and then the Taliban, had earned him the nickname "Sher-e-Panjshir," "the Panjshir Lion." (A suicide bomber posing as a reporter killed Massoud on September 9, 2001, two days before al Qaeda attacked the United States.) Then we all piled in the car (David, Nik, and I in the back, with David in the middle), and our new bodyguard finally spoke.

"Which guarantees can you give me," he asked, "if highway robbers take my gun?"

Something must have been lost in translation. I asked the interpreter to request that Nik repeat his question. That didn't help.

"Who's going to pay for the gun if bandits take it from me?" Nik asked.

If the bandits took his gun, we would be too dead to reimburse him,

David explained. That notion saddened our bodyguard. He pulled his knees up to his chin, rested the muzzle of his rifle against the window, put his head on David's shoulder, and promptly fell asleep. He did not speak for the remainder of our trip together.

The road to Kabul lay through heavily mined wastelands, gorges reigned by bandits, and the Salang Tunnel: at 11,000 feet above sea level, one of the highest in the world. Today, the tunnel, which straddles the country's principal north-south artery, carries daily car and truck traffic, as Soviet engineers had intended in 1964, when they carved the serpentine, mile-and-a-half-long engineering marvel into the Hindu Kush. But in the fall of 2001, the first time I traveled through Salang, the wreckage of the tunnel and the galleries chiseled into the mountainside immediately to the north and south of it represented the greatest monument, both in its size and in the scale of devastation, to Massoud, the esteemed mujahedin leader and hero.

Massoud had made it his trademark to blow up bridges, mountain passes, and tunnels along the front line to keep the Taliban from entering his stronghold in Afghanistan's eastern Panjshir Valley. (One Afghan joke tells of Mullah Omar praying that Allah lets him die before Massoud. When his friends ask why he would come up with such a strange wish, Mullah Omar explains that if Massoud dies first, he would blow up the Sirat Bridge—which, according to the Koran, spans the fire of hell and leads to the entrance to heaven—barring the Taliban leader forever from entering the shaded gardens of paradise.) Salang was an awe-inspiring masterpiece of Massoud's strategic genius.

The damage to the tunnel forced travelers headed south toward Kabul to leave their cars about a mile from the tunnel's northern end, where paved road ended in an enormous crater filled with a muddy soup of snowmelt, engine oil, and the dung of saddle mules and donkeys. Porters swarmed the parking lot, offering to carry travelers' bags through the pass for one or two dollars per piece of luggage. We sent Nik Mohammed back to Mazar-e-Sharif along with the car—he didn't look like he would have been able to survive the four-hour trek that lay ahead. Besides, once we got inside the tunnel, we definitely could not guarantee his gun's safety: while our translator was negotiating a price with our future porters, we overheard a group of men in the parking lot saying: "Here comes a foreigner. Let's rob him and kill him." Nik looked relieved when we said good-bye. Then we proceeded to traipse through icy high-altitude slush, away from the parking lot and into the gaping black void of the tunnel. Enormous slabs of blown-up concrete blocked the road, foreshadowing the havoc contained within.

The walk through the tunnel was grueling and terrifying. In pitch-black darkness, the passage grabbed onto travelers' clothes with jagged steel rods that stuck out of every surface and slashed our faces with sharp pieces of metal pipe dangling from the ceiling. Shrapnel and debris from the aerial bombs Massoud had detonated inside the tunnel barely reflected the meager glow of our flashlights, the only source of light. Unexploded rockets and mortars lay in wait somewhere beneath tons of concrete rubble. There seemed to be no flat surface anywhere at all, and no ventilation. In one spot, a group of porters had started a small fire to keep warm, choking everyone in bitter smoke. Halfway through the tunnel, David, who was walking in front of me, tripped and fell face-down, steadying himself with his arms at an awkward, twenty-degree angle to the ground. When I caught up with him, my flashlight illuminated a steel rod pointing at his chest. The rod's sharp tip was less than an inch from David's heart.

On the other side of the tunnel, Wahid, who had been translating for a succession of *Globe* reporters in Kabul, was waiting for us with the driver, Yarmohammad, in the beige Toyota minivan. In the car there was also a plastic bag full of food *Globe* reporter Lynda Gorov had put together for us: flatbread sandwiches with pasteurized Laughing Cow cheese and tomatoes, a thermos of hot tea, sugar-coated almonds. A montane homecoming feast.

But by the time I arrived in Kabul, three hours later, it became clear that I was not staying there long. Outside Jalalabad, American forces were trying to roust bin Laden from the caves of Tora Bora. I had to get to Spin Ghar, and the only way to get there was to break the Death Road rule.

David and I hired an enterprising young man to provide our security from Kabul to Jalalabad. I never caught the man's real name. We nicknamed him Prince, for his short stature, perfectly coiffed hair, and skinny jeans adorned with an enormous Playboy bunny belt buckle. We met Prince at the Kabul residence of our friends from *USA Today*: a spacious, two-story house that clung to the side of one of the mountains cupping the Kabul Valley. From here, the city looked like an ocher, indented beehive.

Prince immediately established his authority by unceremoniously dipping his hands into the bowl of unwrapped sugar candy set on our colleagues' long, polished dining table. He spoke English like a gangster, sputtering endearing comments such as "Shut up, woman, I'm in charge here," and "Listen to me if you wanna live."

We wanted to live, so we listened. Prince set the rules: we were to pay the money up front; we were not to be late; we were to make sure that our car tires were in order and that the car had an extra canister of fuel in the trunk. The price for this ninety-mile, one-way journey? Two thousand dollars, which seemed like a lot until we saw what we had purchased. The morning of our departure, Prince showed up outside our Kabul compound with a pickup truck full of young men carrying one heavy machine gun, several rifles (one or two for each man), three or four handguns, and three bouquets of rocket-propelled grenade launchers. Prince's crew had enough weapons to take and hold a small village for a few days.

When we set off, however, I realized that if they were going to take and hold a small village, they were going to do so without us. Our bodyguards spent most of the trip speeding out of our sight on the once-upon-a-time paved road that curved along the tempestuous Kabul River; when we would finally catch up with them, they would yell at our driver for not being able to squeeze out more miles per hour from his family-friendly minivan. As soon as we reached the Jalalabad city limits, Prince's men took off. They were ethnic Tajiks, and they did not feel comfortable in an almost exclusively Pashtun city, which was full of gunmen of its own. Our guards had not warned us about that wrinkle when they took the two grand. Prince, how could you just leave us standing alone in a world so cold?

Spin Ghar—White Mountain in Pashto*—is the name of the 15,000-foot-high mountain range that forms a natural frontier between Afghanistan and Pakistan and is straddled by the Khyber Pass: a blood-stained "sword cut through the mountains," in Kipling's words. It is also the name of the first Western-style Afghan hotel I had stayed in: a spacious, Soviet-era affair on Jalalabad's main road, with a check-in counter, laundry service, a restaurant, and furniture. Like the mountain range, the hotel came with its own fleet of anti-Taliban gunmen. Now that the regime they had been fighting had been deposed and Washington had sent American ground troops to scour Tora Bora's caves for surviving al Qaeda fighters, the mujahedin were largely unemployed, and spent most of their time playing chess and smoking hashish in an overgrown and neglected peach orchard outside the hotel's hushed foyer. Most major business operations in Afghanistan's wartime economy were owned by local warlords, and the Spin Ghar Hotel was no exception. Like his counterpart in Mazar-e-Sharif, Spin Ghar's warlord-cum-manager was using the fighters to bring in some extra revenue.

As soon as we checked in, we were told to pick a gunman. Several strung out young men in plastic flip-flops shuffled unenthusiastically toward us across the cement floor tiles of the foyer.

"Take this one here," suggested the uniformed commando behind the counter, pointing out a hauntingly beautiful gunman with a wild reddish-black beard. A grey *paqul* hat crowned this man's long, matted, almost dreadlocked hair. He looked to be in his mid-twenties. He was talking to himself. The gunman would follow us on all of our trips outside the hotel, "for safety," explained the commando, who had draped a bandolier with machine-gun bullets around his neck and over a shoulder, like a wartime boa. The price was twenty bucks a day. I did not ask how much of that the gunman would keep. The young fighter scowled. He looked deranged. This was Najibullah.

For the next several days, Najibullah rode shotgun (or should I say,

---

*Pashto—like Dari, one of the two official languages of Afghanistan. It is spoken by Pashtuns, Afghanistan's largest ethnic group. Pashto is also spoken in the tribal lands of western Pakistan.

semiautomatic rifle?) in the front passenger seat of our minivan. From the point of view of security, his presence was largely decorative: the first time he climbed into our car he confided in Wahid that he would not risk his pinkie for us if things got heated (Wahid translated this; I was not sure if I should have been happy I knew). Nonetheless, no one was particularly displeased with the arrangement.

Najibullah got whatever his commander allowed him to keep of our daily payments, which was more than he had ever been paid to go to war, since in Afghanistan, rank-and-file rebels usually fought for free. In return, he sang in the car; graced us with his gorgeous smile whenever he got high, which was most of the time; and offered us something we, as journalists, valued far more than the bullets in his battle-worn Kalashnikov: a guided tour of the complicated alliances and intertwined histories of the people who lived around Tora Bora, and an insight into the hardships and the troubled mind of one proxy foot soldier of America's war against terror.

Najibullah first fought against the Soviet invaders in the mid- and late 1980s. That was when he met bin Laden, who, at the time, was importing foreign fighters and weapons to Afghan mujahedin under CIA supervision and funding. Of the Saudi terrorist, Najibullah only remembered that he was a "fearless fighter" and "America's agent" (undisputed facts, both of them). In Dara-e-Nur, Najibullah's hometown, about an hour north of Jalalabad, he showed us one of the caves where he and bin Laden had once stayed and fought together: an unassuming, truck-size fissure in the mountainside sandstone deposit. The cave bore no sign of any kind of recent presence, offered no insight into the life of the man who had killed David's father. There weren't even sheep droppings on the ground. No one had used it for ages.

"We had no idea he would turn into a terrorist," Najibullah said, shrugging. Neither, presumably, had the CIA.

Then again, how do we tell freedom fighters (what we called rebels in Afghanistan, including bin Laden, when they were waging war against the Soviet Union) from terrorists (what we called the very same rebels in Afghanistan when they began to wage war against the United States)? Were the members of the armed uprising in Chechnya freedom fighters who rose up against Russia or terrorists if, supported by international Islamist groups seeking to establish a caliphate that would stretch from the Pacific to the Atlantic, they soon took the fight for their freedom beyond the borders of their nation? And what about the Shiite militias in Iraq, who hailed the defeat of Saddam Hussein in the spring of 2003, but by that fall had begun to take up arms against American forces, whom they viewed as occupiers and apostates?

And what was Najibullah, who had fought first with bin Laden, then against him, but always for the cause of Islamic jihad? A broken man, a suffering man who knew no peace. In 1992, Najibullah briefly became an Islamic mercenary in the former Soviet republic of Azerbaijan, which is mostly Muslim, joining a jihad against Christian Armenian troops over the disputed enclave of Nagorno-Karabakh. His recruiters had told him that the Armenians he would be fighting were backed by the Russians; he had remembered, from the eighties, that fighting the Russians was a good thing. Besides, he was broke. He fought for a month, but never was paid. Frustrated, he returned to his homeland and got married. Peaceful life did not last long. Soon, the Taliban came to power and imprisoned Najibullah because he, during the skirmishes that had followed the Soviet occupation, had fought alongside Ahmad Shah Massoud, who had since gone on to become an anti-Taliban rebel leader.

In the Taliban prison, Najibullah's captors flogged him daily on his head, neck, and chest for a month. They released him after his family sold part of its land to pay a chunk of a seventeen-hundred-dollar bribe (the rest of the money—twelve hundred dollars—Najibullah still owed to neighbors and friends when we met). When Najibullah got out of prison, he decided that the only way to protect himself was to go back to war.

For five years, Najibullah had fought against the Taliban and his former comrade-in-arms, bin Laden. For the last fifteen days and nights of that war, in November and early December 2001, he and a group of fellow mujahedin had shivered in an unheated barn on a snowed-in plateau in the Spin Ghar. They had clutched their rifles with bluing fingers and waited for the order to mount an offensive against al Qaeda guerrillas holed up in a heavily fortified command center on the other side of a narrow valley.

The order never came. Instead, the men were ordered to wait for American bombs to flush out bin Laden's men so that the mujahedin could then kill them on the white cold coulee floor.

Najibullah had stayed awake the entire time. He was afraid that al Qaeda fighters would kill him while he slept. He and other rebels smoked cigarettes and hashish. When the planes finally dropped their payload on the command center, the explosion was so powerful that the shock wave injured several of Najibullah's comrades.

When the smoke cleared, the mujahedin found among the wreckage scores of al Qaeda fighters and their wives and children, all dead.

I met Najibullah four days after that. Around us, Jalalabad and its suburbs appeared to be blooming, as if awakening after a long winter. Women in sky blue, mustard yellow, and olive green burqas, finally allowed to walk to the market unaccompanied by male relatives, haggled through the thick mesh covering their faces—the only aperture in their full-length cloaks—over the price of mutton and small, locally grown bananas. Bollywood show tunes, which had been illegal just a week earlier, seemed to blare from every rolled-down car window. (Pashto speakers can somewhat comprehend Hindi, which explains, to a certain extent, the bizarre popularity of the overly romantic pop tunes in this seemingly unsentimental, bombed-out place.) Trucks painted with colorful, dreamy scenes of cool turquoise mountain lakes and lush emerald and fuchsia orchards, and decked out in truck-size crocheted iron necklaces, rattled up and down mountain roads. Rickshaws on pink, baby blue, and orange motorbikes zipped through crowded markets, where old, stooping *jelebi* vendors competed for customers with boys selling juicy chunks of freshly cut sugar cane.

Najibullah found it difficult to fit in amid this jubilant revival of color and sound. He had insomnia. He felt restless. He self-medicated; it did not help. The notion of going home to his wife and three small children made him depressed. Images of the devastation he had witnessed haunted him, particularly the recent memory of al Qaeda wives and children trampled like dead flowers into the mountain snow.

So did the persistent thought that he had squandered his life in the vicious cycle of jihad.

"This war has gotten the better of me," he lamented, wiping *jelebi* syrup off his fingers on his shirt, popping another Valium (which Afghanistan's pharmacies sold over the counter), and folding his slender hands over the barrel of his rifle. "Even before I grew up, I started fighting. I've seen people murdered. I've seen mothers widowed. I am not normal. I have a mental problem. I have not had a single happy day in my poor life. I am sad all the time."

Like most Afghan fighters—indeed, like most Afghans—Najibullah could not read or write. His only training was in guerrilla warfare. His only skills were in staking out the enemy in the rugged mountains along the Pakistan border, surviving without sleep in snow-swept caves and bombed-out houses, and watching his friends get killed.

And his only stable income came from the finger-thin spiraling rows of poppy flowers his wife, the bony-faced Begham, tended on a slope beneath their family compound.

Seven months a year Begham would rise before dawn to pull weeds from the fields until sunset; after the harvest, she would dry the seedpods, overflowing with opium resin, under the hot mountain sun. The work, she told me, was backbreaking. Every June, Pakistani drug dealers would pay her twenty-four hundred dollars for her plot's annual crop of ninety pounds of dried seedpods, and still that was not enough money to feed her children and ailing father, repair the rickety house that a Taliban rocket had partially flattened in the 1990s, and pay off Najibullah's debt to friends who had bailed him out of prison.

I had dated a heroin addict once. I had been sixteen, seventeen, and many of my friends from that time—artists, musicians, poets, some talented, some not, many just hangers-on—had since died: of overdose, of kidney failure, of blood-borne diseases they had passed on to each other in needles carelessly shared in soiled doorways. How ironic, I thought, that heroin should begin its journey to the veins of the people I had known and loved, and to the artists' colonies, ghettos, and university campuses of Europe and the United States, in this decrepit, unhappy family farm of a fighter on whom the Pentagon had relied to help defeat the Taliban—and whom I was paying to protect me.*

Najibullah saw no irony there.

"We know that opium has a bad effect, causes great grief in the West," he said. "But look around! Everybody is growing it to live."

Crisscrossed by slippery stone paths, the neatly furrowed poppy fields of Najibullah's family and his neighbors cascaded down from his mountainside house to terraced valleys below, as far as the eye could see. Tufts of fog clung to the illicit harvest; in the distance, leaden thunderclouds gathered over the war-wracked Spin Ghar. The view was the epitome of all Afghan landscapes—indeed, of most places I have traveled that were shattered by conflict: tragedy and misery may have been sown in those fields, and yet the scenery was dizzyingly beautiful. Suddenly, Najibullah balanced his Kalashnikov on his left shoulder and began to sway his sinewy body, humming a Bollywood tune we had heard in the car on our drive to his house. His thin arms flew up like wings, his fingertips pinched together and waved this way and that, like poppy-flower petals, opening and closing, pointing, keeping time. His eyes were shut and he was smiling: a warrior at peace, at least for the moment.

I watched Najibullah dance above his wife's opium fields. His graceful movements mesmerized me. And I thought that I, too, would not want him to risk for me those pinkies that could dance so well.

———

He didn't.

When the time came for us to leave Jalalabad, the commando at the hotel reception desk selected four somber mujahedin from the chess-playing crowd outside the foyer to accompany us, alongside Najibullah, on our return trip on the Death Road to Kabul. I agreed to pay a hundred dollars to each security guard, payable upon our arrival at the capital. We set out at dawn, they in a pickup truck, we in Yarmohammad's vener-

---

*In fact, after the fall of the Taliban regime, poppy production in Afghanistan skyrocketed. In 2001, 75 percent of the world's supply of heroin came from Afghanistan; by 2009, according to the Brookings Institution in Washington, the number had jumped to 93 percent.

able Toyota minivan. As we took off, David and I gloated over the mark-down from Prince's exorbitant fee for the one-way trip to Jalalabad.

Right around the spot where the four journalists had been murdered a month earlier, our armed escort pulled over outside a rest stop: a cin-der-block roof stacked on top of three cinder-block walls with smoke coming out of a pit in the back, a local take on a 7-Eleven. The gunmen announced it was time to get lunch.

We protested that we did not want to stop. We said we were not hun-gry. We pleaded with them to keep driving. We offered them candy and crackers from our personal stash of food. The guards were unmoved.

"Ramadan is over," said their leader. "We are not fasting. We are going to have lunch. You can wait for us in the car if you want."

David and I sat in the back of the Toyota for the better part of an hour. Like a lot of Afghan vehicles, this van came with cotton curtains strung up on its windows; we closed them. I was nauseous with fear. To comfort me, and to help pass the time, David started a game: we would come up with ideas for flashing neon signs we should have put on the minivan before we left Jalalabad.

"Taliban Bait Here," David proposed.

"ATM on Wheels," I shot back. "Wealthy Infidels."

And for the 7-Eleven: "Al Ambush Rest Stop," "Dead Foreigner Tavern."

It was tasteless, gallows humor. But making light of dark circum-stances is another secret to how war reporters get by. This morbid en-tertainment lasted until our escort finally reappeared from the rest stop.

A mile outside Pul-e-Charkhi, the checkpoint at the eastern entrance to Kabul, our guards pulled over again. Like Prince and his Tajik gun-men before them, these Pashtun fighters did not want to cross into the territory of another ethnic group. The leader of the guards strolled over to our car, motioned for me to roll down my window, and gestured that it was time to pay. I handed him five hundred dollars. The fighter counted the money, folded it, put it in the chest pocket of his long shirt.

Then, with a metallic clang that sounded like one of the last things I was ever going to hear, he loaded a bullet in the chamber of his Kalash-nikov and pointed the gun at me.

"Baksheesh," he said. In this particular case, the universal phrase translated as "highway robbery." The gunman showed on his fingers that he wanted another hundred-dollar bill.

I looked beyond the gunman, at Najibullah. My beautiful friend appeared absent, not paying attention to the shakedown scene. His body swayed to a rhythm I could not discern, his fingers tentatively fluttered in the air. I thought I could hear him hum a song in a falsetto. He must have been stoned.

Just give him the fucking money, instructed the quiet voice of reason inside my head. Or maybe it was David.

"No way," I said to the gunman at the car window. Suddenly, I felt angry: at this man, for putting us through the scariest forty minutes of my month in Afghanistan while he and his men were having lunch; at Najibullah, for making true on his promise not to risk his pinkie for my life; at myself, for having foolishly thought that giving money to gunmen meant I was being protected, and trusting my life to rent-a-guards who had transformed into highway robbers. For trying to tell the story of this unforgiving land and its people who—this is what I believed at that moment—couldn't care less whether I lived or perished on the Grand Trunk Road.

Anger is a dangerous sentiment anywhere because it can consume you with such ease. But in a war zone, where emotions run high all the time and the trigger is always pressing up against somebody's forefinger, anger can spell your undoing in no time. This is a truth about war that I, at that particular moment, had chosen to ignore.

Forgetting that this was a good way to become, eponymously, dead on the Death Road, I wagged my finger at the gunman, and said in my best schoolmarm voice: "I'm going to call your commander and complain."

We all knew, of course, that there was no telephone at the Spin Ghar Hotel. There were no working telephones anywhere in the country.

"Baksheesh," the gunman repeated. His gun advanced through the window. I studied it. Bright pink, yellow, and blue Pakistani candy-bar wrappers, wrappers from Hubba Bubba bubble gum, and Donald Duck gum comics screamed at me from the barrel. The fighter had glued them onto the metal to beautify his weapon. A Kalashnikov barrel heats up very quickly when the rifle is fired, but the candy wrappers bore no sign of charring. This gun had not been fired since the wrappers went on, which, judging by the yellowing epoxy that coated them to hold them in place, had been a long time ago. Was I really going to be the first victim of this candy-wrapped Kalashnikov?

The next scene was straight out of a Hollywood western, if you can picture O.K. Corral transplanted into arid Central Asian foothills. A group of Northern Alliance soldiers—Tajiks—appeared out of nowhere, pointed their guns at our guards-turned-bandits, and told them to leave us alone and clear out. I had been wrong: here were complete strangers who were not going to let us die. Without a word, the Pashtun fighters got into their pickup truck and drove off. The Tajiks waved at us to drive on and left, too. The whole episode took less than a minute. Najibullah didn't come up to say good-bye.

I never saw him again.

Jelebi

Serves 10

Upscale Afghan cuisine has adopted a lot of British and Indian desserts—divinely delicate flans, rice puddings flavored with rose water. But in most poor Afghan towns and villages, the dessert I ate most commonly consisted of sugar-coated almonds, green raisins, and caramels imported from Iran. *Jelebi* was the first locally prepared sweet dish ordinary Afghans ate that I had tried; it is popular in Afghanistan, Pakistan, and parts of India. It's supersweet, and probably should be served with a glass of milk or unsweetened hot tea. *Jelebi* is supposed to be eaten so hot it burns the roof of your mouth (which kind of goes against the idea of something that is supposed to be a treat, but that's life in a war zone, I suppose), but in Jalalabad, our crew would often buy a couple of pounds of the rings, put them in a big plastic bag, and then pick at them during our long daily drives around the violet and yellow filigree of mountain roads, listening to Najibullah's war stories and laments, sound tracks to Indian movies, and distant explosions of American ordnance outside Tora Bora.

2 cups all-purpose flour
½ teaspoon baking powder
1 cup plain nonfat yogurt (any kind will do)
2 cups sugar
1 stick cinnamon
Sunflower or canola oil or ghee, for deep frying
A plastic bottle for squeezing out dough, like a
    clean ketchup or mustard bottle

1. Make the dough: Mix the flour, baking powder, and yogurt together into a batter and set aside for 24 hours to ferment at room temperature.

2. Make the syrup: Combine the sugar with ½ cup water and cinnamon in a small saucepan and boil for several minutes. The syrup is the right consistency when, as you carefully dip the tip of your index finger into the syrup (don't burn yourself!), touch it to your thumb, and gently pull them apart, a thread is formed between the finger and thumb. Remove the cinnamon stick. Keep warm.

3. Heat the oil or melt the ghee in a wok-type deep frying pan. Drop a tiny bit of batter in; if the batter sizzles and rises to the top, the oil is hot enough. Pour the batter into the plastic bottle. Squeeze the batter into the oil in circles, 4–5 inches in diameter, several at a time. Try to keep them from touching when you pour them. When the rings are golden, move them from the oil into the syrup with a slotted spoon. Let them soak in the syrup for 2 or 3 minutes, then remove and stack them in a pyramid or arrange them on a plate.

↜

Baklava

Serves 10

*I*f you cannot conceive of consuming that much deep-fried sugar, this one is for you. It is a popular treat from Greece to Afghanistan; my favorite baklava comes from Palestinian shops in Jordan. If you have leftovers, refrigerate them; baklava is delicious cold.

Note: Defrost the phyllo dough in its plastic packaging. Do not remove the plastic until all the other ingredients and the baking pan are ready. Otherwise, the phyllo will dry out and crumble.

2 sticks unsalted butter or margarine
8 ounces walnuts or pistachio nuts, shelled and crushed
(put them in a Ziploc bag and crush them with a rolling pin)
1 cup sugar, white or light brown
1 teaspoon ground cinnamon
8 ounces phyllo (fillo, depending on who's selling) sheets
½ cup honey

For the syrup:
1 cup sugar
1 stick cinnamon

1. Preheat the oven to 350°F.
2. Melt the butter. Mix the crushed nuts with the sugar and cinnamon. Open the package of phyllo. If necessary, cut the sheets in half so that each sheet fits the bottom of the baking pan (this depends on the size of your baking pan. I use a 9 by 14-inch pan). Generously butter the bottom and sides of the pan and place the dough, 1 sheet at a time, in the pan. Generously spread butter all over each sheet of phyllo as it is placed in the pan. Every 6 to 8 sheets of phyllo, spread a layer of the nut and sugar mixture on the dough. Pour some honey on every 4 to 6 sheets. Continue layering phyllo sheets and nuts until there is no more dough. Pour any remaining butter over the top of the baklava. The secret to good flaky baklava is to have each sheet of dough well buttered so that the sheets do not stick together.
3. Cut the baklava diagonally to form diamond-shaped pieces. Bake for 35 to 45 minutes, or until golden brown on top.
4. In the meantime, prepare the syrup: Combine the sugar and cinnamon with 6 tablespoons water in a small saucepan and boil for about 5 minutes. Remove the baklava from the oven and pour the syrup over it. In about 10 minutes, take the baklava out of the baking pan, gently separating the pieces, and arrange on a serving plate. Serve at room temperature or cold.

Five

Dumplings at Café Titanic

O ne snapshot in my photo album baffles me for a few seconds each time I stumble upon it. It shows a woman in a blue burqa standing next to four men beneath a white, overcast sky, with the backdrop of an empty clothesline and a single leafless tree. I recognize the men right away: one of my Afghan translators, Beijan; Yarmohammad, who drove me to the fringes of the Battle for Tora Bora; and Mullah and Zabi, the cook and the guard who worked at the guesthouse in Kabul where I stayed in 2001 and 2002. Whenever I see the snapshot I wonder why it ended up in the album. It has no artistic value whatsoever; it depicts no remarkable activity that I can see; and for the life of me I do not remember who that woman is or why she is in the picture.

Just as I am about to yank the photograph out of the album and relegate it to some spider-infested cardboard box in the basement, I realize—wait!

I know who that woman is.

She is me.

When the United States went to war in Afghanistan, one popular misconception was that the Taliban was single-handedly responsible for the subjugation of Afghan women. Among the rallying cries for those who supported the war in 2001 was that the United States would "liberate" Afghan women and girls. Everyone knew that during the five years it had ruled Afghanistan, the Taliban had officially excluded women from public life, banned them from attending schools and public baths, regulated what kind of shoes they could wear, ordered them to cover their faces and bodies in the presence of strangers, prohibited them from appearing in public without the escort of a male relative, and created the infamous Police for the Protection of Virtue and the Prevention of Vice to implement these rules and subject to public beatings (or, in some cases, execute) the women who dared disobey. Many Westerners assumed that after the Islamic government fell, Afghan women would immediately swap their burqas for Converse shoes and bikinis and throw keg parties in the streets of Kabul. After the Taliban had been banished—at least for the time being—to the tribal highlands of western Pakistan, I returned to Afghanistan to write about what had changed, and what had not, for the country's women.

Afghan men did immediately busy themselves shaking off the legacy of the oppressive regime and rebuilding a boisterous lifestyle. The government that had ordered all men to wear beards was gone, and now barbers were sharpening their straight razors on leather belts in crowded squares. Their freshly clean-shaven clients clogged city bazaars, selling and buying another formerly forbidden commodity: bootleg videos of Western films and cassettes of Bollywood songs and tunes by the legendary Afghan singer Ahmad Zahir (the Nightingale of Afghanistan, who looked like David). Male shoppers, some wearing jeans and Westen shirts, reveled in the cacophonous combination of Britney Spears and South Asian pop music that blasted out of car windows, restaurants, and shops without fear that the Taliban's virtue police would jail them for their impious behavior and appearance.

In short, the end of the Taliban spelled freedom for the Afghan man.

But for the Afghan woman, freedom remained as much of a pipe dream as manicured golf courses in downtown Kandahar and Swiss-style ski resorts in the Hindu Kush. Much of the Afghan society had for centuries based its attitudes toward woman around the conservative notions of shariah, the Islamic law that sets distinct boundaries for women in public life. The Taliban may have been gone, but parents continued to sell their daughters to future husbands. Husbands continued to prohibit their wives from showing their faces, let alone talking, to strange men. Nargiz, the younger wife of Mahbuhbullah the Tomb Raider, my host in northern Afghanistan, had told me during our first meeting, in October 2001, that she hated wearing the burqa. (She also told me she hated being the second wife.) Even though she had lived in a part of the country where the Taliban had never set foot—and what she wore was dictated by Dasht-e-Qal'eh's rural mores, and not by the government in Kabul—she had somehow tied her hopes of taking off the covering to the fall of the regime. Three months after the Taliban was no longer in power, Nargiz continued to wear the sky blue sack designed to conceal every part of her body except for her feet, fittingly made of a synthetic fabric that seemed designed to trap heat in the Afghan sun.

To find out what it was like to be a faceless, faux-silk silhouette, I decided to wear one for a day. I dispatched Wahid, my interpreter and guide, to a Kabul bazaar (buying a burqa is a man's job in Afghanistan), and he returned with an embroidered, pale blue nylon covering with a tiny rectangle of mesh in the front.

Along with the burqa, Wahid also delivered my first compliment of the day. As soon as I put on the garment, he smacked his lips and said:

"Nice!"

It was the best burqa comment I had heard for only a moment, because Beijan, the other translator, piped up:

"You look better in a burqa than without."

In an attempt to lighten things up—perhaps a lifetime of looking women in the mesh and finding the right words had taught him that Beijan's comment was not exactly what one would call flattering—the gray-haired Mullah the Cook offered this consolation:

"The burqa is your size."

Indeed, how does one compliment a woman in a burqa? Say that it matches her eyes?

"It matches your eyes," David, ever the gentleman, pitched in.

The burqa was uncomfortable. Loose threads on the inside—from the embroidery—tickled my nose and made me sneeze. The ribbon on the top intended to keep the garment on my head was too tight and hurt my forehead (dear Mullah: I appreciate the compliment, but maybe it wasn't my size after all). The mesh in front was at the level of my eyebrows rather than my eyes, so I could not see anything that was not directly in front of me and level with my head or higher. I had to feel my way down the stairs, prompting this delighted remark from Zabi:

"She can't walk!"

To prove the guard wrong, and to demonstrate that I could be perfectly agile in my new getup, I rushed—and banged my forehead against the metal gate of the compound, like a blindfolded slapstick character in an old silent film. On the other side of the gate, I immediately slipped in the mud. Salvation would finally come when I got into our car, I hoped, but as I was crossing the street, a flatbed truck I had not noticed (because I could not see through the mesh) nearly ran me over.

When I reached the car, the tail of my burqa got caught on the door handle as I was trying to climb into the backseat. I wanted to smoke—I could think of no better rebellion from within my polyester prison—but decided against it. The burqa definitely was not a flame-retardant garment. If it ever caught fire, it would probably burn like a torch.

We were on our way to Wahid's house. Our translator's family had invited us for a lunch of *mantwo*, my favorite Afghan dish—giant, spicy meat dumplings served with garlicky yogurt, tomato sauce, and yellow peas. I was hoping to ask Wahid's mother and two sisters for tips on how to cope with the burqa. But first, we had to stop at a photo shop in Kabul's downtown Karte Parwan neighborhood to pick up some film. The owner overheard me explaining to Wahid, in English, which film to buy. The merchant was pleased.

"Finally," he said, "even the foreigners have come to understand that a burqa is the best thing for a woman."

During that trip, David shared with me his favorite wisdom about war zones: most people you meet want to take you in, share their food with you, tell you their stories, put you up for the night, and send you on your way a happier person than you were before you met them.

It is true. The fact that most people want to help, rather than harm, is what allows war correspondents to return to conflict zones, again and again, despite being unarmed, mostly ignorant of local language and culture, only superfluously familiar with the geography and the politics of each new place, and famously loaded with cash and therefore an easy target for scorn and robbery.

But, as much as people in Afghanistan wanted to render assistance, some had trouble conveying their desire to help. While they did give me a new appreciation for an alternative use of bright candy wrappers, the bodyguards who had tried to rob me at gunpoint outside Pul-e-Charkhi had had an undermining effect vis-à-vis my faith in the benevolence of strangers in war zones—so much so that after that incident, I decided that it was safer not to pay for any more security.

After that decision, our entourage began to disintegrate. The driver, Yarmohammad, said he could not drive us all the way to the Tajik border, citing some urgent maintenance that needed to be done on his Toyota minivan, an ill grandmother, and a terminally impassable, snow-clogged mountain road that lay ahead. (I surmised that the real reason he quit was that my reckless attempt to negotiate at gunpoint with guards-turned-highway-robbers had disturbed him, but that his polite manners and impeccable sense of Afghan hospitality prevented him from bringing it up. Either way, I couldn't hold it against him.) Yarmohammad delivered us to the soot-black yawn of the Salang Tunnel, and drove back to Kabul.

During the time we had spent in Kabul and Jalalabad, international contractors had cleaned up the tunnel quite a bit. Gone was the perilous jumble of concrete rubble, sharp steel rods, and fragments of exploded bombs. The tunnel had not yet opened for transport, and its depths were still pitch-black, but compared to our southward journey through it two weeks earlier, our three-hour trek north was less of a potentially life-ending experience and more of a walk in a very cold, very dark park at nosebleed altitude.

At the parking lot outside the tunnel's northern end (no sign of the porters who had so animatedly discussed taking our money and throwing us over the five-hundred-foot abyss during our trip south—they had vanished with the war debris), we hired a different driver. I don't remember that we ever learned his name. He said very little as he sped us toward Afghanistan's northern boundary, past abandoned and gutted Soviet tanks training their forevermore silent cannons at distant hilltops, past toddlers with careworn faces clinging to the blue burqas of their mothers, past men bent with age and hard labor ambling next to donkey-pulled carts laden with kindling.

The road back to the Tajik border, where that auspicious old ferry would float us out of Afghanistan, lay through Taloqan—the very same Afghan town on a dusty plateau in the northern foothills of the Hindu Kush where the Swedish television journalist Ulf Strömberg had been murdered on the first day of this trip, prompting our initial decision to hire bodyguards. On a Taloqan street corner across from the bazaar, a group of former Taliban fighters in dark turbans stood, talking with visible excitement. The driver pulled into a deserted side street nearby, and stopped the car. He opened the trunk and unloaded our bags onto the cold ground in silence. Then he announced that he was going back south, and sped off.

We must have looked really confused, so Wahid patiently explained that the driver had left in such a hurry because he had thought the place was creepy. We had to agree that it was a good instinct. We, too, wanted to get the hell out of Taloqan. So we dispatched Wahid to the bazaar to find a different driver while we guarded our bags full of computers and satellite equipment. For extra protection, David and I each had a copy of a pale green pocket English-Dari dictionary printed in Kabul in 1965 by one S. Sakaria, who I am sure was, or is, a top-notch linguist and scholar. The dictionaries, among other things, instructed us how to pronounce in Dari such crucial expressions as "My husband is very ill," "I see two donkeys," "Thou wentest" (I kid you not), and, perhaps the most useful

of all, "Are you a camel?" Just imagining what it would be like to wander
up to a mujahedin armed to the teeth with 7.62 rounds—to say nothing
of a recently pacified Taliban chieftain—and bounce that one off him
generated enough mirth to last the whole afternoon.

An hour went by, then two. There was no sign of Wahid. As our
phrase books helped us explain later, when we finally made it to Mahbuhbullah's house in Dasht-e-Qal'eh (by asking people for directions to
Mahbuhbullah *tajer,* or Mahbuhbullah the merchant, because Dasht-e-
Qal'eh had no street names or addresses, and because our dictionaries did
not provide the Dari words for "tomb raider" or "vodka smuggler"), our
tarjuman nabud shodan: "translator to become not to be."

Because the page dedicated to verb agreement had been printed back-
ward and could only be read through a mirror, we had to make do with
the infinitive form.

David was right, of course: most people we met wished us no harm
and wanted to help us out. That did not mean I could burden anyone I
met with my presence, my needs, and expect them to follow me loyally
to every wretched place my job required me to go. Waiting for Wahid,
as I stood astride my duffel bag in Taloqan's pale December sun and
the former Taliban fighters continued their loud argument two blocks
away, provided a moment for reflection on our relationship. Perhaps, I
thought, the young translator who had become my trusted guide in Afghanistan's physical and political minefields had also had his fill of my
crazy demands.

(I was wrong about Wahid. His dedication to David and me—whom
he saw as first and foremost his guests and his wards, and not just two
deranged foreigners looking for trouble and paying him to tag along—
was unparalleled, with the exception, perhaps, of my Jordanian friend
and driver Bassam, to whom I dedicate another part of this book. Later
I learned that Wahid had found a driver, who had needed to perform
some minor repairs on his car. Instead of returning to us and telling us
about the delay, Wahid went with the driver straight to the auto shop to
wait for the car to be fixed—a logical move, unless you consider that we
were standing there on the street in a foreign, unknown town the whole
time. But that was our problem, not his. The car repair took five hours,

and when our loyal translator and the new driver finally arrived to pick us up, we had left. Professor S. Sakaria had helped David utter the syllables necessary to hire a friendly man named Qandahar to take us across what we later discovered was a well-known minefield.)

No, that winter in Afghanistan my communication with people upon whose life I was intruding, as my job dictated, was not working very well. But the theory of the well-meaning, botched encounter between host and guest might explain those awkward moments when the men in Kabul tried to say something nice about my burqa. After all, my role, as a woman who was paying them, and therefore was in charge of them, was the biggest misunderstanding of all. Not one of my Afghan companions, who were all men, knew how to handle it. Their clumsy compliments to me in the burqa were only the tip of the iceberg. I was a woman in a land of men, a female employer in a place where men conduct all business. And that was a lesson I kept learning, over and over, from everyone I met that winter.

The education began at the very start of the trip, after we had taken, one more time, the ferry across the Pyandzh River and, at an austere Afghan border outpost slapped together with mortar and rusty sheets of corrugated metal, hired a translator named Engineer Fazul (Wahid was in Baghdad at the time, working with the *Globe* reporter Lynda Gorov). Engineer Fazul—he preferred to be called by this honorific, which identified him as a man with a college degree in a country where 85 percent of the population could not read or write—was a thin, sullen man in his early forties who had studied at a technical university in the Soviet Union. He had retained the thick beard the Taliban had forced him to wear, and also the Russian he had learned in college. He spoke it almost perfectly, though with the occasional mistranslation of a language student who has not had a conversation with native speakers in years. "Gunnerers are scouring in the barns," for example, was Fazul's way of saying "Soldiers are showering in the barracks." It was a hell of a lot better than my Dari, which tended to become not to be whenever I needed it.

The problem with Engineer Fazul's translation was not the presence of these endearing misnomers. The problem was that despite the fact that I was paying half his salary (for which he signed a page in the back of my notebook every two days), he almost never spoke—or misspoke—to me. Whenever David addressed Engineer Fazul, the man would respond eagerly, with long, thoughtful, and detailed tirades. Whenever I asked him a question or tried to strike up a conversation, a strangely vacant expression would fall over the engineer's face like a shroud, or a burka, and silence would issue forth from his lips. In fact, it may have been just me, but I was pretty sure he actually pursed his lips tighter together every time I spoke to him.

In most situations, an Afghan woman does not speak to a man unless she is spoken to first. She is very much her man's property; most women are essentially locked away in their husbands' or fathers' compounds. Men often treat women worse than animals: in Kabul, where women travel by car more frequently than by donkey, I once saw a man first stuff two sheep into the back seat of a taxicab and then stuff two women into its trunk. Given all this, it was hard to tell if Engineer Fazul found it beneath his dignity to address me. He may also have been trying not to upset his relationship with David. Or maybe he didn't want to embarrass or compromise me?

Unlike Engineer Fazul, many Afghans I encountered did not appear to be sure that I was a woman (this may have been an advantage that made it possible for me to conduct any interviews at all). For one thing, I had a crew cut. I also exhibited many characteristics of what in most circles of Afghan society was considered exclusively male behavior: I wore pants; I sat cross-legged next to men in roadside taverns and smoked cigarettes while I waited for my order of lamb kebab; and, unlike most Afghan women, who were expected to turn their heads away whenever they saw a stranger, I arrogantly approached fighters and warlords and asked them questions directly, without shame. Someone once asked David if I were his son. In a land where it was common for boys to go to war before they turned fifteen, men often assumed that I was just another teenager who had joined the workforce.

Once, in Kabul, I developed laryngitis and my vocal cords became so irritated I could not produce a sound. We were sitting on a mattress in a room full of elders who were studying me in a way that suggested they were trying to figure out what I was. I had a question, so I leaned over to David and whispered it in his ear. He repeated the question to Wahid, prefaced by the words: "Anna asks." Ah! Everyone in the room nodded at each other with a sort of relief when they realized that I was asking David to address the men for me. Gender conundrum solved: clearly, I was a woman.

With the help of the difficult Engineer Fazul, David and I arrived at Shibirghan Prison in northern Afghanistan. We were there to interview some of the 3,014 suspected Taliban and al Qaeda prisoners—mostly Pakistanis, mixed in with some Arabs, and a few Uzbeks, Tajiks, and Russians—who were slowly dying of infection, starvation, dehydration, and wounds from recent battles in the prison's thirty crammed, unheated, unlit, and unventilated rooms designed to hold no more than 800 internees.

At the prison gate, four Northern Alliance gunmen frisked us before letting us inside. David went first and was ushered through the gate, then Engineer Fazul. Predictably, the young fighters thought I was a young man, like them. They were disabused of their assumption when, much to their delight, in the process of patting down my torso they discovered my breasts. David and Engineer Fazul were already inside the gate. The search quickly became a fondling session at gunpoint.

They were younger than me, in their teens—boys who grew up climbing up and down the hulls of burned-out Soviet tanks instead of jungle gyms, dreamers who grew up with no dreams other than of things exploding. I had spoken to such young Afghan gunmen before. One, a somber sixteen-year-old, had told me gravely: "Whenever you face the enemy, you have no choice other than to shoot." His first kill had been on September 11, 2001: a Taliban soldier in a rock-strewn field. The boy had let the soldier come so close he could smell the man's sweat. Then he fired. That boy had not yet started shaving, but his eyes were tired, hollow, and reflected nothing, as though the war had taken his youth and his soul.

The young guards outside Shibirghan Prison had the same eyes. But now that they also had me, their faces wore expressions of impatience and hunger: children about to unwrap a new toy. In rural northern Afghanistan, few children had ever gotten toys. I was a rare treat. One of the teenagers squeezed my breast, hard. The others trained their guns on me.

I was rescued. A passing Northern Alliance officer, whom I had interviewed on some front line a month earlier, recognized me and told his gunmen I was off-limits. I slipped into the prison yard, where David was already interviewing the warden. I felt sick. Engineer Fazul laughed when I asked him to translate my story to the warden. The warden laughed, too.

The incident at the gate could have become a very brutal lesson about another role women played in war-torn Afghanistan: that of trophies, loot, targets of one of the most humiliating weapons men have always wielded over women in conflicts everywhere. The benevolent officer saved me from learning it. Maybe he simply was afraid of creating an international incident.

No one was there to save little Bibi Amina.

She was ten. A month after I visited Shibirghan, five gunmen broke into the girl's house with a domed roof shaped like a woman's breast. The men were ethnic Uzbek fighters of the Northern Alliance: at the time, America's proxy ground troops in the war. They took turns raping Bibi Amina, her two sisters—twelve-year-old Bibi Aisha and fourteen-year-old Fatima—and her mother, Nazu. They raped them for hours, all night. They took turns with the woman and the girls, and they took turns training a Kalashnikov assault rifle on the girls' father, a crippled cauliflower farmer named Jamaluddin. Before they left, taking the family's life savings and a carpet that had kept down the dust on the earthen living room floor, the men explained to Nazu why they had chosen her and her daughters.

"They told me I was a Pashtun," recounted Nazu.

Pashtuns, the largest ethnic group in Afghanistan, had made up the core of the Taliban. In the northern province of Balkh, where Nazu's family lived, Pashtuns were a minority. Now that the Taliban had fallen, Northern Alliance fighters—mostly ethnic Uzbeks and Tajiks—were taking revenge, and Pashtun girls and women were the spoils of choice.

In preying on the women of a vanquished nation, the fighters continued a millennia-old tradition that proliferates in all wars. Japanese troops raped Chinese women in Nanking in 1937 and early 1938; Allied troops raped all the women they could lay their hands on in defeated Nazi Germany in 1945; Hutu men raped Tutsi women in Rwanda in 1994. In this century, Sudanese nomads called the Janjaweed raped women farmers in Darfur. In Iraq, I have interviewed Sunni and Shiite Muslims, Christian and Sabean women who had been raped by men of other sects or religions. Rape is a common front line of war, a front line that often remains hidden because of the stigma attached to sexual violence by many societies, and because in many societies, the targets—women and girls— are considered less important than men, the fighters. Twenty-three hundred years before Uzbek gunmen raped Nazu and her daughters on the outskirts of Balkh, Alexander the Great, the Greek emperor, laid siege to this city, defeated its king and married his sixteen-year-old daughter, Roxanne. History suggests that the union—which now, serendipitously, was contributing to the financial well-being (and the garden décor) of my Dasht-e-Qal'eh tomb raider friend, Mahbuhbullah—was not quite consensual.

When I spoke to Nazu, her daughters crouched beneath the breastshaped clay roof of their home. Fatima's kerchief partly concealed the scars on her face from where the rapists had hit her against the wall. Bibi Amina, a tiny, fragile child, played with the fringe of the giant red scarf that covered her head: her security blanket. I could not tell whether she had understood what had been done to her. But she did understand this much: one of the men who had hurt her, her sisters, and her mother lived right down the street.

The morning after the rape, the men had returned with a simple warning: if Jamaluddin and his family told the authorities, the gunmen would kill them. The family did not press charges. They knew that the gunmen had the backing of a powerful warlord, whose men had so intimidated the local police force that the police chief, an ethnic Tajik, told me that although Northern Alliance gunmen had raped hundreds of Pashtun women and girls in the area, he was not going to confront the rapists.

"We cannot do anything," he said in an office thick with cigarette smoke and chagrin.

The Northern Alliance fighters who had assaulted Bibi Amina's family, and the fighters who had groped me in Shibirghan, were members of the Junbish-e-Milli militia of General Abdul Rashid Dostum—that feared Uzbek warlord, Mahbuhbullah's former commander, known for his fondness of whiskey, his penchant for switching sides depending on who was winning in the convoluted and bloody chess game of Afghan politics, and his brutal rule in his native northern Afghanistan.

Dostum and his men had become infamous for raping women and children during the carnage that engulfed Kabul in the early 1990s, after the Soviet troops had pulled out of Afghanistan and withdrawn their support of the unpopular Communist government there. Dostum was one of the leaders of different mujahedin groups who had proceeded to fight for power in the capital. Tellingly, it was not the rapes of hundreds of women that earned Dostum's wild militia their nickname but their penchant for looting the homes of their victims after they had raped them.

Dostum's men became colloquially known as *galamjam,* or carpet thieves.

How come your little green phrase book says nothing about euphemisms, esteemed Professor S. Sakaria?

Accusations of war crimes perpetrated by the Junbish resumed after the Taliban fell. At Shibirghan, a Pakistani prisoner named Umar told me how Junbish fighters had packed him and about three thousand other captured foreign Taliban fighters into ten or so airtight metal cargo containers for transportation by truck to Shibirghan. The men were given no food or water, and the only air for the prisoners came from holes that the Junbish fighters shot through the walls from the outside—after the prisoners already had been immured. If the bullets did not kill the men in the containers, the heat and dehydration did. Of the two or three hundred prisoners in Umar's container, he said, only six men survived the trip to Shibirghan. I don't know whether they have survived the prison itself. Umar had an infected shrapnel wound in his leg; it was beginning to stink. His cellmates were dying of gangrene. Rancid, insidious smells filled the prison.

Umar's story of the mass killing of hundreds or even thousands of Taliban prisoners of war in the span of three days in 2001 was later substantiated by other witnesses and human rights researchers, who had unearthed the mass grave in the desert of Dasht-e-Leili, a fifteen-minute drive from Shibirghan, where Dostum's men had buried the bodies of their victims. The massacre, documented by many American newspapers and magazines and investigated by the Cambridge-based Physicians for Human Rights, may have constituted the first landmark atrocity in America's war against terrorism.

Umar and his cohorts were not good men. They were Taliban fighters—the ones who had beaten or publicly executed the women whom they had perceived as violating the strict laws of shariah, and jailed the men for wearing their beards too short. But the Junbish, it seemed, were more interested in revenge than in wartime justice. They were probably emboldened by what appeared to be the tacit approval of Dostum's American patrons. The United States saw Dostum as a crucial ally in the north; in the beginning of the war in Afghanistan, the Uzbek general was on the CIA payroll—much like, years earlier, Osama bin Laden had been. Around the time I interviewed Umar and Bibi Amina's family, several men from a U.S. Special Forces unit would ride alongside Dostum in white pickup trucks wherever he traveled in northern Afghanistan. The State Department mentioned Dasht-e-Leili in a couple of its annual human rights reports as a place "where international experts found evidence of summary execution and death by suffocation," but took no further action, and the Bush administration discouraged government investigators from looking into the massacre. When the United Nations helped form the first post-Taliban Afghan government, Dostum joined it. In 2009, he was serving as the military chief of staff in the government of President Hamid Karzai.

After I visited Bibi Amina's house, some Junbish gunmen approached Wahid in front of the Mazar-e-Sharif hotel where we were staying. The gist of the conversation: we had overstayed our welcome in the land of Dostum. The warlord, the gunmen said, "can no longer guarantee your safety." (Incidentally, according to the State Department, Dostum would later tell the same thing, verbatim, to the international investigators who had wanted to probe the Dasht-e-Leili killings.) We had to leave Balkh province the next day. So we did.

Nazu and her daughters, on the other hand, had no other place to go. Squatting on the dusty porch of their ransacked, violated house, these women were heroines for speaking to me about their rape—in a culture where the black mark of dishonor associated with sexual abuse usually muzzles the victims; in a country where women are expected to fall quiet in the presence of strangers; in the land of Dostum, where the police had given up on protecting women from rapists, and Pashtuns from everybody else. They were unlikely and unwitting dissidents in a land where most women appeared to be barely more than fixtures of the landscape, shapeless and mute smudges of pale blue scampering down dirty streets.

"In the beginning, you'll have trouble walking," Khadija, Wahid's older sister, instructed me. Halfway through my day in a burqa I had finally arrived at Wahid's family apartment; through the blue mesh of my garment I could not discern much about the outside of the compound apart from the typical, for Kabul, pale yellow, mud-brick walls and a small tiled yard. I complained about my experience in the burqa to Khadija, who was twenty-six and had been wearing the thing for twelve years. In response, she suggested that I be patient and give it a few more months.

"Little by little, you'll become used to it," she assured me. "Now that I've worn a burqa for a long time, I'm used to it. Whenever I walk in a burqa now, I feel as free as if I didn't have it on."

The room was empty apart from several mattresses, transparent pink curtains, and a heaping pewter tray of hot *mantwo* on a plastic *dastarkhan* spread over the carpet on the floor. Wahid, his two sisters, his mother, his brother, David, and I sat around the *dastarkhan*. This was my first meal in Afghanistan during which men and women other than me sat down for a meal together. In all the other houses I had visited, women and children ate separately from men and their guests (which included me), usually picking at our leftovers.

This was also a meal that had been cooked specifically for me: Wahid, knowing how much I liked *mantwo,* the Afghan dumplings, had asked

Khadija to prepare them. Wahid and Khadija's father died when the siblings were still young, and their older brother, Adyl, had moved to Iran to study Islam, so Wahid had become the household's sole breadwinner and de facto head of the family. His word to Khadija was law. She had spent the whole morning in the kitchen, slaving over yellow split peas and dough and spiced ground beef. As I shoveled fistfuls of the food into my mouth, I could not feel too bad about it. She was a fantastic cook.

The first time I had tried *mantwo* was in Mazar-e-Sharif, in Restaurant Row, a startling and delightful oasis for well-off travelers starved for culinary diversity after weeks of lamb kebab and bread. Restaurant Row is a narrow alley where the air in the evening grows thick with the mix of smoke from lamb grilling on skewers in front of eateries, whiffs of mint and garlic chefs whip up with yogurt in open-air kitchens, the yeasty blast wafting from the freshly baked, flat bread boys carry on trays mounted precariously on their heads, and the vinegary glop of discarded tomatoes and herbs running in the deep, black gutters along the sidewalks.

Everything about that visit was emblematic of the vibrant, post-Taliban Afghanistan. Noisy crowds filled the restaurants, oblivious to the echoes of intricate syncopated rhythms as the ancient muezzin of the Blue Mosque called for prayer in exquisite improvisations that evoked John Coltrane high on the Koran; both the restaurant goers' shirking of their religious duties, and the muezzin's untraditional, jazzlike phrasing were sins unthinkable just a few months earlier, when the Taliban had run the city.

The restaurant we had picked was called Café Titanic, an homage to the movie that seemed to have invaded every Afghan heart. Even under the Taliban, which had banned all movies, *Titanic* somehow circulated on bootleg video cassettes and swept Afghanistan off its feet. Everything became *Titanic*. The most popular hairstyle for teenage boys and young men, with a long fringe and cropped back, à la Leonardo DiCaprio, was called "Titanic" (the Taliban had imprisoned several barbers for giving the haircuts). A giant street market that sat astride the Kabul River in the capital was nicknamed Titanic for its unwieldy size. Wedding cakes were baked in the shape of the luxury liner. In 2003, when Afghans no longer needed to fret about retribution for evoking the forbidden movie, Kim Barker wrote in the *Chicago Tribune* about finding in a Kabul market Titanic Mosquito Killer, Havoc on Titanic Perfume Body Spray, Titanic Making Love Ecstasy Perfume Body Spray, and Just Call Me Maxi Titanic Perfume (not to mention Titanic baseball caps and T-shirts). Café Titanic in Mazar-e-Sharif was among the first of the hundreds of establishments to celebrate the sinking of the Taliban by naming itself after the movie and crudely painting the outline of the legendary passenger steamship on its mortar walls.

A smiling restaurant manager in a velvet vest embroidered with silver thread and mirrors over a loose *shalwar kameez* suit ushered us up a flight of wooden stairs to a large, smoke-filled lounge where men sat on wooden dining podiums along walls freshly painted with a *Titanic*-themed mural (a stormy sea, a blob of gray representing an iceberg, and a few uneven white streaks that could have been seagulls, or maybe drowning crew members; it was hard to say). A small group of women in burqas shuffled up the stairs ahead of us. But they were not led to the lounge; they kept climbing the stairs upward, to the third floor. A thick canvas curtain hung in the doorway at the top of the stairs, and, as I watched, the women disappeared behind the flowery drapes. At Café Titanic, the world's most popular romantic drama may have defied the Taliban, but it was not powerful enough to allow the mixing of the sexes. Our orders of *mantwo* arrived, bathed in spicy sauces of white, red, and orange. I imagined that in the secret room upstairs, the women had thrown back the front flaps of their burqas, baring their chiseled cheekbones and elegant arches of plucked eyebrows, and a boy hoisting a large aluminum tray had courteously served them their dumplings.

Khadija, Wahid's sister, was eight years old when, long before the Taliban took power, an Afghan man decided her role in society. Khadija's mother had wanted her to go to school, but Khadija's eldest brother, Adyl, who was living with the family at the time, and therefore served as head of the household, refused to allow the girl to study. Khadija rationalized Adyl's decision for me:

"At that time, women were very liberated. They didn't wear burqas and their legs were bare. My brother didn't want me to go to school and become like that." Khadija's education, therefore, was limited to verses from the Koran and cooking. Six years later, when Khadija reached puberty, Adyl bought the girl her first burqa.

Khadija's sister, Samiya, the baby of the family, was seventeen when the U.S.-led war unseated the Taliban regime. Adyl was in Iran by then, and, emboldened when she saw some women in Kabul unveil their faces, Samiya doffed her burqa and began to go outside wearing a long dress, pants, and a large, loose-fitting scarf over her head. This decision came at some expense: Samiya's brother Zamorai told me, in front of the girl, that he had stopped liking her because she had become too emancipated.

"It's okay, she'll understand," he told me when I suggested that perhaps it was not the nicest thing to say about his sister. "Our sisters know their place."

What was the place of women in this Kabul household? I asked. Zamorai began to answer, but I told him I wanted to hear it from his sisters. Khadija responded so quietly I could barely hear her voice.

"Because I love my brothers so much, if they tell me, 'Go to your place,' I understand," she said. "I don't become angry with them. My tears come out, but I leave the room."

We finished the *mantwo,* scooped up the last of the split-pea sauce with the crispy half-moons of home-made *nan,* and Khadija and her sister cleaned up the dirty dishes and rolled away the *dastarkhan.* I put on my shoes, wriggled back into my burqa, and gingerly made my way across the uneven tiled yard of their compound.

"Open your face," the women called after me from the doorway. A feminist call for freedom from the veil this was not.

"Open your face," they shouted, "or else you'll fall in the mud!"

◈

Mantwo

Serves 8 very hungry people

I once had *mantwo* at an Afghan restaurant in Cambridge, Massachusetts (Helmand, so called after the home province of its owners, who happen to be close relatives of President Karzai; it is the same restaurant that serves the pumpkin with yogurt sauce from the second chapter of this book). I had not come armed with S. Sakaria's phrase book, but I decided to show off nonetheless and ordered in my very limited Dari. The waiter ignored me completely. I was beginning to wonder whether I was getting the Engineer Fazul treatment when David came to the rescue and asked the man, in English, whether he, too, hailed from Helmand.

"No." The waiter smiled. "I'm from Peru."

The dough for *mantwo* is a bit messy, but I suggest that you roll up your sleeves and make it from scratch. You can also use wonton wrappers from the Asian foods section of your local supermarket. If that's what you do, get at least 52 wrappers, but know that in my book, that's considered cheating.

For the dough:
8 cups all-purpose flour
3 teaspoons salt

For the split pea sauce:
1 cup dried yellow split peas
2 teaspoons ground coriander
½ teaspoon ground cumin
¼ teaspoon cayenne pepper
3 cups water or broth

For the yogurt sauce:
1½ cups plain yogurt, nonfat,
  any style
4 teaspoons chopped fresh mint
4 medium cloves garlic, crushed

For the *mantwo* stuffing and meat sauce:
1 tablespoon olive oil
2 pounds ground beef
  (or 1 pound ground beef and
  1 pound ground lamb)
4 medium onions, chopped
2 carrots, peeled and grated
2 tablespoons salt
1 teaspoon ground cumin
1 teaspoon black pepper
1 tablespoon ground coriander
½ cup chopped cilantro
½ cup chopped parsley
2 tablespoons tomato paste
¼ teaspoon cayenne pepper

1. Make the dough: Pour the flour into a large bowl and stir in the salt. Slowly add 3 to 4 cups warm water to the center of the flour; add enough water to make the dough not stick to your fingers but also be pliant. Knead for 5 minutes, cover with plastic wrap, and refrigerate for 30 minutes.

2. What makes *mantwo* special in my mind is that it is served with three different sauces. While you're waiting for your dough to come out of the fridge, make the split pea sauce first. Combine all the ingredients in a saucepan. Bring to a boil, then reduce the heat to a simmer for about 45 minutes, or until the peas mash easily.

3. While that's cooking, whip up the yogurt sauce: Combine all the ingredients and refrigerate.

4. Make the stuffing: Heat the oil in a large skillet. Cook the meat and onions over low heat until all the meat is browned, stirring so that the meat doesn't clump together. Drain the fat.

5. Stir in 1 cup water, the carrots, salt, cumin, black pepper, coriander, cilantro, and parsley and simmer for about 30 minutes, or until all the water evaporates.

6. If you've made your own dough, remove the dough from the fridge. Cut it in half, then halve each piece until you have 52 pieces. Roll out each piece into thin rounds about 2½ to 3 inches in diameter. Lay them out on a lightly floured surface. (If you're using wonton wrappers, lay them out.)

7. Mound 2 large spoonfuls of the meat mixture in the center of a dough circle. Dip a finger in water and trace it around the edge. Lay a second piece of dough on top and press around the edge to seal. Roll up the edge. Repeat until all the dough is gone. You should have some meat mixture left over. Steam the *mantwo* for 40 minutes.

8. In the meantime, make the meat sauce: Combine the remaining meat mixture, 2 tablespoons water, the tomato paste, and cayenne pepper. Simmer for about 10 minutes, or until the water has evaporated.

9. To serve, spread the yogurt sauce on large serving plate. Put the *mantwo* on top. Pour the split pea sauce over the *mantwo*. Top with the meat sauce. Serve hot.

Six

Vodka at Gunpoint

The Russian colonel waved his Makarov pistol and nodded at our chipped twelve-ounce glasses on the wobbly picnic table. He had just replenished them for the second time, filling them again to the brims with vodka. His nine-millimeter handgun was loaded and the safety was off, and he wagged the weapon left and right, like a sinister magic wand, casually allowing us to glimpse the ominous void of its muzzle. That kept me sober even after two glasses.

"Drink, American spies," the colonel hissed dramatically, slurring, at my colleagues. "And you," he wrinkled his forehead to help focus his watery eyes on my face, "you, whore of the American spies, also drink."

A stifling late-September afternoon smothered the outdoor café in southern Tajikistan, a few hundred feet north of the Pyandzh River that marks the border with Afghanistan. The café—from the looks of it, a local dive, a raggle-taggle constellation of plastic and metal tables teetering atop an unevenly poured sheet of asphalt—was empty except for the five of us sweating in plastic chairs: Alan Cullison, a reporter for the *Wall Street Journal,* Robert Cottrell of the *Financial Times,* and me, a freelancer on assignment for the *Boston Globe* and the *San Francisco Chronicle,* plus two very drunk colonels of the Russian border guard, whose base stretched from the café to the river. The merciless Central Asian sun was at its zenith, and the old asphalt pavement was melting in blotches where it was not shaded by the tall poplar trees that lined the otherwise deserted street. Even the café owners, a family of Afghan refugees, had vanished after delivering our second bottle of vodka. There was not a soul around to rescue us from the colonels, their booze, and their cocked guns.

The year was 2001. Two weeks earlier, terrorists based in Afghanistan, on the other side of the Pyandzh, had attacked the United States. I was in Tajikistan to try to hop onto that ancient rope ferry across the river, cross into Afghanistan, and write about the impending war. But Afghan opposition officials in Dushanbe were slow to grant foreign reporters visas to the section of the country under their control, and dozens of journalists from all over the world were stuck in Tajikistan's capital, waiting for our paperwork to be processed. Dushanbe had a languid, postcolonial feel to it. It was home to two good restaurants; widespread poverty; an immensely corrupt, quasi-authoritarian regime; and a half a million friendly and put-upon locals too wary of the government to talk to foreigners. One morning, Alan, Robert, and I decided to travel south, to the Afghan border. We would write from there about the prospects of war, and, possibly, about Afghanistan's bustling narcotics trade.

By 2001, Afghanistan produced an estimated three-quarters of the world's opium, and drug traffickers used the impoverished former Soviet republic of Tajikistan as one of its main smuggling routes. When the United States announced that it would go to war with Afghanistan's Taliban rulers, antinarcotics officials worried that a full-scale war would accelerate the drug trade, because the world's attention would be focused on bloodshed, not on trafficking. Later, it turned out that they were right.

———

On the Tajik side of the border, the guards were Russian. Crippled by a recent civil war that had brought forth warlords with such winsome nicknames as Hitler and Four-Fingered Ali, and hamstrung by a flailing economy—the monthly salary in Tajikistan at the time averaged four dollars—this former Soviet republic did not have enough money or manpower to secure its own boundaries. The Kremlin, whose imperial ambitions had not abated with the 1991 collapse of the Soviet Union, was happy to lend its troops and thus maintain a foothold in a land that had been within Russia's sphere of influence for decades. The Russian guards successfully prevented the Taliban and the Afghan civil war from spilling into Tajikistan. But they were less effective in stopping the drug cartels that transported most of Europe's—and the world's—opium supply from Afghanistan across the Pyandzh River, along a route that was informally known as the Great Drug Road. There was talk that some border guards were complicit in the drug trade. At one point, twelve Russian soldiers based in Tajikistan were caught trying to ship seventeen pounds of narcotics to Moscow.

Most of Afghanistan's opium was produced in the south, on the territory controlled by the Taliban. A year before the United States attacked Afghanistan, the Taliban had banned drug cultivation, declaring the activity un-Islamic, although one Tajik official told me the ban really was aimed at jacking up the prices for the opium that had already been produced and lay stockpiled in different parts of Afghanistan. When the war appeared imminent, the Taliban lifted the ban and told Afghan farmers that they could plant opium poppies again in case the United States attacked (and they did). The price of heroin in the country immediately dropped from about two hundred and twenty dollars per pound to forty.

But not all the opium came to Europe from Taliban-controlled lands. Leaders of the Northern Alliance, the anti-Taliban resistance fighters and the future foot soldiers of the U.S.-led war, were also involved in drug production and trade, which trafficked up to fifteen hundred tons of narcotics across Tajikistan in a year. There was also speculation that the Northern Alliance was using heroin to pay for the weapons and ammunition they received from Moscow.

In Dushanbe, my colleagues and I hired a taxi: an ancient Lada with no seat belts. Rectangular iron patches had been soldered onto particularly rusted spots of its hull, and a crackly radio blasted old Soviet pop songs. We drove south, past women in ankle-length dresses of turquoise and fuchsia velvet picking cotton in parched fields and unshorn goats denuding poplar saplings. Just before noon we arrived at the gate of a Russian military base, where two very drunk and hostile colonels immediately detained us, ordered us to the café across the street, and forced us to drink vodka at gunpoint.

Every American elementary school kid knows the story of young George Washington and the cherry tree. Every Russian elementary school kid knows the story of Grand Prince Vladimir and the drink: the prince, the medieval ruler of ancient Rus, was searching for a monotheistic religion to help him unite his heathen land in the late tenth century, so he sent his emissaries to talk to Jewish, Christian, and Muslim clergy to see which religion would work best—or so the legend goes. Vladimir dismissed Judaism outright: the Jews' loss of Jerusalem, he had ruled, was clear evidence that God no longer favored his previously chosen people. Islam, on the other hand, was quite appealing—until someone pointed out to Vladimir that Muslims are not allowed to drink beer or mead.

The Russian ruler could not tell a lie.

"Drinking is the joy of Rus," the prince legendarily pronounced, and the fate of Russia was sealed.

It is possible that none of it was any more true than the myth about the Pilgrims stepping off the Mayflower onto Plymouth Rock (no mariner in his right mind would pull up a ship that close to a rock in an unfamiliar harbor; the pilgrims had actually waded onto the sand dunes of what today is Provincetown—but the myth, and the tourist attraction of the Rock, in downtown Plymouth, the port of my own American landfall, persevere). True or not, the story, which is taught in elementary school social studies class as early Russian history, has helped generations of Russian kids get their priorities straight: drinking, and drinking hard, is such a crucial part of Russia's national identity that the habit is believed to have played a decisive role in determining the religion that to this day shapes the country's domestic and foreign policy.

Fast-forward to the mid-sixteenth century. Binge drinking is a problem; Ivan the Terrible, Russia's mercurial first tsar, forcibly—and counterintuitively—replaces the sale of beer and mead with vodka at Russian state-run taverns, and restricts the serving of alcohol to a handful of holidays. The idea is that fewer doses of the stronger libation will somehow sober up the land. The vodka sticks, but the "handful of holidays" part does not, and so, this early attempt at prohibition backfires. Drinking vodka becomes a national pastime. Today, no gathering is complete unless there is a bottle of vodka on the table, and Russian hosts ply their guests with the innocuously clear, extremely potent drink the way American hosts . . . actually, there really isn't a comparison.

Russia's etiquette is full of vodka-related rules (the interval between the first and second shots of vodka at any gathering must not exceed five minutes, and if it does, the first shot doesn't count and the participants must start anew; an empty bottle of vodka must be promptly removed from the table—and, preferably, replaced with a full one—or else bad luck is guaranteed to befall all those gathered around it) and regulations (no one stops drinking until the entire bottle is consumed; vodka must be shot, not sipped; women—who, according to a popular proverb, are not quite human—are allowed to skip a few shots whereas men are not).

It is the drink of choice for birthday celebrations and mourning ceremonies. It is a fever reducer: rub your feet with vodka at the onset of a cold or the flu and the chills will let go of your aching body. It is a cure for sorrow: after you split up with your girlfriend, dive into a working-class *ryumochnaya**—usually a narrow basement with no chairs, where men (for the customers of a *ryumochnaya* are almost unchangeably men) drink hard liquor standing up along walls steeped in the sour fumes of yesteryear's alcohol and lost second chances—and the soothing, warm murkiness will envelop your mind. It is an ideological weapon: in Chechnya in 2002, a Russian army lieutenant colonel plied me and four other foreign correspondents with vodka on a rare, tightly controlled tour of the separatist region organized by the Kremlin. He somehow thought the toasts—"To your objectivity!"—would make us report the news his way: that, despite the daily reports of ambushes, bombings, arbitrary detentions, and summary executions, the war was over and happy Chechens were rebuilding their republic.

Vodka is at the heart of grotesque fights over whose turn it is to clean the grimy bathroom of a cramped communal apartment. It is also a peacemaker: when the *kommunalka* bathroom is finally clean, one neighbor will pour the other the traditional one hundred grams, to make up.

---

*Ryumochnaya—a Russian vodka and cheap brandy bar. Usually, only vodka and brandy are served there (no beer or wine), typically in warm, wet, chipped, poorly rinsed glasses. The term comes from the word *"ryumka,"* which means "shot glass" in Russian.

Simply put, vodka is a traditional way of life. Café Idiot (named after the Fyodor Dostoyevsky novel), my favorite restaurant in my hometown, St. Petersburg, serves a shot of vodka free as an aperitif before any meal you order, even if it's just a cup of tea; if you order a liter of vodka and a selection of cold appetizers (for one), the restaurant owners promise to deliver you to the nearest hospital free of charge.

The price Russia pays for its love affair with the drink is devastating. Some studies suggest that two out of three Russian men die drunk. Russian police records attribute to binge drinking at least half of all murders committed across the country's nine time zones. Hundreds of thousands of Russians die each year of alcohol-related diseases. In 2004, health officials blamed alcohol abuse for 70 percent of all accidental deaths across Russia that year. Vodka is the cause of scores of industrial accidents, thousands of unwanted pregnancies, and countless divorces.

When I was little, Communist party leaders, having apparently forgotten Ivan the Terrible's failed efforts, tried to stem alcoholism by limiting how much vodka a person could buy. Each family would get a monthly quota of vodka coupons, redeemable at government-owned liquor stores. This did not so much interfere with popular drinking habits as shifted them, and people began to drink rubbing alcohol, cheap eau-de-cologne, and a fluorescent green astringent aftershave that smelled like cucumber. Some of the poorer alcoholics died after drinking varnish removers and paint thinners. Real vodka became a luxury, and my parents and grandparents, who did not drink much, would pool their monthly vodka coupons and then use the alcohol (or the coupons) to appease plumbers, car mechanics, and electricians whose services would not be available otherwise. The logic was that having a drunk plumber fix a leaky sink was better than the alternative, which was having no plumber at all—even if as a result the sink did not stay fixed very long. Vodka became a coveted form of currency.

I never was a big vodka drinker, even though I am from Russia. (I also don't like the cold. Why do people have this idea that Russians must like the cold? First of all, a lot of Russia is warm; and those of us from the colder parts of the country did not ask to be born just a few degrees south—or, in some cases, north—of the polar circle.) The little taste for vodka I did have, I lost during four years with an alcoholic boyfriend. But this I know for sure: nothing better than a shot of hard liquor to make you think you are warm during a long, cold Russian winter. In fact, hundreds of Russians die in the streets each winter after making this mistake. They get drunk and fall asleep in snowdrifts, coddled in the soft blankets of white; their frozen bodies are discovered in the spring when the snow melts. Russian cops have coined a tender, delicate name for them. They call them "snowdrops."

But enough of that. Whatever its strengths and weaknesses, vodka is the great equalizer, the best mixer, and the surest way to friendship with a Russian—and some non-Russians, too.

With that in mind, on my trip to Afghanistan in February 2002, I brought along the closest thing to vodka I could find in Moscow that fit in my coat pocket: a flask of Johnnie Walker. (Russian vodka makers might consider packaging Stoli in a flat vessel.)

"What's this?" asked Wahid, the intrepid translator, who was watching me rummage through my bag at our rental house in Kabul—the one with Zabi the guard and Mullah the cook. A sleeping bag, a transformer with alligator clips to charge my laptop from a car battery, wool socks, maps, and endless containers of fifth-generation antibiotics rolled onto the woolly kilim rug covering the poured cement floor of the bedroom. I passed the bottle for Wahid to examine, and went back to unpacking.

I had met Wahid on my very first morning in Afghanistan. Having survived the Grand Foxhunt Adventure on the nocturnal drive from the Pyandzh River to the Northern Alliance foreign ministry guesthouse in Khojabahauddin, David and I were shown to a small room where someone was already sleeping on a single cot next to one of the walls. (During the few nights we stayed at the guesthouse, the number of guests in the room would range from three to eight.) We unfolded our sleeping bags as quietly as we could, and when we woke up, several hours later, our neighbor was sitting on his cot, cross-legged, studying us. He was in his early twenties, clean shaven, with Paul McCartney hair (circa the *Abbey Road* period), and he was dressed in blue jeans, slippers, and a *payraan tumbaan,* a traditional, knee-length cotton shirt.

"I hope I did not interfere with your sleep last night," said the man, in English. And then: "Do you have a translator?"

Wahid spoke Dari and Pashto, the two main Afghan tongues. I once heard him speak to a very gratified Indian journalist in Hindi. He also spoke Urdu, which he had learned in Pakistan, where he had spent several years as a refugee from the Taliban. He had fled to Pakistan after the Taliban government had arrested him for draft dodging. Apart from having no desire to fight in Afghanistan's protracted civil war, Wahid explained, he simply could not afford to quit his job as a pro boxer to become a poorly paid Taliban foot soldier. He was the second of five children and had become his family's sole breadwinner after his soldier father had been killed and his older brother—the one who had banned Khadija from attending school—had fled to Iran to become a religious scholar. If Wahid had joined the army, his mother, younger brother, and two sisters would have been left to starve.

He said that the prison guards had beaten him with sticks and thin metal rods on his back and feet. Other than that, he told me nothing else of his arrest, or the terms of his release.

The trials of torture or exile had not robbed the young man of his essential inquisitiveness. He had questions about everything: Muslims in Moscow, Americans and al Qaeda, horseback riding and health care. Working with journalists seemed like the perfect job for him, and his natural curiosity made us a perfect match: we learned about his tormented and beautiful country together, and after the interviews were over, we would ask each other about the things we had not learned. How long can an average Afghan house of mud, manure, and straw stand before it requires thorough renovations? (No more than twenty-five years.) What do Russians eat for breakfast? (Hot cereal, sandwiches, hardboiled eggs, or leftovers from last night's dinner, although I prefer a fruit salad.) What about Afghans? (Tea, flat bread, honey or jam, and eggs, if they've got them. Many Afghans cannot afford any breakfast.)

When Wahid asked me about the Johnnie Walker bottle, I assumed his question was part of our never-ending Q&A.

A couple of hours later we left the compound to interview an elderly imam at the shrine of a little-known nineteenth-century Sunni mullah. The shrine—a boxy stucco building painted dark green and no larger than a garden shed—sat in the heart of Kabul.

I had noticed the shrine during a previous visit to the capital. All around it, Afghanistan was basking in the new era of secular rule. Across the street, a movie theater had reopened and was advertising reruns of old Bollywood flicks. A poster vendor had taped large, colorful prints depicting sultry Indian movie stars with deep décolletage and bare midriffs to the cinder-block wall of a house adjacent to the shrine. A small group of women clicked by in high heels, unaccompanied by men; a couple of them had cautiously swapped all-concealing burqas for pastel-colored head scarves. The shrine sat in the middle of it all, green and dark, like a void.

The saint of the shrine was a mystic who was believed to have been clairvoyant. As such, he was not revered by the Taliban. At one point, the conservative Islamic government had ordered the shrine shuttered. Now it was open again, but no one except its eighty-two-year-old imam seemed to care. The old man, Hamir Jan, sat wrapped in an ancient wool blanket on the filthy floor in the lobby of the shrine. His eyes were fixed on the open door, but no one came in.

I wanted to sit down with the old imam and ask him what he thought about the fall of the government that had banned his shrine, and about the corruption of Muslim values that had followed that fall—the wave of secular behavior that was gushing through Kabul's streets, past his open doors. Our minivan was bouncing along a potholed alley when Wahid turned to me from the passenger seat.

If I were making a movie, I would use slow motion to replay what happened next: flashing a disarming Robert Redford smile in my direction, Wahid, my sole guide through the combustible ethnic and religious labyrinths of post-Taliban Afghanistan, reached into the inside pocket of his leather jacket, fished out the whiskey bottle, nodded at me, raised the bottle to his lips, took a large gulp, and held out the bottle for the driver, motioning for him to try some, too.

"Wahid!" I lurched forward and yanked the bottle out of his hands (revert to normal speed here). The bottle was less than half full. "Omigod. Did you drink all that by yourself?"

"Do not worry, Anna," Wahid reassured me. "The guard at the house drank most of it."

The next day, when everyone had sobered up, I did get to talk to Hamir Jan. The imam was broke. His camel wool blanket had bald patches. No one had given alms to his shrine for weeks. He invited me to sit on his thin, stained carpet. The tea he offered me was weak. The sadness in his eyes seemed to pertain not just to the decline of the shrine, but to the degradation of some moral standard to which this man had continued to hold his country, despite a lifetime of war, fratricide, and rape.

"I have one request for you," the tragic-eyed imam told me. "Please don't tell Afghan women to uncover their faces and throw away their burqas. First, they will throw out their burqas, then they will lose their scarves, and then they will bare their arms and legs. Then they will become like prostitutes and forget their faith."

Wahid translated. I did not tell Hamir Jan about the burqa the translator had bought for me, or about the whiskey he had drunk. Before we left, I kissed the imam's hand. Its wrinkles smelled like moss.

The Russian border-guard colonels in Tajikistan insisted that the press badges issued by Tajik and Russian foreign ministries were merely a cover. In reality, they said, Alan and Robert were American spies. Because I was Russian and a woman, and therefore could not have been trusted with a real job, I was either a local liaison for the CIA or a hooker, or both. Torture by vodka seemed to be just a prelude for our executions.

Hours passed. We drank and drank. There were no chasers: no goose-skinned pickles; no green, juicy strings of marinated wild garlic; no moist black bread smothered with butter and sprinkled with salt; not even an onion. No water. I managed to skip a few sips of vodka, claiming the gender exemption. I could feel Robert fading in the chair to my right. Fueled by the drink, my imagination was churning out various scenarios of what was going to happen next: the colonels rape me, then throw us all in jail. The colonels kill us all. The colonels throw us into a stinky, moldy dungeon where they torture us, extracting all sorts of idiotic confessions, whereupon they kill us and dump our bodies into the yellow water of the Pyandzh River. Or simply keep us in the dungeon forever. No matter how I looked at it, drinking that vodka was going to be the last thing I would ever do as a free woman.

All of a sudden, one of the colonels—the one who had been waving his pistol at us the most—reached under the table and planted his hand firmly on Alan's crotch.

Hah! So they'll rape him first, I thought.

Then Alan turned and slapped the colonel across the face with the open palm of his hand.

Everyone froze. The colonel stared at Alan. The second colonel stared at his comrade. Robert's hand, holding a vodka glass, stopped in midair. I held my breath. The silvery leaves of the poplar trees paused from moving in the slight wind. Everything in the southern Tajik street, it seemed, readied itself for the one-sided act of bloodshed that was about to unfold.

The colonel's head bobbed slightly. His eyebrows tied into a knot as he evaluated what had just happened. The dull, short barrel of his Makarov quivered.

Then he roared with laughter.

"*Muzheek!*" he yelled, bestowing upon Alan the title that in Russian means, at once, a commoner and a tough guy worthy of macho camaraderie.

"I like this guy! You're the man!" He poked Alan's shoulder with an unsteady finger. Alan started laughing, too. The second colonel leaned back in his chair, roared, and merrily winked at me. Robert put down the vodka glass without taking a sip. The poplar trees shifted their branches in relief. I exhaled.

Then, just as suddenly as he started laughing, the colonel dropped his face on the table and instantly fell asleep. His buddy reached over and thoughtfully removed the pistol the colonel still was holding in his hand, returning it to its holster on the colonel's hip. Then he rose from the table, holstered his own gun, and motioned for us to follow him.

"Come on, American journalists," he whispered when we were a dozen yards from his sleeping comrade. He tripped, steadied himself by flapping his hands in the air like wings, and gave a conspiratorial giggle. "Come on, you CIA spies. I'll take you to a village where opium smugglers live."

~

Zakuski
Russian Appetizers

*G*ood vodka, you will discover once you get past the initial shock of ingesting eighty-proof alcohol, has a delicate flavor. That flavor will change depending on what you put in your mouth after your drink. Some vodka snobs (yes, those do exist!) argue that true aristocrats consume only hot appetizers with their vodka, but your typical Russian host will most likely offer a selection of gherkins, onions, pickled mushrooms, salted fish, or yeasty black bread to chase down your drink. Here are a few traditional chasers for you to choose from.

P. S. Some of these are really good appetizers even if you don't like to drink.

Hot Appetizers

Mushroom "Julienne"

Serves 4

½ medium onion, diced
1 tablespoon olive oil
8 ounces sliced mushrooms
½ cup sour cream
4 ounces (or more) grated sharp cheese
  like cheddar: the more, the better
Pinch of fresh dill
Salt and pepper, to taste

*P*reheat the oven to 400°F. In a small skillet, lightly brown the onion in the oil. Mix with the remaining ingredients in a bowl, divide among 4 ramekins, and bake in the oven for 10 to 15 minutes, or until the tops are golden brown and bubbly. Serve immediately. Eat with teaspoons.

Blini

Serves 4 (will yield about 20 blini)

*D*espite many a restaurant menu in the States, *blini* is the plural form of *blin,* the ultra-thin, large pancake. There is no such thing as "blinis."

1 cup all-purpose flour
Pinch of salt
Pinch of sugar
2 eggs
1½ cups milk, more if needed
2 tablespoons olive oil, plus more for frying
Sour cream, salted butter, lox, honey, or jam. Or, depending on
  your budget, caviar. (And if you can't get that, IKEA carries
  a decent low-cost surrogate, lumpfish roe.)

1. Combine the flour, salt, and sugar. Add the eggs and milk and mix well until the batter is perfectly smooth and the consistency of a smoothie.

2. Heat the oil in a frying pan (I like cast iron). Turn the heat to low. Pour some batter—about 1½ tablespoons—into the pan and tilt the pan so that the entire bottom is covered with batter. When tiny craters begin to appear on the surface, in about 1 minute or less, use a knife to separate the edges of the *blin* from the pan, then flip the *blin*. (If you have already started drinking, don't be a show-off: use a spatula. That thing they do in the movies where they swiftly jerk the pan and throw the blin into the air, and then it lands perfectly on the uncooked side—that probably won't work.) Fry the other side for about a minute or less, then move the cooked blin to a plate. Repeat with the remaining batter, adding more oil as necessary.

3. When you eat this sober, you place a *blin* on your plate, center some sour cream, butter, lox, honey, jam—or caviar—on the *blin*, roll it up using your fork and knife, and cut it into small, elegant pieces. But since you are drinking, most likely you will pick your *blin* off the communal plate with your fingers, juggle it in the palm of one hand as you ladle in the condiments with the other, and then shovel all of it into your mouth at once. Either way is traditional.

Cold Appetizers

Caviar

*W*ait.
    You got caviar? Can I come over?

Gherkins

Serves 4 or more

*I*f you have more than four guests, simply slice the gherkins into smaller pieces.

1 jar lightly salted gherkins

Drain the liquid from the jar of gherkins and empty the gherkins into a plate. Serve. If there are pickled garlic cloves in the jar, serve those, too. They are delicious.

తో

Herring in a Fur Coat
Selyodka pod shuboi
Generally serves 4 or more, but I can eat this entire thing by myself

1 pound salted herring, deboned and cut into ¼-inch pieces
1 large onion, diced
8 ounces boiled carrots, chilled and diced (about 6 carrots)
8 ounces boiled potatoes, chilled and diced (about four medium
    potatoes)
8 ounces boiled beets, chilled and grated (about 2 medium beets)
4 hard-boiled eggs
Mayonnaise
4 or 5 sprigs parsley, minced

1. On a large plate, arrange the herring in a layer. Spread the diced onion over the herring. Spread the diced carrots over the onion. Spread the diced potatoes over the carrots, and the grated beets over that.

2. Peel the eggs and cut in half, separating the whites from the yolks. Grate (or mash) the whites and the yolks separately. Sprinkle the whites over the beets. Spread mayonnaise on top of the whites. Sprinkle the yolks over the mayo and dust with the parsley. You should have a layered, colorful dish. Cut and serve with a wide metal spatula, ladling onto your guests' plates. The trick is to keep the layers intact as you serve the dish, which gets more difficult the more vodka you drink. In fact, you can turn it into a drinking game.

Black Bread

As with gherkins, cut into as many pieces as you see fit.

½ loaf pumpernickel bread
8 tablespoons salted butter (1 stick)
    at room temperature, optional
Salt, optional
2 garlic cloves, crushed, optional

Smother the bread generously with butter, then sprinkle some garlic and salt on top. Or simply get a piece of bread. Exhale, down the vodka, toss the bread into your mouth after it, swallow, inhale. *Muzheek!*

Onion

*T*his is a very traditional (and probably the cheapest) chaser. Like the gherkins, it's also low-carb.

Serves 4

1 medium yellow onion

Peel the onion. Cut into quarters. Serve.

Note: For the sake of those who are not drinking with you tonight, make sure you don't have any social obligations afterward. If there is anything that smells worse than vodka breath, it's the vodka-onion breath combo. Don't even bother with gum or Tic Tacs. They won't help.

Seven

Borsch During Wartime

We tore into the dark rye bread with our clumsy, shaking fingers, spilling black, moist crumbs onto the linen tablecloth embroidered with bright red and yellow roosters. We sank our butter knives into the large lump of opaque, garlicky white *salo,* the lard spread that gleamed whitely from a glazed saucer of hardened clay next to the woven-straw bread basket. We washed our bread and lard down with cold vodka from two short, glistening shot glasses. Greedily, we spooned out of our earthenware bowls the hot, thick borsch, inhaling its earthy fragrance and watching the dollops of sour cream slowly melt, starlike, into the deep scarlet brew of chunky meat, sliced beets, and shredded cabbage, pliant and springy like seaweed. There we sat, huddled inside the pinewood booth of a Ukrainian chain restaurant: two exhausted, shivering, crushed reporters searching for the elusive therapy of rich, Slavic food.

Outside, cold October rain slashed Moscow's streets, as it had for the last three days. The three seemingly never-ending, dark days that we had spent sinking in black puddles and slipping on fallen leaves in a courtyard of faded, gray concrete apartment blocks, where we had waited with dozens of other reporters behind a small grove of defoliated trees and a police cordon. On the other side of the trees and the police line loomed a blocky, Soviet-era theater building of sandblasted concrete. Inside it, a group of Chechen men and women armed with explosives and guns were keeping hostage more than 750 actors, theater employees, and members of the audience who had come to watch *Nord-Ost,* a musical about war, courage, betrayal, and love during the early decades of the Soviet Union, based on a popular coming-of-age novel written more than half a century earlier by the Soviet writer Veniamin Kaverin.

In the middle of the performance on October 23, 2002, five masked men wearing camouflage fatigues and carrying Kalashnikovs and a woman in a black hood jumped onto the stage and fired several rounds from their semiautomatic rifles into the ceiling. They announced that the theater hall was packed with explosives, and that everyone inside was a hostage.

At first, the audience did not know whether all this was part of the production. There were many armed people in the play *Nord-Ost,* which honors the triumphs of the Soviet army in World War II. The public sat in their chairs, looking at the stage and waiting for what was going to happen next. Then one of the gunmen shouted:

"Don't you understand what is going on? We are Chechens!"

The hostage takers promised to release their victims if Russia immediately withdrew all of its troops from Chechnya, a small Muslim region that had unsuccessfully but often fiercely resisted Russian colonial rule for almost three centuries. In the latest iteration of the on-again, off-again war, the Kremlin had been fighting Islamic separatists since 1994, with three years of cease-fire in the late 1990s. Up to 300,000 people, mostly Chechen civilians, were killed in that war. If their demand was not met, or if Russian forces attempted to storm the theater, the hostage takers would detonate their explosives and level the theater, killing everybody inside (and, possibly, in the surrounding apartment buildings). The rebels, some of whom wore belts fashioned from explosives, had sent a videotape to al Jazeera. In the recording they called themselves the "Islamic Suicide Squad" and said that they were ready to die for their cause. Georgi Vasilyev, one of the creators of the musical who was among the hostages, would say later that the rebels told him they had chosen to target his show because they found insulting its spirit of Russian patriotism and its celebration of Russia's air force. In the grand finale of the epic musical, a fighter plane with a wingspan of forty-nine feet descends onto the stage. Since 1994, Russian bombers and fighter jets had strafed tens of thousands of people and decimated dozens of towns and villages in Chechnya in air raids that were part of the Kremlin's latest campaign to subdue the breakaway region. By October 2002, Chechnya's capital, Grozny, looked like Dresden after World War II.

The takeover, which insolently thrust the war in Chechnya into the heart of Moscow—the theater was less than three miles from the Kremlin—is now known as the siege of Nord-Ost, or the Moscow theater hostage crisis. It lasted fifty-eight hours. Before dawn on October 26, 2002, a Russian counterterrorist unit sneaked into the theater, pumped poisonous gas into the building through its ventilation system, and then waded through the theater aisles, gunning down the subdued rebels at point-blank range. Soon thereafter, the Kremlin issued a statement celebrating what it described as a victory over "an inhumane and ruthless enemy."

But that day, it turned out that the people of Russia had no enemy more ruthless than their own government. Within minutes, the horrifying consequences of the raid that had ended the hostage crisis blotted out the temporary feeling of euphoria brought on by the end of the crisis itself. The gas the commandos had used to disorient the rebels was killing scores of the hostages it had been meant to save. Some staggered out of the theater; some crawled. Some were dragged by their hands and feet. Most were brought out on stretchers, unconscious. Standing outside the theater in the predawn gray, I saw the freed hostages' waxen shapes pressed against the fogged-up windows of the buses into which rescue crews had piled them: mouths open, faces tilted upward at unnatural angles, high-heeled shoes and dress slacks pointing ominously at the low sky. Many of these people would suffocate on the way to the hospital or in their hospital beds, drowning in their own vomit.

Preferring to keep its counterterrorism tactics secret, the Russian government had not warned Moscow's hospitals about its plan to poison the hostage takers and their hostages. Doctors in the city had been preparing to treat victims of gunshot and shrapnel trauma, not gas. Now they had to detoxify close to four hundred men, women, and children. But they did not know which antidotes to use: in a hideous display of the cynicism that has been the hallmark of most Russian governments, the Kremlin refused to disclose the name, or even the main properties of the poison the commandos had employed—this, the government said, would have amounted to disclosing top-secret counterterrorism methods—leaving the hospitals to a grim guessing game.

While they were in control of the theater, the Chechen rebels had released more than seventy of their captives. They had killed, according to different accounts, one or two. At least one hundred and twenty-eight more people—one out of every six remaining hostages—died of poisoning following their rescue. The Russian government never did release the name of the toxin it used, other than to say, many days later, that it was an opioid. Nor did it ever explain why its commandos had decided to execute, rather than capture and interrogate, all of the stricken hostage takers.

Some of the most flagrant human tragedies I have witnessed in the course of my work took place in failed states, countries where the governments were too weak, or too corrupt, or simply too nonexistent to take care of their people—places like Afghanistan, where millions of refugees clung to life in houses made of burlap sacks, or like Somalia, where there often was no authority higher than a band of teenagers armed with Kalashnikovs. Sometimes, the government stood by inertly as people withered—for example, in Kenya, where drought was threatening to wipe out hundreds of thousands of nomadic herders. But here was a strong, viable, even prosperous government that had made the chilling choice to purposely kill, in cold blood, more than a hundred of its own citizens—theater goers, stage crew members, actors—in the name of declaring victory over a handful of rebels. No Afghan refugee camp had prepared me for this. Around me, a small crowd of reporters stood in the frigid Moscow rain in crushed, funereal silence as the buses slowly pulled away from the theater: we had just witnessed government-sanctioned, quiet mass murder.

After the last bus carrying weak, dying, and dead victims of the siege rolled away, we called in updates to our news desks on our cell phones. David and I flagged down a cab and took Dima Shalganov, a freelance photographer working for the *Globe,* to a small clinic run by Western doctors (the Russian hospitals were overwhelmed with the poisoned hostages) across town. Dima had managed to sneak into the theater right after the Russian special forces took over, and the commandos had beaten him up, kicking him all over his body. We needed to make sure they hadn't broken Dima's ribs.

Then we drove home, listening to radio reports about the mounting death toll from the gas.

Sixty-seven.

Seventy.

Eighty.

Ninety. We got to our enormous, twelve-story apartment building and, instead of going home, shuffled straight into Korchma, the Ukrainian restaurant on the first floor, let a willowy waitress in a traditional long, dark skirt and white, embroidered apron lead us to our pine-lined booth, and did what generations of Russians, betrayed by their government over and over, have done to heal: we ate.

It is not for nothing that Russians celebrate everything—New Year's, birthdays, funerals, wedding anniversaries—by sitting down to an enormous feast. Sure, Americans have Thanksgiving, but, let's face it, that holiday is 65 percent football and only 35 percent turkey, and it doesn't come close to the level of gastronomic indulgence of a Russian holiday repast. In Russia, the table is the traditional place for sharing candid interaction among friends, arguments about politics, and underground poetry readings, and Russian holidays are all about the food.

When I was growing up, my parents kept a separate set of china, stemware, silverware, and serving plates for the holidays (we celebrated birthdays and the New Year). They stored these treasures on different shelves in various rooms of our narrow, three-bedroom apartment, and it was my job to retrieve them several hours before the guests arrived, so that then dad, armed with a special linen dish towel—this one also would only emerge on holidays, creased and stiff from several months of patiently sitting in the back of a closet—could inspect them before setting them on a special folding table we would unfold for the occasion. Some of the plates and silverware were family heirlooms that had survived the Bolshevik revolution of 1917, with a light patina of cracks over the intricate glaze to attest to their venerable age. A silver Fabergé salt bowl, an ethereal art nouveau affair we had inherited from my mother's great-grandfather, a craftsman who had worked for the tsars' famous jeweler, would emerge from behind a glass door in my grandmother's bureau (the salt bowl moved with me, first to my own apartment in St. Petersburg, then to Moscow, then to Massachusetts). A silver vodka snifter engraved with a delicate snowdrop—it had once belonged to dad's long-deceased mother, and now, like the salt bowl, belongs to me—would come out as well.

The stately, century-old, large white-and-blue basin was for *salat olivye,* the fabled Russian potato salad with bologna, sour pickles, onions, boiled carrots, hard-boiled eggs, and green peas drowning in mayonnaise. (*"Salat olivye"*—you say it and it evokes the calorific, decadent pleasures of a Russian holiday, the way the puritanically stark green beans of Thanksgiving never will.) The oval plate painted with delicate pink flowers and slightly chipped on one side was for smoked redfish, which would not be sold in any ordinary Soviet stores, but which dad's father, the heart of any party and an orchestra conductor of some renown, would "obtain" through his "acquaintances."

My grandfather would also "obtain" black Greek olives, pits still in. The olives came in gallon-size, rectangular tin cans and were served exclusively on holidays in a small cut-glass bowl; the rest was somehow preserved or distributed among friends and family. Jellied meat cooked overnight by my grandmother arrived on a tray of white porcelain; *cheremsha,* pickled, crunchy shoots of wild garlic, sat in a cut-glass bowl, like the olives, next to a crystal vase laden with the sauerkraut grandma made each fall and kept, for freshness, in huge glass jars between the doors of our kitchen balcony. Boiled potatoes were kept hot in a pot wrapped lovingly in layers of *Pravda*—the daily newspaper (published, as all Soviet newspapers were, by the government) that our family did not read, but to which the Kremlin forced everybody to subscribe, lest they be suspected of harboring anti-Soviet tendencies—and, after that, a woolen blanket. These tasted best with pickled mushrooms, which I would help collect each August in the birch-and-pine woods outside our summer house, and which emitted an enticing silvery gleam in old china.

Since most of our birthdays came in late fall, after the Soviet Union's managed economy let the last of that year's fresh vegetables rot or disappear from the stores, we rarely ate fresh produce at those holiday meals. But mom's signature beef dish—thin strips of tenderized meat baked under a coating of onions, cheese, and sour cream; she called it "the beef"—waited its turn in the oven and would be served on one antique tray, and the giant sheet of mom's egg-and-cabbage pie would be sliced into neat squares and piled onto another.

These meals would last for hours, with new courses arriving from the kitchen and new bottles of sweet Georgian wine being uncorked and passed around the table. It was as if the abundance of food and the ceremony were meant to at least temporarily stave off the dreary Soviet reality that reigned outside our apartment, starting with the unlit, damp stairwell. The stairwell smelled like cat piss and was frequently populated by the casualties (or beneficiaries, depending on your outlook) of Russia's favorite pastime: drunks who would often fall asleep halfway in, halfway out of the elevator, its unoiled doors clanging shut like pincers at the pale, exposed waist, then opening again, futilely, for hours. In Leningrad, "the elevator is out of service" was a common metonymy.

Big, tasty, fat- and cholesterol-intensive meals—and food in general—were our coping mechanism, the reward for making it through another year in the dictatorship, up another breath-stealing flight of mismatched, M. C. Escher-esque stairs to our sixth-floor apartment. We were not celebrating the settlement and prosperity of our land, the way many Americans do at Thanksgiving; we were celebrating ourselves for having survived our land for another year. Pumpkin? Cranberry sauce? We had *solyanka,* the soup made of beef, pork, lamb, poultry, at least three kinds of cured meat, barley, beans, carrots, potatoes, and pickles, and served hot, with half a cup of full-fat sour cream. Such unapologetically glorious nourishment—here, have another gargantuan dollop of sour cream, some more lard spread for your bread—was invented by a nation that needed something to compensate for the brutality of life in a country perpetually at war with its own people, at war with itself.

For me, a child growing up in the Soviet Union, the deserted grocery stores were the first skirmish lines of this war. The country spanned ten time zones; it could grow oranges in the Black Sea subtropics of Ajara; raise sheep and grow melons in the windswept steppes of Kazakhstan; cultivate tomatoes and eggplants in the foothills of Tajikistan; pick grapes and fruit in the vineyards and orchards of the Caucasus; troll for crabs, shrimp, and fish in the stormy depths of the Pacific, the frigid waters of the Arctic, and the many rivers that veined the country's sprawling topography; raise cattle and harvest grains in the fertile fields of the central Russian plains and the western republics. Using its railway system of more than ninety thousand miles of tracks—the world's longest, our school textbooks never failed to remind us—the Soviet Union could then deliver all of this bounty to its 290 million citizens.

Instead, it starved us.

I am not talking about a lack of the cheap, gratifying snack foods that Americans are used to. Peanut butter and popcorn were luxuries that we only recognized as mysterious references in the rare Hollywood films that had made it past watchful Soviet censors. Life during wartime did not allow for such creature comforts, since their nature is to tell a society: "Hey, you deserve it, you've earned it, have some."

No: the Soviet rulers, through cruelty, ineptitude, or probably both, had literally stripped the stores of everything apart from the bare necessities. The government's notion of what constituted those necessities tended to change from one month to the next, so that in February, say, Soviet citizens could stock their shelves with Chinese canned ham, eggs, foot powder, crab sticks, and gallon-size glass jars of year-old prune juice with marshes of green mold around the rim (where was this juice a year ago?), but most of those would mysteriously vanish from the store in March, and in their place would appear chicken (its feet, head, and guts still in place, and a lot of its feathers still clinging to the yellow skin reminiscent in its thickness of a Soviet general's leather boots), potato starch, dried peas, and Roquefort cheese. (Are you surprised, dear reader? That Roquefort—$13.99 a pound at the grocery store in Plymouth, Massachusetts—cost the ruble equivalent of probably a quarter a pound and was cheaper than cheddar. Even so, no one wanted it, for which self-respecting Soviet citizen would buy something that was so blatantly moldy when most of us already had to clean our other purchases of fungi that were, we hoped, unintentional?) Bananas usually showed up in November or December; I grew up convinced that this was when they were harvested. They were sold green and hard as coconuts (which I had never seen, but I knew from nursery rhymes and Soviet cartoons that they were hard), and my parents would stand in an hour-long line so that they could buy a boxful and let it sit on top of a kitchen cabinet for at least a week before the fruit were suitable for eating.

There was a way to get something special to eat, even for those of us who had no "connections." The occasional *gastronom,* the Soviet parody of a supermarket, had a department where customers could splurge on a treat such as salami if they were willing to also pay for food they decidedly did not want, usually something the state had zealously overproduced or misguidedly imported and now was desperate to unload—say, four large boxes of "Hercules," the Russian word for oatmeal that stuck so firmly to the plate, the spoon, and the teeth of the mortals who dared cook it that the Greek hero himself would not have been able to summon all the powers of Olympus to unglue it. Such extras were aptly called *nagruzka,* or extra weight, and they tended to accompany anything of value that a person would want to buy, not just food. A rare translation of Jorge Luis Borges carried with it the punishment of the most recent edition of *Das Kapital,* with a foreword by the current Communist Party leader.

The process of purchasing food in a *gastronom* seemed designed to ridicule and humiliate the buyers. All food in every store sat behind counters vigorously guarded by hostile salesclerks; the counters were arranged by food type. Each counter had a number we had to memorize each time we went shopping at a new store—although you had to order your food at the counter, you had to prepay for it at the cashier. To buy that thick-skinned, fluffy chicken, some Roquefort, and, say, half a kilo of hard candy, you needed to stand in three different long lines at three different counters, where, if your food of choice was still available by the time it was your turn to order (remember the line for toilet paper in *Moscow on the Hudson?*) the salesclerk would weigh your order and bark out the price. After repeating the process at the other two counters you then shuffled to the line for the cashier, where, for the twenty minutes you awaited your turn, you repeated the mantra of your purchase: "two rubles, seventy-three kopeks to department number one; one ruble, twenty-eight kopeks to department number three; two rubles, five kopeks to department number four." The cashier would then take your money (and swear at you venomously if you didn't produce exact change), and, in return, give you three separate receipts, one for each department. But heaven forbid you mixed up the department numbers or forgot the exact amount of money you owed for your candy, because then you would have to repeat the whole process over again and face the wrath of the overworked, frustrated salesclerks. This ain't no party, this ain't no disco. You got some groceries to last a couple of days, now get out.

When you finally had all the food you could find, and you lugged it out of the supermarket in old plastic bags you reused over and over, washing them with dish soap (a suspect, solid brown brick that somehow still retained the feel of the animal bone of which it had been made; definitely no artificial fragrances)—not because you cared about the environment, but because you never knew whether you would clap your hands on a new plastic bag again—you felt as though you had accomplished something, a feat almost heroic in scope. Stand down, Hercules! I got chicken fat!

And that, right there, was something to celebrate.

In lieu of justification for all this mind-boggling hardship, each subsequent cadre of Communist rulers invoked the never-ending revolutionary struggle of the proletariat (supposedly, us) against the subversive agents of the bourgeois, capitalist counterrevolutionaries, ever prepared to sink their anti-Soviet claws into our great nation and always lurking nearby (and therefore, potentially, also us). In the United States, revolution spelled independence from Britain and then ended, paving the way for the slow establishment of a civil society. In the Soviet Union, revolution never ended: its continuous battle was the way of life. And we all were hostages in that war.

So we ate what we had managed to buy, mixing chicken with canned ham and potato starch, hoping that the carbs and the fat would, at least for a while, insulate us from the knowledge that it might be us in the sights tomorrow. With much of the literature forbidden and much of the music banned, eating was one of the few ways we had to manage our intake of pleasure.

On the third day of the hostage crisis at Nord-Ost, several hours before commandos raided the theater, I briefly spoke with an anguished young woman who said she was the daughter of a man being held inside. She gave only her first name, Aglaya: tormented for generations by their governments and the governments' spies, people in Russia to this day feel uneasy about identifying themselves fully to strangers. We talked in the courtyard outside the theater. It was hard to tell whether Aglaya's face was wet from rain or from tears. She had joined several dozen other relatives of hostages who had gathered near the police cordon. These people believed that their vigil would somehow prevent the police from storming the theater and provoking the hostage takers into detonating their bombs.

None of them harbored any illusions about the benevolence of the self-titled Islamic Suicide Squad. Before the Nord-Ost siege, Chechen rebels had famously orchestrated at least two large-scale hostage takings that had ended with the deaths of dozens of civilians. During one, in June 1995, men led by rebel commander Shamil Basayev—whom some Chechens saw as a liberator and most Russians saw as Chechnya's own Osama bin Laden—took twelve hundred hostages and holed up in a maternity hospital in the southern Russian town of Budyonnovsk. More than a hundred people were killed in the battle for the hospital between Russian forces and Basayev's men; Basayev was allowed to flee.

The following January, Chechen insurgents seized more than three thousand hostages in the Dagestani town of Kizlyar and escaped with many of them to a tiny village called Pervomaiskaya, a constellation of adobe shacks on the border with Chechnya. There, Russia's special forces, backed by thousands of regular troops, battled the rebels for days, leaving dozens of hostages to die in the crossfire. Once again, many of the rebels—including their commander, Salman Raduyev—escaped into

Chechnya. Several months later, in 1996, after Chechen forces brazenly stormed Grozny, surrounded or captured the Russian troops garrisoned inside the city, and forced Moscow's army to withdraw, Russian president Boris Yeltsin declared a cease-fire that effectively halted the war with the breakaway republic for more than three years.

The attacks on Budyonnovsk and Kizlyar were nefarious, horrifying raids, tailored to demonstrate to the Kremlin—and the rest of the world—that the rebels would stop at nothing to get what they wanted. In 2002, in the October downpour outside the besieged Moscow theater, relatives of the hostages understood well that lives of civilians meant little to their captors.

"I hope seven hundred lives mean something to Putin," Aglaya said. "Otherwise, why live in this country?"

It is a refrain I hear often. Surely, the president (the prime minister, the king, the warlord) would protect his subjects if only he knew they were suffering. Surely, a leader of people would not leave them behind. I hear this in Russia, in Chechnya, in Jordan, in Iraq. I don't say anything, the same way I did not say anything to this girl with a wet face, Aglaya. It is not the reporter's place to kill people's hopes.

Meet Vladimir Putin: the former colonel of the KGB, the Soviet secret police, the name of which had become synonymous with disregard for human life; the man who, after he first became president in 2000, brought back the Soviet national anthem nine years after the Soviet Union had ceased to exist, unveiled a plaque in Moscow commemorating the Soviet dictator Josef Stalin, and authorized the issue of special silver coins bearing Stalin's portrait, glossing over the small detail that up to twenty million people had been executed without trial or starved or worked to death in the labor camps of the gulag during Stalin's Great Terror.

(Stalin, incidentally, had specifically targeted all Chechens. When Nazi Germany attacked the Soviet Union, Chechen separatist rebels seized upon the turmoil to rekindle a full-fledged insurgency against the Soviet rule; in parts of the mountainous region, by some accounts, up to 80 percent of all fighting-age men joined the revolt. In 1944, Stalin sought vengeance. During a campaign the Soviets had dubbed "Chechevitsa"—

the Russian word means "lentils," but sounds a little like "Chechnya"—the Soviet army and security police rounded up the entire population of Chechnya, half a million people, put them on freight trains, and shipped them off to Kazakhstan. Between a quarter and a half of the Chechens died on these trains of disease, dehydration, and starvation. The survivors and the children born to them in exile were allowed to return to Chechnya only in 1957, four years after Stalin died. It is possible—in fact, it is likely—that Saddam Hussein, who famously admired and emulated Stalin, modeled his al Anfal campaign against Iraqi Kurds on Stalin's Chechevitsa.)

Putin rose to power in the most dire of circumstances. Eight years after the Soviet Union broke up, millions of workers were going months without paychecks while a tiny group of Kremlin insiders, who had snapped up most of Russia's industries for peanuts from Yeltsin's post-Soviet government, famously bought British mansions and Swiss chalets. Unable to pay their electric bills, nuclear weapons facilities had switched off their security features. Impoverished soldiers abandoned their posts to pick mushrooms in the pine-and-birch forests of my childhood to supplement their diets. A hungry recruit broke into my parents' summer cottage north of St. Petersburg to steal two cans of corned beef. Gangland-style assassinations became the choice method of settling business disputes. People longed for someone who could rein in the oligarchs, curb crime, restore Russia's self-esteem as a great military power, and provide for the common man.

In the summer of 1999, rebels operating out of Chechnya (free of Russian occupiers after the 1996 cease-fire) attacked Dagestan, seized several villages and towns, and pronounced the creation of the "Independent Islamic State of Dagestan." Chechen gangs were holding for ransom hundreds of hostages taken from Russian cities. And, most ominously, someone had blown up four apartment buildings in Moscow and two other Russian cities, killing more than three hundred people. The Kremlin, which had been portraying the small Muslim nation in the Caucasus as a nest of terrorists incapable of civilized behavior or of governing itself, immediately blamed the bombings on the Chechens.

This paved the way for Putin, who had been plucked from the shadows by the inner circle of the ailing President Yeltsin, to pledge, in shockingly blunt jargon that seemed taken straight from a Soviet gangster flick, that he would "wipe out in the outhouse" the perpetrators, and launch a full-scale invasion of Chechnya. For the second time since 1994, Russia occupied the region, scoring quick victories, taking back Dagestan, and recapturing Grozny in a campaign that propelled Putin, as the candidate who would restore law and order, to the Russian presidency several months later.

Several Russian and Western observers and critics called the apartment bombings a cynical provocation, staged by the government to put Putin in the Kremlin. Several of the Russian critics were later jailed, forced into exile, or killed. (Remember Alexander Litvinenko, the former Russian spook poisoned by polonium-laden sushi in London?) To silence dissenters more effectively, the government quickly took over much of the national media, including all three television channels with countrywide broadcasting. Putin was so wildly popular, and his government so firmly in control of the news programming, that it barely mattered that the war raged on for years, and that violence in the Caucasus continues to this day.

Was it true that Putin and other Russian leaders were willing to blow up their compatriots—mostly blue-collar workers and military personnel—in order to create a pretext to subdue Chechnya and galvanize support for the future president? I don't know. Any thorough investigation into the apartment bombings quickly withered. All evidence was promptly ordered classified for seventy-five years, long enough for people to forget that they had ever cared. But the very notion, the acceptance bordering on resignation, that Putin and his friends could have sacrificed Russian civilians so lightly—and the fact that the government did nothing to dispute that theory other than to forcibly silence the few domestic dissenters who dared give voice to it—illustrated the greatest disillusionment of Russia's creeping transformation from a fake socialist state ruled by indifference toward its subjects to a fake democracy ruled by indifference toward its subjects. After a brief flirtation with the notion of building a civil society, the country easily fell back on its long-standing tradition of treating its own citizens like enemies and hostages in the name of keeping its rulers in power.

All that had changed, it seemed, was that the perks of power had grown from special stores and hotels to Mercedes S-600s and summer homes on Cyprus and Capri, prized oilfields and refineries, factories and gold mines. The scraps thrown to the subjects had grown from ghastly *gastronom* fare to imported goods (hello, peanut butter and popcorn! *konichiwa,* sushi!) available, to those who had the cash, in Western-style supermarkets in major cities such as St. Petersburg and Moscow.

The morning after Aglaya and I spoke, before sunrise smeared with ghostly yellow the heavy clouds over the wet, cold capital, President Putin reminded the young woman and the rest of us that, eleven years after the fall of Communism, Russia continued to operate on the premise that disregard for human life could always be justified by the needs of the state. And if it could not be justified, then the state stopped talking about it.

And so did everyone else.

In this environment of apprehension and betrayal, when you could not trust your own government with your life, borsch was the great leveling force. It was the dish we all had grown up with: the soulless apparatchiki, the indifferent elite, the enduring, perpetually betrayed nation. As the filling, nourishing soup of the Soviet Union, borsch was not just a miracle drug for anyone struggling to survive Russia; it transcended regional borders and boundaries of class. When I lived in Moscow, I could (when I was feeling really flush) get borsch at Pushkin, one of the capital's classiest restaurants, named after Russia's most celebrated nineteenth-century Romantic poet, where courteous and solemn waiters in period clothes elegantly glided from table to table, ferrying flambé desserts and bowls of sparkling black caviar on ice. In St. Petersburg, I could warm up with a crimson bowl of the hearty, vegetarian brew at the Idiot, the one that serves a shot of vodka with every meal (vodka goes really well with borsch, by the way), or, for the ruble equivalent of fifty cents, at a tired canteen near the wharves into which longshoremen would pile, stomping gray slush off their boots at the door, after a diesel-choked day at the docks—and it would be just as good, just as hearty, just as crimson with beet juice. Out of desperation after a day of trying to report in Chechnya, I could buy it at the claptrap Assa Hotel, the only lodging available then in Nazran, an Ingush town where foreign journalists—and Russian spooks spying on these journalists—stayed whenever they were going to or coming from the rebellious region.

And, exhausted, disheartened, and starved after watching a night in the capital descend into three days and nights of unutterable horror, I could get it at Korchma, the Ukrainian joint that was so fortuitously located on the ground floor of my Moscow apartment building. Borsch was the great equalizer, the therapy most readily available, the gastronomic apotheosis of comfort in a country where comforts were so hard to come by—a country that made no promise that it would stand by you.

~

Russian Soul Food

*P*eople often ask me if I miss Russia, and I always struggle to find the correct answer. I left in 2004, after working as a foreign correspondent in Moscow became too difficult. Ex-KGB (or KGB-trained) minders from the Foreign Ministry had tapped my phones, tracked my movement around the country, and ordered me to inform them each time I wanted to travel abroad. At the same time, the wave of xenophobia that had helped propel Putin to power had engulfed Russia; in the playground, an elderly lady forbade her little grandson from playing with Fyodor, who was six at the time, because she had overheard him speaking English.

What I do miss is the food. Some of it—the pickled mushrooms in their gooey aspic; the half-sour garlic tinted pink with beet juice; and the salted herring with onions and boiled potatoes—I can probably find in some specialty shops in the States. Some of it—the crunchy chunks of marinated lamprey and the battered bits of deep-fried *koryushka,* a tiny, smelt-like fish that smells like cucumber and is caught in St. Petersburg only in the middle of spring—is all but impossible to find here.

But some of it—the famous borsch, or the decadent *solyanka,* or the beloved *salat olivye*—I can re-create quite easily. And so can you.

❧

Borsch

Serves 8 to 10, and you'll probably have leftovers

B orsch is the pride of every Russian cook—even though (or maybe because) each cook prepares it differently. My grandmother, a refined professor of German from St. Petersburg, makes a mean vegetarian borsch with prunes. The mother of my artist ex-boyfriend, a daughter of Cossack horsemen from Central Russia who worked as a telephone operator by day and brewed atrociously putrid moonshine in her bathroom at night, prepared hers with large beef bones and chunks of uncured bacon (to be fair, she prepared pretty much everything with chunks of uncured bacon, even apple pie). I am going to go with a leaner version of beef-based borsch here, but you can always skip the meat and add some kidney beans instead (alternatively, if you're feeling like some Cossack food, sauté the carrots in bacon fat instead of olive oil). And yes, the beans can come from a can. Borsch is the closest Russia has ever come to a democracy.

You'll need a really large pot.

1 pound lean beef, cut into thin strips, or one 15-ounce can kidney
    beans, rinsed and drained (or 1½ cups cooked kidney beans)
Salt and pepper, to taste
3 large carrots, peeled and grated
Olive oil or bacon fat
1 medium cabbage, white or red, cored and shredded
1 medium onion, peeled but not cut
3 large beets (just the roots, no greens), peeled and grated
1 large bell pepper (any color—everything will end up being
    a shade of red in the end), halved and cored
4 large potatoes, peeled and cubed
4 tomatoes, halved
6 prunes
2 tablespoons ketchup
1 tablespoon ground coriander (or seeds)
Sour cream and chopped parsley, for garnish
Minced garlic, optional

1. Fill a large soup pot halfway with water and bring to a boil. The proportion of water to solids should be about one to one. If you're cooking with meat, add the meat to the cold water and boil it for 10 minutes, then pour out the broth, fill the pot halfway with fresh water, add salt, and boil for 10 more minutes. If you're going vegetarian, boil the water, add salt, and skip to the next step.

2. While your water (or broth) is boiling, sauté the carrots in olive oil (or bacon fat) until tender. Add the cabbage, sautéed carrots, and onion to the water (or broth), in this order, and wait for it to boil again. Add the beets. Remove the onion, discard it, and reduce the heat to a simmer. Simmer for 15 minutes.

3. Add the bell pepper, potatoes, tomatoes, prunes, ketchup, coriander, and pepper. If you are making vegetarian borsch, add the beans now. Simmer for 10 to 15 minutes, or until all the vegetables are tender.

4. Serve the borsch hot, with a generous dollop of sour cream in the middle and a sprinkle of parsley on top. Some people also like to put minced fresh garlic into their borsch plate; it gives the soup an extra kick. Borsch tastes perfect with dark rye bread (with or without butter or lard) and with ice-cold vodka. You can serve leftovers for up to 5 days if you keep them in the fridge. Definitely reheat before serving.

❧

Solyanka

Serves 8 to 10

*S*olyanka originated as a peasant leftover soup—a Slavic version of the Tuscan *ribollita*—but over the years it has become a staple soup in most restaurants serving Russian food. Like *ribollita, solyanka* is also a meal in and of itself. The key to making a good *solyanka* is to use as many different meat products as possible, cholesterol be damned.

4 ounces each of lamb, pork, beef, and chicken, cubed
Salt and pepper, to taste
2 bay leaves
1 cup barley
¼ cup tomato paste
2 large carrots, peeled and cubed
4 large potatoes, peeled and cubed

Oil, for frying the onion and garlic
1 large onion, finely chopped
4 cloves garlic, minced
4 ounces each of salami, pastrami, pepperoni, and baked ham
3 large sour pickles, finely chopped
1 tablespoon paprika
One 15-ounce can cannellini beans, rinsed and drained
   (or 1½ cups cooked cannellini beans)
1 cup pitted black or kalamata olives
Sour cream, chopped parsley, and 8 lemon wedges, for garnish

1. Combine the raw meat in a large soup pot, fill the pot halfway with water, and bring to a boil. After 5 minutes, pour out the water, fill the pot halfway with fresh water, add salt and the bay leaves, and bring to a boil. Add the barley. Reduce the heat and simmer for 15 minutes. Add the tomato paste, carrots, and potatoes and simmer for 5 minutes.

2. Meanwhile, pour enough oil to cover the bottom of a skillet and heat the skillet. When the oil is hot, add the onion and garlic and sauté until the onion is translucent but not brown. Remove the skillet from the heat and add the onion and garlic to the simmering soup. When the barley and vegetables are tender, add the salami, pastrami, pepperoni, ham, pickles, paprika, pepper, beans, and olives. Simmer for 5 minutes.

3. Serve hot, with a dollop of sour cream and a sprinkle of parsley. Serve lemon wedges on the side, to squeeze into the soup.

   Skip dessert.

꙳

Salat Olivye

Serves 8, and if you have leftovers, have them for lunch the next day

O pinions differ on how much mayonnaise goes into a good *olivye*. Some say the salad is prepared right only when a metal serving spoon being pulled out of the *olivye* capriciously acts as though it wants to stay in the salad forever. Lara Vapnyar, a writer who had emigrated to the United States from Russia ten years before I did, beautifully writes, in her collection of short stories *Broccoli and Other Tales of Food and Love,* that the best *olivye* occurs if you "add more and more" mayonnaise "until the salad makes a wet slurping sound while you mix it, similar to the sound of the

snow slush on the streets of Manhattan when you step in it." Others say
there should be only enough mayonnaise to lightly coat the ingredients. I
leave it up to the chef: if you want to drown your *olivye* in mayonnaise, go
for it. My personal belief is that the trick to perfecting *olivye* has nothing to
do with the mayo: it is to be generous with your bologna and pickles, and
cut your vegetables and meat very finely into cubes of the same size.

In some households, *olivye* is called "the bucket salad." Not because you
die from eating it (it's not *that* bad for you), but because of all the meals on
the holiday table, it is the one made in the largest quantities—by the buck-
etful. One reason for this is that the salad takes a long time to prepare (it is
common for the host's entire family and even some guests to pitch in, cutting, peeling, and opening cans), so why not make a whole lot of it at once?
The other reason, of course, is that it's so damn good, keeps well, and tastes
even better the next day, after the mayo and the juice from the pickles have
had a chance to saturate everything.

6 large potatoes
6 large carrots
8 hard-boiled eggs, peeled
2 pounds bologna, finely cubed (some food snobs use pastrami
    or ham or even smoked turkey breast instead, but as far as I'm
    concerned, no food snob should be indulging in something as
    delightfully unhealthy as *olivye,* so to hell with them)
Two 8 ½-ounce cans green peas, drained
2 large onions, finely chopped
2 large bunches parsley, finely chopped
6 large sour pickles, finely chopped
1 medium apple, optional (apples belong to the *olivye* that
    features pastrami, not bologna)
Lots of mayo

1. Boil the potatoes and carrots, unpeeled, in a large pot until they can be
pierced easily with a fork. Move them immediately from the boiling water
into ice-cold water (this should make them easier to peel), then pat dry. Peel
them and dice into really small cubes.

2. With a fork, crumble the eggs into a large serving bowl. Add the remaining ingredients and mix well. If you can resist the temptation of eating
it immediately, refrigerate for at least 1 hour before serving; that will allow
the mayo to mix with the pickle juice and permeate the concoction.

Eight

Mezze in Jerusalem, Mansaf in Al Quds*

I f you look southwest from the limestone summit of Mount Nebo in Jordan on an exceptionally clear day, then, across the oily surface of the Dead Sea, you can see Jerusalem. Sprawled on the lazy hills like a swatch of red-and-white lace, even from this spot almost thirty miles away, Jerusalem tells a tale of two cities entrenched in their contrasting visions of the world. The white dots are the flat roofs of the mostly Arab East Jerusalem. Palestinians use the roofs to string laundry on taut rope lines; to collect the rare Middle Eastern rain into water barrels that heat up in the scorching daytime sun; and to sleep on rolled-out mattresses on stifling summer nights. The red dots are the homes of West Jerusa-

---

*Al Quds—Arabic name for Jerusalem.

lem's Jews, who slant their roofs and cover them with terra-cotta tiles, the same way generations of their ancestors had done to protect their homes against snow and rain in the shtetls of Eastern Europe. The Ash-kenazim* must have brought the habit of being prepared for inclement weather to the desert along with yellowed family photographs and mem-ories of pogroms and the Holocaust.

In the Old Testament, Mount Nebo is the place in the Land of Moab from which Moses beheld the Promised Land for the first time. When Moses scaled the twenty-six hundred feet of bleak limestone and grass after wandering the desert for forty years, the Bible says, he saw "all the land": past the hills of Jerusalem, all the way to the Mediterranean Sea. I envy the old man's eyesight, and the fortuitous weather. More often than not, a layer of thick haze clings to the Jordan Valley and the low hills beyond it. Most visitors to Mount Nebo have to satisfy themselves with a glimpse, almost directly across the river, of just one biblical attraction: the West Bank city of Jericho, the lowest permanently inhabited place on earth, its blood-steeped walls sheathed almost always nowadays in curvy layers of maroon and heather smog.

One windy December evening in 2002, when harriers glided over the Jordan River in low circles, searching the reed beds for supper, the lights of Jericho were all that Israel was willing to reveal to us, two dusk-time visitors to the sacred site: a Soviet-born Jew who had recently returned from a reporting trip to Israel, the West Bank, and Gaza; and a would-be Palestinian terrorist.

Bassam Shream was a Jordanian driver, a tour guide, a heavy drinker, an even heavier smoker, and—like Wahid, my Afghan translator—a for-mer boxer. We met in 2002 at the Marriott in downtown Amman, where I was staying during an assignment for the *Chronicle*. Bassam was work-ing as a hotel driver. This was my first trip to Jordan, where I knew no one; he had a friendly smile, and I hired him to work for me. He spoke inelegant English, which would improve only slightly in the six years of

----

*Ashkenazim—European Jews.

our friendship, and he wrote in English phonetically, with a thick Arabic accent. Once, before a trip to Jordan, I sent Bassam a text message asking him if he wanted me to bring him anything from the States.

"Barf m," he texted back. Excuse me? "For smell," he elaborated. Clearly, I wasn't getting something. The next text message cleared it up: "Xpensiv lebl," it read. My friend was asking for a bottle of nice perfume.

Of course, I spoke no Arabic. It is thanks to Bassam's English that I can write this chapter.

I had come to Jordan to finagle an Iraqi visa ahead of the impending invasion by the United States and the "alliance of the willing" it had cobbled together to topple Saddam Hussein. I spent two weeks waiting for that visa to be denied. While consular officials behind the turquoise-and-ocher replica of Babylon's Ishtar Gate that guards the Iraqi embassy in Amman deliberated what to do with my application (although it is just as likely that they had simply tossed it in the trash can the day it arrived), I bided my time reporting from Jordan.

On the eve of the war, this kingdom, with a pro-American foreign policy but a geopolitical reality firmly wedged between Iraq on the east and Israel and the West Bank on the west, had found itself facing a curious conundrum. On the one hand was Jordan's desire to be a friendly neighbor to Israel, and an American ally in the fight against international terrorism. Dollars had a lot to do with it: Jordan depended on tourism, and an open border with Israel—so that pilgrims to the Holy Land could cross the Jordan River as easily as Elisha and Elijah did it—made at least as much economic sense to Amman as it did to Tel Aviv. As for the United States, King Abdullah II did not need his Harvard education to understand simple math: in 2008, the tiny kingdom received over 680 million dollars in American aid, behind only Israel, Egypt, and Pakistan.

On the other hand was Jordan's Palestinian population. Approximately six out of ten Jordanians are Palestinian, and decades after they had fled or were forced to leave their homes following the Arab-Israeli Six-Day War* of 1967, tens of thousands of these refugees were still liv-

---

*Arab-Israeli Six-Day War—the war between Israel and the forces of Egypt, Jordan, and Syria, June 5–10, 1967. Israel launched strikes against Egypt, Syria, and Jordan, and ended up in control of the Sinai, Gaza, the West Bank, the Golan Heights, and Jerusalem.

ing in the suffocating, squalid, and barely sanitary warrens of refugee camps where families cramped into claustrophobic cinder-block dwellings ran power lines illegally from one rusted roof of corrugated metal to the next, and children played near slimy rivulets of open sewage.

One such site, Baqa'a Camp, on Amman's outskirts, was home to at least a hundred thousand people. Two of them were Bassam's parents.

They had not seen their old homes for almost half a century. Yet, they were still hoping to return to their former towns and villages one day. And in 2002, they linked their hope for reclaiming their ancestral lands to Saddam Hussein, who dreamed of destroying Israel and returning Jerusalem to the Muslims, like his twelfth-century compatriot, Saladin, had done during the Crusades. Saddam had fired Scud missiles at Israel in 1991, and had reportedly awarded multithousand-dollar handouts to families of Palestinian *shahid**—men and women who died fighting the Jewish state in the name of a free Palestine. The Palestinians in Jordan believed he was the man who would bring them back home.

During the first Gulf War, Jordan did not join the U.S.-led coalition against Iraq because King Hussein, Abdullah's father, did not want to alienate Jordan's Palestinians. By 2002, King Abdullah was willing to take the risk.

He was for the most part successful in preventing dissent through a well-balanced combination of overwhelming nationalistic propaganda (every building, billboard, bus, and taxi seemed to be plastered with the country's red, white, green, and black flag and portraits of King Abdullah: alone, with his gorgeous wife, with their picture-perfect children, in a suit and tie, in tribal red-and-white-checkered *kuffiyeh*,** or in military uniform), discrimination (with a small exception, the most prestigious and politically meaningful jobs were distributed among the elite Hashemite clan, leaving behind the Palestinian majority and the barely literate bedouins), and the use of a well-informed

---

*Shahid—Arabic for "martyr." Palestinian suicide bombers are often called *shahid*.

**Kuffiyeh—an Arab word for a traditional head scarf worn by men. The color and pattern of a *kuffiyeh* can reflect the country of origin, tribe, and status of the wearer. In the Middle East, the most commonly worn *kuffiyehs* are red-and-white or black-and-white checkered scarves.

and well-metastasized security apparatus called, like its Iraqi counterpart, the Mukhabarat.

But Jordan's security police and exuberant nationalism did not prevent the rise of homegrown Islamic fundamentalists who aligned themselves with international terrorist groups (the most famous, Abu Musab al Zarqawi, would ravage Iraq as the head of al Qaeda in Mesopotamia until an American air strike killed him in 2006). Nor could they stop the weapons smugglers from trafficking handguns, rocket-propelled grenade launchers, Kalashnikov assault rifles, and ammunition from Iraq across Jordan's basalt desert to the West Bank and Gaza, arming the Palestinian intifada that was bleeding Israel. Similarly, the government's official policy toward its neighbors to the east and to the west did little to change the way Jordan's Palestinians felt about Iraq, Israel, and the impending war.

Few in Jordan dared to openly criticize King Abdullah's friendship with Israel or his support of the American war in Iraq, especially in interviews to the press. After a day of trying to get people to talk on the record about the war, I asked Bassam what he thought. With the lit Marlboro Light pinched between his index and middle fingers, the driver pointed at three invisible points in the western darkness that sprawled beneath Mount Nebo.

"Qalqilya is there. Nablus is there. Al Quds"—Bassam used the Arabic name for the city that is as sacred to Muslims as it is to Christians and Jews—"is there." Was he being a tour guide now, showing me the marvels of the Holy Land, or a stateless Palestinian, homesick for the little West Bank village that his parents had been forced to flee years before he was born? The sun had set over the West Bank in an agony of green and mauve, and the lights of Jericho blinked at us from across the invisible river.

"People here like Saddam very much," Bassam said. He took a drag, and the tip of his cigarette mimicked the coruscating hills on the other side. "They think he is a great man, and I agree."

It would be several years before Bassam told me that he also had been trained to kill Jews.

Take the American debates over same-sex marriage, abortion, gun control, and the teaching of evolution in public middle schools, amplify the emotional charge that accompanies these topics by ten billion times, and you still won't get anywhere near the level of combustibility that commonly accompanies discussions about the Arab-Israeli conflict. In fact, "Arab-Israeli conflict" is not even the correct name for the seemingly eternal hostilities that harrow this tortured land. But the subject is so volatile, so entrenched, and so complex, that any name I use to describe it, its major participants, and the contested land at its heart is bound to give someone to understand that I am taking a side in the battle.

"Israel and Palestine" suggests that I believe two states exist; "Israel and the Palestinian territories" suggests that I believe they don't. "Arab-Israeli conflict" unnecessarily includes countries like Jordan and Egypt in the camp of nations formally opposed to the existence of Israel; "Israeli-Palestinian conflict" unnecessarily excludes countries like Syria. And what about Iran? To avoid any potential hassle over semantics, journalists often resort to politically correct names that sound like cumbersome lists ("Israel, West Bank, and Gaza"); or, if we are looking for shorthand, to euphemisms ("the Middle East").

Add to this the fact that across most of the Middle East (the real one) and parts of Central Asia, the Jewish state is a country That-Must-Not-Be-Named, and that the very mention of the I-word is bound to rile someone. That is why Western reporters in Afghanistan, Iraq, Iran, Syria, Egypt, Lebanon, and the Gulf State refer to Israel among each other as "Dixie"—as in, "Justin Sullivan from Getty Images and I worked together in Dixie in 2002."

Many reporters who cover the Middle East (the real one) carry two passports, since most countries on the Arabian Peninsula will not accept any visitor with a Dixie stamp. And yet, even though everyone knows that it is impossible to enter the Palestinian territories without Israel's permission—unless you cross the border illegally (perhaps alongside a shipment of rocket-propelled grenades)—most Western journalists who work in the region frequently hear people in Arab countries complain that we do not spend enough time recording the hardships of people living in the West Bank and the Gaza Strip.

Eight months before Bassam and I watched the sun set over Dixie, I was trying to do exactly that.

One April afternoon in 2002, I was hanging out with some teenage boys on Omar al Mukhtar Street, the main shopping street of Gaza City (the street is named after a slain leader of the Libyan resistance to Italian colonists who captured and hanged him in 1931). Most shops seemed to have been closed for the intifada, the Palestinian uprising that is always brewing just below the surface but that had intensified since 2000. But three things that appeared to be the city's permanent fixtures were readily available: construction rubble, which lay everywhere in conical piles (the dirt would make easy stuffing for the sandbags the residents used to block the streets when Israeli troops arrived, and the rocks were good for hurling at Israeli soldiers); rusted fingers of bare steel rods that pointed skyward from the unfinished top floor of almost every building, like some architectural warning to the heavens, or perhaps an admonishment; and, plastered to cinder-block walls spray-painted with anti-Semitic slogans and pictures of exploding buses and bleeding Israeli soldiers, countless garish posters of local *shahid.*

The posters looked as if they had been slapped together by the same designers who make single-use, paper place mats for many American diners—the kind that advertise the local taxidermist, the funeral home, and the chain-saw rental. In each poster, the young man (and, rarely, a woman) who had died trying (though not always succeeding) to kill Jews looked sternly at the camera, often clutching a Kalashnikov. Behind the dead foot soldiers of the Palestinian liberation movement, photoshopped into every picture, exaggerated orange-to-purple sunsets loomed over Jerusalem's al Aqsa Mosque.*

These posters were the objects of worshipful envy among my pals:

---

*Al Aqsa Mosque—the third-holiest place in Islam. The mosque is located on the Temple Mount in Jerusalem, the holiest site in Judaism. The al Aqsa Martyrs Brigade is the name of one Palestinian militant group.

talkative, earnest kids no older than fifteen who one day would make—
and by now, many of whom probably already have made—a bountiful
harvest for Hamas, the anti-Israel political party and paramilitary organization with a stronghold in Gaza, which would pluck them off the
streets and train them to kill Jews. The boys were catching their breath
after running behind a funeral procession Hamas was holding that day
for several *shahid*. A couple of the kids were throwing rocks at the picture
of an exploding bus scrawled on the wall of one building: getting some
target practice "for when the Jews come," one boy explained. I liked
these boys a lot. They were romantics, full of the arrogant invincibility of
youth. War had not yet hollowed out their eyes.

"Who wants to be a martyr?" I asked the kids, through an interpreter.

It was like asking a group of Boston kids who wants to be the starting
center fielder for the Red Sox.

Dozens of fists flew up into the air:

"Me, me, me, me!" the kids all yelled.

"I want to be like them!" from the back row.

"Me, too!" someone shouted, jumping up and down.

Final answer?

"I want to blow myself up!"

This was, formally, the second intifada, known as the al Aqsa Intifada. The trigger for the second intifada was the visit in September 2000
to the Temple Mount*—home of the al Aqsa Mosque—by Ariel Sharon:
a belligerent former general, an Israeli hero of the Arab-Israeli Six-Day
War, and, depending on your side in this eternal conflict, an indomitable
defender of his people or a despicable war criminal. Sharon's military exploits, and his willingness to stop at nothing as he bluntly pushed ahead to
achieve his goals, had earned him the nickname "the Bulldozer" among
the Israelis. (That nickname took on a special meaning in a country that
uses bulldozers to demolish houses of suspected Palestinian militants—

---

*Temple Mount—the area of Mount Moriah in the Old City of Jerusalem where, according
to the Old Testament and the Koran, Abraham (Ibrahim) offered his son Isaac (Ishaq) as a
sacrifice to God. Muslims believe that from the Temple Mount, the Prophet Mohammed as-
cended to heaven. Jews believe that from a rock on the Temple Mount, the world was made.
The Temple Mount is also the location of the Dome of the Rock and al Aqsa Mosque. All this
on thirty-three and a half acres of land. If this doesn't explain why the Arab-Israeli conflict is
so difficult to solve, what does?

sometimes killing people in the process—and where the bulldozer has become a symbol of crude violence.) His acquiescence to the massacres of hundreds of Palestinian and Lebanese civilians at Sabra and Shatila,* when he led the Israeli invasion of Lebanon in 1982, had generated the Palestinians' name for Sharon: "the Butcher of Beirut." Soon after the 2000 visit to the Temple Mount, he became prime minister.

The first intifada, in protest of the Israeli occupation of the Gaza Strip and the West Bank, officially lasted sporadically from 1987 until the signing, in 1993, of the Oslo Accords, a mutual declaration of agreement that "it is time to put an end to decades of confrontation and conflict" and "strive to live in peaceful coexistence." Of course, although scholars, politicians, and journalists refer to the first and the second intifadas, it is not as though someone had ever blown the whistle (or the shofar) on a conflict that still is not resolved—much like in Chechnya, where the insurgency has truly never ended since the Russian empire forced the mountainous region into its fold in the late eighteenth century. The Palestinian uprising began in 1948, after the creation of the independent state of Israel was announced, and will not end as long as the war that dare not speak its name continues. The hostilities dwindled down in February 2005, when Sharon and the Palestinian leader Mahmoud Abbas declared a truce. More than three thousand Palestinians and more than a thousand Israelis were killed between September 2000 and February 2005.

The *Chronicle* sent me to cover the intifada and Israel's unsparing effort to defeat it in April 2002. From my Jerusalem hotel I had the view of the television towers of Ramallah, where the Palestinian leader Yasser Arafat was under siege by the Israeli Defense Forces; of the pale walls of the Old City of Jerusalem; and of Israeli helicopters hovering over

---

*Sabra and Shatila—Palestinian refugee camps in Beirut. On September 16, 1982, the Lebanese Christian Phalangist militia, with a go-ahead from the Israeli defense forces, entered the camps looking for some Palestinian fighters who were believed to have been hiding among the refugees. For sixty-two hours, the Phalangists, who blamed Palestinian fighters for the assassination of their leader and president-elect, Bachir Gemayel, on September 14, raped and murdered Palestinians inside the camps. It is believed that the massacre was tacitly approved by the Israeli troops who were stationed around the perimeter of the camps and were led by Ariel Sharon. The number of victims is disputed. Israeli intelligence says between seven and eight hundred people, including women and children, were murdered in the camps; Palestinians claim that the death toll is as high as thirty-five hundred people.

Bethlehem. These landmarks were confined to a proximity that felt almost claustrophobic, and seemed to make the intractable conflict even more intense, more inexorable.

This density overwhelmed me. Centuries of suffering and violence steeped every square inch of contested soil, flowed in the juice of every lemon, radiated from every pebble. Decades of superb reporting from this conflict intimidated me. I did not know where to begin. David reminded me.

"Your readers aren't there, you are," he told me over the phone from Moscow. "You are the only eyes they have." My job was to make the teenage wannabe suicide bombers from Gaza heard in the delis of San Francisco, to deliver the grief of an Israeli mother whose child was killed by a terrorist to a family in Marin County. Onward.

By then, Palestinian militants were launching almost daily attacks on Israeli civilians and troops. Israeli forces responded by kicking off what they called Operation Defensive Shield, which looked less like a shield than a double-edged sword. The Israelis drove their tanks and armored personnel carriers into the West Bank, reoccupying the six largest towns and rounding up scores of young men. In Ramallah, the Palestinian political center (since Palestine technically is not a country—although it has a permanent mission with an observer status in the United Nations—we cannot call the seat of its government a capital), Israeli troops surrounded Arafat's compound, putting the president of the Palestinian National Authority under house arrest. In Bethlehem, Israeli soldiers battled Palestinian gunmen holed up in the Church of the Nativity, which Christians believe to be the birthplace of Jesus. For six straight days, Israeli artillery shelled the refugee camp in Jenin, leveling almost all buildings and killing at least as many civilians as they did militants; some died of wounds and sepsis because no one was allowed to leave or enter the camp, not even medics. (When I tried to walk into Jenin with a group of Palestinian doctors—they were wearing scrubs and were unarmed apart from a few syringes; I was waving my pen and notebook like a white flag—a Merkava Mk3 tank fired a 120-millimeter shell in our direction as a warning shot. We got the hint and scrammed.) The UN secretary general later reported that 497 Palestinians and 29 Israeli soldiers were killed during

Operation Defensive Shield and in the immediate aftermath. Some of the Palestinians were killed when they accidentally tripped the booby traps set by Arab militants and meant for Israeli troops. Like the Afghan mujahedin who mined their fields without leaving a map, the fighters who had set the mines in Jenin—usually trip-wired to doors of civilian homes—were either arrested or killed, and were not there to warn the civilians returning to their homes.

Curfews that lasted for days and severe restrictions of commerce Israel imposed during Operation Defensive Shield meant that international relief agencies could not bring humanitarian aid to the most impoverished parts of the West Bank and Gaza. In Gaza, which was already crippled by poverty and unemployment, prices of staples such as eggs and bread went up by a third. In Jenin, when the siege was finally lifted and the agencies and journalists were allowed in, I saw a sea of people mob and nearly topple an aid truck carrying cooking oil and flour. People shoved, elbowed, dragged each other out of the way. This, too, brought to mind Afghanistan, with its wars for American food aid—although in the food-aid fights in Jenin no guns were involved, as far as I could see, and definitely no tanks. The United Nations reported that one out of five residents of the Palestinian territories did not have enough to eat.

In Israel, where parents in crowded emergency rooms and suddenly eerily quiet homes were mourning children wounded and killed by the ruthless bombings in public places, there was no shortage of food. But accessing the supply that was there had become a life-threatening extravagance. Terrorists targeted grocery shoppers and diners.

On August 9, 2001, a man carrying a guitar case walked into a busy Sbarro pizzeria in downtown Jerusalem during the lunch hour. Inside the guitar case was a twenty-pound homemade bomb packed with screws, nails, and bolts. When the man detonated the explosive device, killing himself, he also took the lives of fifteen people. One of them was Yokheved Shushan, a ten-year-old girl with golden curls. She was eating lunch with her mother and older sister, Miriam. The bomb drove hundreds of tiny metal fragments into the bodies of 130 diners, including

Miriam; nineteen months after the explosion, the teenage girl remained confined to a hospital bed. The shock wave from the explosion ruptured Miriam's spleen. Pieces of burning furniture broke Miriam's hips and ankles and burned her stomach. Metal splinters forever lodged under her skin.

"The family is not what it once was," the girls' mother, Ester, who had six other daughters, told me. After the bombing Ester had stopped leaving her apartment, even to shop for her surviving girls. She had stopped cooking. She could not eat. In her living room, an oily trace of Ester's lipstick, a single farewell kiss, clouded the glass on the picture frame over the photograph of Yokheved's smiling face.

"We feel scattered," Ester whispered. "We are all like parts."

Around the time I arrived in Jerusalem, the litany of suicide attacks had taken on the feel of a sinister pub crawl:

March 9, 2002. A suicide bomber detonated his bomb at the crowded Café Moment in central Jerusalem, killing eleven late-night diners and injuring fifty-four.

March 27, 2002. A suicide bomber in Netanya set off an explosive device in the dining room of the Park Hotel, where two hundred and fifty guests had just sat down for their Passover seder.* Thirty people were killed in the attack, which became known as the Passover Massacre.

March 29, 2002. A suicide bomber killed a shopper and a security guard in a supermarket in Jerusalem.

March 30, 2002. A suicide bomber in Tel Aviv killed a customer at My Coffee Shop.

March 31, 2002. A suicide bomber, this one a woman, detonated her explosives in the packed, beach-front Maxim restaurant in Haifa, killing nineteen people.

---

*Passover seder—a traditional Jewish feast that celebrates the beginning of the Passover holiday. Passover takes place during the Hebrew month of Nissan, usually in early spring.

April 12, 2002. Another female suicide bomber attacked Mahane Yehuda food market in downtown Jerusalem on Friday evening, when poor Jewish families were doing their last-minute Sabbath shopping. Six people were killed. Broken vegetables and fruit lay scattered everywhere.

Israelis who studied this roster of violence offered contradictory advice about where it was safe to eat. One of my fixers—who helped me set up interviews in Israel, the West Bank, and Gaza—told me that I should only eat at restaurants that had elaborate security guards and metal detectors, because their presence, he said, deterred suicide bombers who wanted to kill as many civilians as they could. The idea was that security guards prevented terrorists from getting deep into the crowd of diners; if these bombers detonated in the doorway, the fixer said, I had a better chance of surviving.

His colleague argued that metal detectors and security guards actually attracted suicide bombers, because their presence suggested that there were enough customers inside to warrant such protection, and that therefore I should only eat at restaurants that were hidden in Jerusalem's mazelike, cobblestone courtyards, because terrorists did not like to wander around looking for their target.

A friendly Russian-American Jewish couple in Jerusalem, who had made the macabre, fatalistic decision to send their two children to school on separate buses—so that one of their children could survive in case the other was attacked—tried to convince me that I should defiantly go out wherever my heart desired and put my faith in God. I thanked them for the advice, but opted not to take it. Somewhere out there, within the ancient walls, street vendors sold hot pita pockets stuffed with falafel, *shwarma** sandwiches dripping with cumin-flavored yogurt and tomato juice, *bureka* triangles with salty cheese or potatoes. I was too afraid to have any of that. Every evening, after I returned from my interviews to my hotel in the Jewish section of Jerusalem, I shuffled to the front desk and ordered the only food they served: hot tea and tiny sandwiches

---

* *Shwarma*—a sandwich with hot, grilled meat or poultry, usually made with pita bread or (especially in Iraq) with a baguette; the pan–Middle Eastern Big Mac.

with stale and sweaty cheese that looked as though they had been transported, across state borders and time, from my Soviet middle school cafeteria.

Then came Friday night, and I discovered that my hotel was kosher and therefore was not serving any food at all on the Sabbath.

Before I had left home, I had promised my family that I would not, not for any journalistic riches, venture into Gaza or the West Bank. David did not believe me for a second, but graciously responded with a noncommittal, "You'll do what you have to do." That was only my fourth time in a war zone, but now I know what he knew then: never make promises as you head off to a war. You arrive in a new place, your danger bar—the little red arrow on the built-in sensor we all have that tells us what is safe and what is not—is at an all-time low, supersensitive. You scan every window for the shadow of a sniper, you watch every piece of upturned dirt for the plastic sickle of a land mine, you resign yourself to another room service dinner of chewy cheese sandwiches because getting a falafel in the street might be too dangerous.

The next thing you know, you are in Gaza City, getting into a taxi with strange, thick-necked men who look like thugs from a B-rated gangster movie, because they have promised to take you to interview a senior leader of Hamas, a group that the State Department lists as number thirteen on its ledger of foreign terrorist organizations. (The list is arranged in alphabetical order, not by degree of terroristness, so Hamas, which wants to destroy Israel but has not really killed a lot of Americans, comes after the Basque Fatherland and Liberty, which does not want to destroy Israel *or* kill Americans, but before al Qaeda, which wants to destroy Israel and launched the worst attack against the United States since Pearl Harbor.)

I could not begin to explain to the *Chronicle*'s readers the biblical proportions of the conflict without trudging through the war debris in Nablus, sitting down with the bereaved relatives of terrorism victims in the hospitals of Jerusalem, listening to militant Soviet settlers in Ariel, or hanging out with aspiring suicide bombers in Gaza City. Besides, I was getting hungry. Quickly, I came up with a rationalization for crossing the lines of conflict, something I could later offer my family as a legitimate excuse: I told myself that to go crawling through the rubble around Yasser Arafat's besieged complex in Ramallah, where the muzzles of Israeli snipers tracked my every move from behind the camouflage mesh strung across the windows of abandoned apartment buildings, was safer than sitting down for a cucumber salad and hummus in a Tel Aviv café.

So I asked a cabdriver to drop off the photojournalist Justin Sullivan and me at the heavily fortified Erez Checkpoint at the northern tip of the Gaza Strip (this was the only conflict I have ever covered where journalists took taxis to a shooting war: one yellow cab from the Jerusalem hotel to an Israeli checkpoint, and then another taxi from the Palestinian side of the checkpoint to whichever West Bank or Gaza town we were headed). We walked across the tarmac to the checkpoint: a concrete building with bathrooms, a metal detector, an X-ray machine for luggage, and a couple of small rooms in which Israeli border guards and police officers sat. One of the border guards, a young French-Israeli kid, twisted his finger next to his temple as he saw us off. We passed the concrete blast walls that separated Israel proper from Gaza, and emerged into a weedy, gravel-strewn lot where Palestinian cabbies idled next to their wrinkled cars, waiting for their next paying customer. I could eat in peace. No Palestinian suicide bomber was going to blow up a restaurant full of his or her own people.

A real Palestinian, Bassam told me as he dipped a slice of pita bread into a bowl of hummus, eats a big lunch. And a real Palestinian lunch, he continued, reaching for a sprig of watercress to fold into his hummus sandwich, has to have a *mezze* plate, or appetizers, and *mansaf.*

Gastronomically, Bassam's Jordan was a mixture of high-class restaurants where he took his clients and the cheapest dives where he took his friends. Although I continued to pay for his services as a driver, I had graduated to the latter category in 2005, and now we were sitting at a small table with uneven metal legs on the second floor of a popular, inexpensive, Palestinian-owned Amman restaurant called, naturally, al Quds. The restaurant occupied two crowded floors on King Hussein Street, in the oldest section of Amman, several sandstone blocks from an amphitheater the Romans had cut into the side of a hill nineteen hundred years earlier, back when the city was called Philadelphia.

This al Quds had squat-over bathrooms and butcher paper in lieu of napkins, and it did not attract the slow-moving tourists floating past clothes shops that glistened with embroidered dresses and chintzy belly-dancer outfits, or the young, bearded religious scholars hurrying to prayer at the city's oldest mosque, around the corner. But the food spread in front of us was without equal: tiny pewter bowls of creamy hummus; steaming balls of falafel stuffed with cilantro and sautéed onions; *fattoush* salad, with tomatoes and cucumbers seasoned with lemon juice; hot, freshly baked pita bread; a plate of mint and watercress leaves and pickled vegetables; and, of course, *mansaf,* a dish of lamb, paper-thin *taboon* bread, rice garnished with almond slivers, and thin yogurt called *jameed.*

"One day, Anna, I will make *mansaf* for you," Bassam promised me, tearing a bit of yogurt-soaked lamb with a piece of *taboon* and depositing it in his mouth.

Once upon a time, *mansaf* was a dish popular among bedouins who grazed their sheep, goats, and camels in the sparsely vegetated valleys and hills of ancient Palestine. Today, Palestinians in the West Bank and Gaza cook it mostly on special occasions—for a wedding, say. Or a funeral. And so it was that the first time I had tried *mansaf* was at a funeral banquet in honor of Ahmat Salmi, a fifteen-year-old high school student who had hung several grenades from his belt, hooked them up to a push-button detonator, and set out to Dugit, an Israeli settlement on the northern tip of the Gaza Strip, about five miles north of his home, to kill some Jews.

Justin and I found ourselves at Ahmat's funeral by chance after we, having hobnobbed with the teenage *shahid* hopefuls in downtown Gaza City, followed a funeral procession that tottered through the streets. After one turn, we came upon an enormous tent blocking an alley in the al Shati refugee camp (population eighty thousand; at the time, most of them unemployed).

A tall electric fence circled Dugit to protect the Jewish settlers from boys like Ahmat—naive revolutionaries whose vigor was deftly harnessed by the savvy older men of the Palestinian militant establishment (and is this not the story of every war ever fought?). Ahmat did not make it to the fence. Israeli forces guarding the settlement had spotted him coming from afar and opened fire. He died right away. He never got to kill anyone, not even himself.

Now his father, Omar, was honoring what he called Ahmat's martyr-dom under the giant tent in a loud, cheerful street festival reserved for *shahid*. About two hundred men—neighbors and relatives—attended the celebration. Justin and I stood out in the crowd, and the men nudged us toward the heart of the tent, making us the guests of honor. These men were generous with their grief. They were inviting us to mourn together.

We were seated in white plastic chairs next to Omar, and soon, a teenage boy—Ahmat's cousin, also about fourteen or fifteen years old—brought out a giant pewter tray of hot *mansaf* and held it in front of us.

"Please. We would be honored if you eat with us," Omar said, tear-ing off two pieces of lamb and handing one to Justin, the other to me. At a *mansaf* party, it is polite to tear pieces of meat and pass them to your neighbors at the table.

We thanked our host and, uncertainly, picked at the food. Ahmat's story didn't make me hungry. It made me deeply sad. I told Omar that I understood if it was hard for him to talk about the loss of his firstborn, but that I would have liked to know more about Ahmat—what kind of kid he had been, what kind of son. I asked Omar whether it disturbed him that Ahmat had died without killing any Jews, or that Palestine was no freer as a result of his death.

The man shrugged. I noticed that he had not touched the *mansaf* on his plate.

"He was killed before he could do anything," he nodded. Then he said: "This time we failed, but maybe next time we will succeed."

Some other time. Some other son. Some other funeral tent.

Hamas had officially claimed responsibility for sending Ahmat to Dugit; it had also paid for the funeral celebration. (In Gaza, where un-employment at the time hovered around 80 percent, Hamas paid for many things: food for the poor, medicine for the sick, kindergartens for the children whose parents were lucky enough to have steady jobs.

Hamas was a terrorist group; it was also a charity. Its handouts bought the organization the respect of the locals—and, when the time came to die for the cause, their lives also.) The day after Ahmat's funeral, I asked Abdel Aziz al Rantisi, the cofounder of Hamas who would later become its leader, whether it bothered him that his foot soldiers were barely old enough to shave.

"We hear the readiness of youth," al Rantisi replied. We were sitting at his office at the Hamas headquarters in Gaza, Justin and I on a squeaky leather couch, al Rantisi in a large swivel office chair. Gunmen with thick arms and necks stood in the hallway just outside the door. They had patted us down before we were allowed into the building.

"Some young people clearly say that they want to be martyrs," the Hamas leader continued. "We hear that and choose from these people."

(A trained pediatrician, al Rantisi harbored a special interest in the young. Famously afraid to pick up a ringing telephone because he believed that the Israeli security services might rig the phone to kill him, the prolific grandfather had his grandchildren pick up the receiver instead. The precaution did not save him. He was killed in 2004, when an Israeli helicopter fired a missile at his car.)

Al Rantisi's son, Mohammad, was in the room during our interview; a tall, slender man of twenty-three, he was a medical student in Iraq, home for spring break. I asked Mohammad if he, too, wanted to become a martyr.

"I would be honored to be chosen," he began. With a dismissive smile, al Rantisi put out his hand, ordering his son to be silent. In the Animal Farm of Palestinian insurgency, some bombers are more suicidal than others.

"He doesn't know what he's saying; he is only saying it because of his youth," al Rantisi said.

"Some men," he looked at his son sternly, "must grow up to become doctors." He turned his face back toward me: a bespectacled man with wide-set eyes, a graying beard, and closely cropped hair. I tried to imagine him in scrubs. "But for that to happen, others must sacrifice themselves and become martyrs."

At the end of my second week in Jordan, I received the long-awaited phone call from Rania, the Jordanian fixer whom I had hired to help me get an Iraqi visa. She was all business.

"Your last name, Badkhen. It's Jewish, is it not?" she demanded.

She had me. A *badkhen* is a fiddler and an irreverent jester-rhymer who performs, usually ad lib, at Jewish weddings—a Yiddish rapper, if you will—but I never got to share this factoid with Rania. She didn't wait for an answer.

"The Iraqi embassy told me they would not be issuing visas to Jews." And she hung up.

After the fall of Saddam, obtaining Iraqi visas stopped being such a problem. For a brief time, Iraq did not require entry visas—possibly because the bureaucracy that would have issued and checked these visas had collapsed along with everything else during the U.S.-led invasion. Later, the visa requirement was reinstated, and with it returned the extortion apparatus that had traditionally accompanied the process. People seem to think that replacing a totalitarian society with one that is governed democratically makes life better, but in fact what makes life better or worse in any society is the degree to which one's ability to complete ordinary civil transactions is based on one's ability to bribe. My problem with Rania, I later realized, had been not my last name but the fact that I had not known how, when, and whom to pay off. Between 2005 and 2009 I bought three visas to Iraq. The cheapest one, which I got through an agency in Washington, D.C., in 2009, cost forty dollars and took two weeks to obtain; the most expensive one, which Bassam had finagled through some obscure connections in Jordan overnight in 2005, set the *San Francisco Chronicle* back seventeen hundred dollars. In 2003, I ended up sneaking into northern Iraq through Iran—the Shiite government in Tehran, anticipating Saddam's fall, was happy to assist foreign journalists in crossing a certain mountain pass where the state border was unmanned on the Iraqi side, as long as we didn't linger in Iran. It was because Rania did not help me, and the Iranian government did, that I ended up in Irbil instead of Baghdad and met Ahmad Shawkat.

I returned to Jordan in May 2003. Saddam Hussein's regime in Iraq was gone, and Jordan became my layover destination on the way to and from Iraq: it was a beautiful country, it was easy to get around, and an entry visa to the Hashemite Kingdom cost sixteen bucks, paid at the airport upon arrival. With Bassam's help, I hired a driver to take me from Amman to Baghdad in a new, shiny Chevy Suburban. I was negotiating the time of my departure when Bassam announced that he needed an extra day to get his passport.

"But you're not driving," I said.

"I cannot let you go by yourself," Bassam responded. "It is too dangerous."

On the Iraqi side of the border, the road to Baghdad lay through a vast sulphuric desert dominated by Sunni tribesmen who would later form the backbone of the anti-American insurgency. Armed gangs had already begun ambushing and robbing journalists traveling on the highway (the kidnappings and executions would start a few months later). Bassam did not carry a gun, which meant that he was just as defenseless against highway robbers as I was; I suppose he was prepared to yell at them in Arabic on my behalf. I imagine that if things had gotten violent, my former boxer friend could always have dusted off his right hook. I knew he would have stood by me no matter what. I postponed my trip a day, and slept in the back seat while Bassam watched the road.

When I was leaving Iraq, Bassam came from Amman to pick me up, this time in a friend's beat-up Mercedes sedan. The friend drove. In the middle of the desert, a powerful sandstorm hit the highway. Sandstorms are common in Iraq in the spring, when the northwesterly *shamal* wind, funneled into the Mesopotamian plateau by the mountains of Turkey, drags through Iraq and Kuwait enormous quantities of sand it picks up in Syria and Lebanon. The *shamal* comes in quickly and silently, like an ocher paint roller, and can blow for several days straight, subsiding slightly at night when the air is cooler. It shrouds everything. It grounds air traffic, shutters stores, and brings cars and trucks to a halt on the fast, straight desert highways.

The *shamal* blew when Bassam and his friend were about halfway to Baghdad. Visibility abruptly dropped to almost zero. Even without the sandstorm, the highway was difficult to navigate: giant craters gaped where American aerial bombs had struck the tarmac during the "Shock and Awe" phase of the invasion. Bridges over dry wadis wobbled and sagged on bent piles crippled by air raids. Now this road was also slick with engine oil from several dozen car crashes. Bassam's five-hundred-mile trip took twenty-one hours instead of eight. After five hours of sleep, he and his colleague were on the road again, carrying to Amman my friend Thorne Anderson, a photographer with whom I had worked in Iraq; my Iraqi friend and translator Thanaa, who hitched a ride with us to visit some relatives in Jordan; and me. By then, the *shamal* had moved on, taking its veil of dust to Kuwait.

The ride was uncomfortable with the three of us squeezed in the back. The Mercedes was no Chevy Suburban. I was irritated at Bassam for not bringing a larger car. Thanaa was nervous—this was her first time traveling outside Iraq. The driver, a Palestinian man in his sixties who went by an honorific, Abu Ahmed, was tired and tense. Thorne nodded off. He clearly had mastered the invaluable technique of wartime survival: when you are in a situation you don't like but cannot control, just let it be. I bet Thorne never would have yelled at robber bodyguards with candy-wrapped Kalashnikovs.

For six or seven hours, no one spoke. The border crossing was humiliating and long. Jordanian border guards made a point of checking every single item in our luggage. I longed for the Pyandzh ferry: at least no one on that Afghan frontier had bothered to stick their fingers inside my aspirin bottles or unwrap my Tampax. The Jordanian border guards made me totter to three different offices to get my passport stamped three different ways by three different men, each of them sipping tea from a glass. They opened my laptop and shook it upside down, as though hoping that something—what?—would fall out from inside the keyboard. Perhaps they were looking for weapons: several days earlier, a Jordanian airport security guard had been killed by a cluster bomb in the luggage of a Japanese journalist traveling from Iraq through Jordan. (The journalist had picked up the U.S.-made bomblet in Iraq and was bringing it home as a souvenir. Ah, the things some of us carried.)

Perhaps they were looking for someone on whom to take out their frustration at being stuck in this outpost, far away from everything, surrounded by black basalt desert, dust storms, and war.

We crossed into Jordan, annoyed and worn out. Several miles along the road Bassam asked Abu Ahmed to pull over. Now what? A checkpoint? Overheated engine? But my friend tuned the radio to a station that blared trashy Egyptian pop music, got out of the car, and began to dance in the middle of the empty highway. This is absurd, I thought. Bassam shook his shoulders and clapped his hands. Then I thought: No. This is perfect.

Soon, we were all out on the tarmac, thrusting our hips this way and that, flinging our hands up and watching our long shadows twist in the setting sun. Abu Ahmed stuck two oranges under his shirt to make them look like a woman's breasts, and belly-danced in front of me and Thanaa, and Bassam laughed harder than I ever heard him laugh, before or since.

The trips to al Quds—the restaurant, not the erstwhile destination of Saladin and Saddam—became a tradition. I would be restless after the eight-hour flight from Moscow or jet-lagged and drowsy after an eighteen-hour trip from Boston when Bassam would pick me up at the airport. We would drive to the guts of Jordan's ancient capital—horns honking, drivers yelling at each other through rolled-down windows— park the car, and walk downhill to the storefront with a concrete balcony and a window shaped like the silhouette of the Dome of the Rock.* (The balcony was used to store large electrical equipment—a generator, or an enormous air-conditioning unit, or maybe both—and unsightly wires usually dangled out of the stencilled likeness of the mosque's cupola, as though some horrid alien monster had built a nest inside the shrine.) A manager—like Bassam, a son of Palestinian refugees—would come with a notepad and Bassam would order *mezze* and *mansaf*.

"To feel the culture," my friend would say.

He would take out his Marlboro Lights and put them on the table,

---

*Dome of the Rock—the Muslim shrine on Temple Mount in Jerusalem that houses the holiest object in Judaism: the rock from which, according to the Talmud, the world was created. The octagonal construction with an arcade of twenty-four piers and columns is topped with a large dome (hence the name) and was erected in the seventh century.

next to the plate of freshly baked pita bread, and we would talk—about my family, about work, about Iraq. But mostly, during our *mansaf* outings, we talked about Bassam's unfulfilled, ill-starred love life.

He told me a sad story about an arranged marriage that ended in a divorce ("She was so cold, always angry at me," he said), and an even sadder story of a love affair with a divorced single mother who killed herself by jumping out of his third-floor window one day while he was at work. He was always brokenhearted over elusive women who disappeared from his life under tragic circumstances: suicides, long-distance relationships abruptly ended, and women who just went away.

Our last trip together to al Quds was in July 2008. I was leaving for Iraq the next morning. Bassam was wearing a blazer, and I noticed, on his lapel, a tiny pin with the Jordanian flag. I asked my friend which identity was more important to him, Palestinian or Jordanian.

That was when he told me how, after returning home from the army as a young man, he suddenly felt appalled, physically revolted, by the way Palestinian refugees were living in the camp where he had grown up, Baqa'a. There was barely any infrastructure. Streets were so narrow that larger cars would inadvertently take off chunks of walls. Tuberculosis struck almost every household. Out of hunger, women became prostitutes. For all of this, and for his parents' interminable nostalgia, which they had managed to pass on to their children who had never set foot in the West Bank, Bassam had blamed the Jews.

Lots of people in the Arab world say things like this, but Bassam wasn't just whistling Dixie. He decided to become a terrorist, to take on Israel. He had served in the Jordanian army and knew his way around weapons. Through a friend, he obtained a recommendation to go to a training camp in Syria, to learn from other Palestinian men how to be a better fighter, a better marksman, a more enduring warrior. He was going to become a *shahid*. Sun setting over al Aqsa Mosque would be photoshopped into his picture. For a month, he was kept in a small, solitary cell, with no entertainment apart from a single book.

"To make me think more," Bassam explained.

The book was Maxim Gorky's *Mother,* a Russian classic and a propaganda masterpiece that tells the story of a young man who, in an effort to protect his underprivileged mother against the injustices of tsarist Russia, becomes a revolutionary. This book would not have been at the top of my reading list: it was pretty much the *Johnny Tremain* of Soviet high school. If you attended, you read it. I remember loathing it. On Bassam, the book had an effect his terrorism coaches had not anticipated: he decided that rebellion was not for him. He quit the training camp, returned to Jordan, and got a job as a tour guide, which eventually led him to befriend an American journalist born in the Soviet Union to a Jewish father.

"Now I am a Jordanian first, Palestinian second," Bassam told me. He scooped some yellow rice into his bread.

"Bassam," I said. "You know that I am, ethnically, Jewish, right?" Bassam shrugged and smiled.

"I am not against Jewish, not anymore," Bassam said. "I am for peace. One day, *inshallah,* I will go to Palestine and there will be peace, no problem. I will see al Quds."

"*Inshallah,*" I said: God willing. "Maybe we can go together."

Two weeks later, when I was in Iraq, a man called me. He said he was Bassam's cousin. He said that Bassam had died of a heart attack. If there was anything he could help me with, he was at my service.

❧

Mezze

Serves 6 to 8

*L*unch is the big meal of the day for Israelis and Palestinians alike, and a big part of a traditional lunch in both cultures is a spread of appetizers called *mezze.*

For all the entrenched hostilities between the two peoples, the appetizers they like are exactly the same. A typical *mezze* includes hummus, tabouleh, *baba ghanouj,* pita bread, and falafel. (All of those are always made at the restaurant where they are served, and although I know few people who make their own pita bread, no self-respecting Palestinian hostess would ever serve you hummus she had bought at a supermarket.) It is easy and quick to whip up the spreads and the salad; falafel takes a little bit more time, but it's not difficult to make, either. You can keep whatever you don't finish in the refrigerator for up to a week. Do it up and enjoy a piece of Middle East peace at your lunch table.

❧

Hummus

Two 15-ounce cans chickpeas or 8 ounces cooked dried chickpeas
½ cup tahini (sesame seed paste, available at most supermarkets)
2 small cloves garlic (or 1 large clove)
Juice of 1 large lemon
½ cup good olive oil, plus 1 tablespoon for serving
Finely minced parsley, 8 to 10 pitted kalamata olives,
    ¼ cup pine nuts, ground sumac (available in Middle
    Eastern groceries), optional, for serving
Pita bread, for serving

1. Thoroughly rinse the chickpeas, running them between your fingers to remove their transparent outer shells (they look a little bit like contact lenses). Discard the shells.

2. In a blender, combine the chickpeas, tahini, garlic, and lemon juice and puree slowly, gradually adding the ½ cup oil. The hummus should be very smooth, silky in texture (totally unlike the hummus you buy in an American supermarket), and almost white in color. If necessary, add 1 or 2 tablespoons warm water. Scoop it out into a bowl. Pour the tablespoon oil on top, and sprinkle with parsley, olives, pine nuts, and/or sumac. Serve with pita bread.

❧

Baba Ghanouj

1 large eggplant
3 tablespoons tahini (sesame seed paste,
    available at most supermarkets)
Juice of 1 lemon
Salt to taste
Pita bread, for serving

1. Preheat the oven to 400°F. Wash the eggplant, incise it on one side, and lay it on a baking sheet lined with aluminum foil. Bake for about 40 minutes, or until the flesh of the eggplant is very soft. Remove the eggplant from the oven and let it cool for about 10 minutes.

2. With a spoon, scoop out the soft eggplant flesh from inside the skin into a mixing bowl. Discard the skin. Add the tahini, lemon juice, and salt. With a fork, whip the ingredients together. Serve at room temperature, with pita bread.

～

Falafel

*M*y favorite falafel is stuffed with sautéed onions, but that's just too complicated to make, so I'm going to go with a simpler recipe. The trick to making falafel is that the chickpeas are not cooked but soaked overnight, so you have to know ahead of time that you're going to be preparing it.

1 pound dried chickpeas, soaked overnight
    in plenty of lightly salted water
1 bunch parsley
1 large onion, quartered
2 or 3 cloves garlic
1 tablespoon ground coriander
1½ teaspoons ground nutmeg
1½ teaspoons ground allspice
Salt and pepper, to taste
Plenty of olive oil, for frying

1. Put the drained chickpeas, parsley, onion, and garlic through a meat grinder or a food processor with a chopping blade. Add the spices and salt. Knead well, as you would dough, with your hands.

2. Pinch off a small amount of the chickpea mixture and roll into a tight ball with your hands. Place on a cutting board or a piece of waxed paper. Repeat until all the chickpea mixture is gone.

3. Pour oil into a large cast-iron skillet or wok, until it is about ½ inch deep. When the oil is boiling hot, carefully add as many falafel balls as will fit on the bottom of the skillet. Cook, turning them with a spatula so they

brown on all sides, for about 3 minutes. Remove cooked falafel balls with a slotted spoon to a plate and cover them so they don't get cold while you cook the rest. Serve hot.

ᵔᴗ

Mansaf

Serves 8

*I*t takes hours to prepare *mansaf,* which is why Palestinians don't usually cook it every day and reserve the meal for special occasions (you've been warned). Traditionally, it is cooked in an enormous stewing pot over an open fire, but for our purposes, a stove will suffice.

4 cups basmati rice
1 tablespoon each of ground turmeric,
    ground allspice, and ground cumin
4 pounds lamb, cut into large chunks, on bone
    (or lamb shanks), trimmed of excess fat
1 large onion, skinned but whole
Salt
Two 1-pound containers plain, nonfat yogurt
    (or *jameed,* if you can get it at a Middle Eastern
    grocery store, thinned with some water)
2 sticks cinnamon
Juice of ½ lemon, optional
16 sheets *taboon* bread, or, if you can't find it,
    very thin Armenian lavash bread
1 cup slivered almonds and/or pine nuts, for sprinkling

1. Combine the rice with 4½ cups water and 1½ teaspoons of the turmeric, and bring, uncovered, to a boil. When the rice is boiling, reduce the heat, cover, and cook for about 10 to 15 minutes, or until all the water is absorbed and the rice is ready. Wrap the rice pot in some newspaper and a blanket to keep it warm.

2. Put the lamb into a large stewing pot (I like cast iron), add the onion, salt to taste, and just enough water to cover the lamb. Bring to a boil and simmer, covered, until the lamb is very tender. Discard the onion. Do not discard the broth.

3. Meanwhile, in a different pot, combine the yogurt, the remaining turmeric, the allspice, cumin, and cinnamon. Turn the burner on high. As the yogurt begins to heat up, start stirring it with a wooden spoon to prevent it from separating—*but always stir in the same direction.* So once you have started stirring clockwise, no turning against the clock, or the yogurt will separate. As soon as the yogurt starts boiling, turn off the heat.

4. Add about 2 or 3 cups of the lamb broth to the pot of yogurt. If the mixture is not tart enough, add the lemon juice. Add the lamb to the mixture and bring to a boil, stirring constantly (in one direction).

5. When you are ready to serve the *mansaf,* for each guest arrange 1 or 2 sheets of bread on a large tray so that the bottom of the tray is completely covered. Heap some rice on top of the bread and sprinkle with nuts. Remove some lamb meat from the sauce and place it on top of the rice. Pour about ½ cup of the yogurt mixture over the rice, to give it some moisture. Pour any remaining yogurt into a serving pitcher or bowl. Your guests will pour more yogurt over their rice or lamb as they see fit; they may also want to dip their bread in the yogurt.

Traditionally, *mansaf* is eaten with your hands or with a spoon, but no one will scorn you for using a knife and fork, as long as you enjoy your meal. If you want to make a culinary contribution to world peace, invite Palestinians and Jews to your table. And don't forget to pass a piece to the person on your right and your left.

Nine

Peanut Butter for Your Donkey

The woman emerged from the thicket of acacia trees that flanked the raw red flesh of the unpaved clay road. She stepped around inch-long thorns and the dung of the donkeys she was herding in front of her in her rubber flip-flopped feet with the measured and even steps of someone who had been walking for many hours and maybe days and who would keep walking for hours or days more. Three empty, beat-up, plastic twenty-quart jugs hung from the donkeys' backs: like most people on the Horn of Africa that brutal spring, the woman was walking to get water for herself and her family back in the bush.

It was 2006. The worst drought in decades had struck Kenya, Somalia, and Ethiopia that year, destroying traditional grazing lands, killing tens of millions of animals, and putting seventeen million people in East Africa on the brink of starvation. Herders orphaned of their livestock were forced to survive on meager rations of water, rice, oil, maize, and flour distributed by relief agencies, and that aid was running out. The *San Francisco Chronicle* had sent Michael Macor, a Pulitzer Prize–winning photographer, and me to Kenya and Somalia to document life without water. Everywhere we went people were walking, with plastic containers mounted on donkeys, on camels, on women's and girls' heads and bony shoulders.

There was no rain in the forecast.

The heat teased the thirsty pilgrims with mirages of lakes and puddles on the vermilion road. The woman's path lay past countless decomposing cattle carcasses, past ghoulish marabou storks that fed on their scarce rotting flesh. The woman looked straight ahead, never changing her pace. If she wanted to reach her destination, she had to spend her energy as parsimoniously as water.

I watched her through the dirt-smeared window of our Range Rover as it rolled down the road. Michael and I had spent most of the day following a rickety truck with the words DANGER PETROLEUM fading from the sides of its rusty tank. At dawn that morning, the truck driver had pulled up in the fourteen-wheeler to a grassy clearing on the north bank of the Tana River, where crocodiles skulked in typhoidal water in the viridescent shadow of mangrove trees. Masking tape and sticks held together a multicolored contraption of thick plastic pipes that looked like something Dr. Seuss had dreamed up for his antiutopian fairy tale *The Lorax* and snaked from the river up the slope of the bank, where it was wired to an old, crank-up generator coughing up clouds of black, sooty smoke. The driver stuffed the free ends of the pipes into two hatches of the fourteen-thousand-quart tank and a pump began to push murky, brown river water into the cistern.

The driver added a pint of chlorine from a blue plastic container. The chlorine, which would treat the typhoid, was supposed to dissolve as the water sloshed inside the tanker while it bumped along the rutted road. This liquid, courtesy of the Atlanta-based CARE International aid agency, would become the only source of water for several days for dozens of nomadic families grazing their dwindling herds of malnourished animals outside Garissa, a provincial capital in northeastern Kenya, one of the areas worst hit by the drought.

In one village, the truck poured some tepid water into a five-thousand-quart black plastic water tank. A dozen miles away, the truck filled an earthen reservoir by the side of the road; ivory-colored film formed and bubbled on the surface as water rose in the pit. Outside another distribution point, women and children, slipping on clay soaked with animal urine and mashed by thousands of hooves and feet, squeezed past camels, cows, and goats to collect drinking water from thirty-foot-long concrete basins, from which the animals were already drinking. It was important to nurture the animals first, the humans explained, but it was also important not to let them drink too much. Goats and cows, particularly, were prone to overdrinking and often collapsed under their own waterlogged weight and died; the herders then had to drag their bloated cadavers away from the basins before the bacteria from their rapidly decomposing tissue could contaminate the water. Someone pointed out two dead goats by the side of the road a few hundred feet away: their greed had killed them.

One aging herder told me he had walked fifty miles to the water from the section of the bush where he lived with his wife and ten children. The journey had taken thirty-two hours.

How much longer did the donkey-herding woman outside our car window have to walk? Suddenly, the rope holding one of her yellow water jugs came untied and the vessel slipped off the back of the first donkey in her small procession. Before she had a chance to stop her animals, the second donkey stepped on the jug, cracking it. Just like that, the container became another piece of useless, shattered plastic littering the roads all over northeastern Kenya. The woman and her caravan kept walking. She did not need to stop to do the simple, brutal drought-time math: now she would be bringing home a third less water than she had planned.

I took notes. The next morning, somewhere in the Bay Area somebody read the Story of the Woman with a Broken Jug. Maybe the reader imagined, for a split second, what life must be like without water. Maybe, feeling momentarily uncomfortable, she shuddered, took another sip of coffee, and flipped to the sports section. When I looked up from my notebook, the woman was gone. Our car kept moving.

———

In the Horn of Africa droughts are frequent and almost expected. We are accustomed to seeing television footage—usually filmed from a helicopter—of Martian swaths of waterless land, cracked into giraffe-hide patterns; close-ups of children with bellies boated from hunger staring at the camera as flies land on their skin; panoramic shots of carcasses of wasted animals lying beneath shadowless thorn trees. These images, and our imaginations, nurture in us the belief that surely there must be no respite from this recurring, brutal natural disaster, nowhere for the millions of East Africans to turn to but international aid agencies, and that no one in that part of the continent is spared by this horrific act of God.

But in the spring of 2006, in parts of East Africa—some just a few minutes' drive from the donkey woman's path—water seemed abundant, and not just in the diseased Tana River, whose mocha-colored meanders sickle through central and eastern Kenya. There was plenty of any liquid, really. The shower in my air-conditioned room at the Nomad Palace, Garissa's thirty-dollar-a-night take on a Comfort Inn, had cold and hot running water. I began each morning with a large ceramic teapot of hot black *masala chai* tea steeped in spices and whole milk, a glass of orange juice, and a can of Coke, all dirt cheap. (An expense account I compiled for the *Chronicle* after the trip shows this entry: "3/27 juice/tea Nomad Palace $1.16." This was the price of juice and tea for me, Michael Macor, and the Kenyan photojournalist Kabir Dhanji, who was accompanying us as a fixer.)

No nomads stayed at the Nomad Palace. At night, hotel chefs stoked up the grill in the large courtyard, Swahili pop music blasted through the speakers, and the Palace welcomed the kings and queens of Garissa: businessmen, city and provincial officials, heads of the local branches of international relief agencies. They gathered around plastic tables for plates of rice with deep-fried potatoes, paper-thin chapati flatbread, and *nyama choma,* the traditional grilled meat. A short walk across a red-dirt road, an outdoor bar served cold Tusker, a crisp local lager, the ultimate thirst quencher, the pride of Kenya. No nomads stopped by that watering hole, either. In Garissa, the disparity between the haves and the have-nots somehow felt deeper than it had in Kabul, Baghdad, or Jerusalem. Perhaps it was because what separated us was such a basic commodity: water.

Some minutes after the Woman with the Broken Jug had vanished from our sight, Michael and I arrived at a village where the CARE truck had not made a stop that day: a small congregation of makeshift *manyata* huts of grass and sticks surrounded by brush. The women and old men of the village stood in a circle and talked about their perpetual and indefinite wait for water and their futile search for food; about how their cattle had died from lack of nourishment; about how even their goats, the most undemanding of farm animals, had become too skinny to sell. Gaunt, apathetic children clung to the women's hips. Then, someone's toddler, red-haired from malnutrition, reached for the bright blue plastic pipe that was dangling over my left shoulder.

"Miss?" a man asked. A wide-bladed knife in a leather sheath hung from the waist of his black-and-lavender *kikoy* sarong. The man's waist seemed barely wider than the blade of his knife. "What's this?"

The plastic pipe was the drinking straw of my CamelBak, a soft, heat-resistant container that still carried about a liter of bottled spring water I had poured into it in the morning, before we had left the Nomad Palace. The container was built to retain temperature long enough that the water was still cool despite having spent most of the day in 96-degree heat. It was cleverly fitted into a small black backpack (which had a few nifty separate compartments where I could keep sunscreen, a hotel room key, some pens, and an extra notebook) that hung from my shoulders on wide, padded straps so that I almost did not notice its weight. American troops in Iraq and Afghanistan carried similar soft bottles; theirs were typically camouflage and clipped onto their flak jackets. Leaflets taped to the walls of chow halls and showers on military bases remind the troops to drink plenty and often and describe the first symptoms of dehydration: fatigue, labored breathing, dizziness, crushing headache.

We are mostly water. Water makes up, on average, 60 percent of our bodies: 20 percent of our bones, 70 percent of our brains, 75 percent of our muscle tissue, 80 percent of our blood, and almost 90 percent of our lungs. To stay healthy, we must replenish, through drinking or eating or both, almost two and a half liters of water a day—and much more if we sweat. Depending on how hot it is around us, we can lose up to three gallons of water, or 12 percent of our water weight, in less than one day—through urinating, sweating, even breathing. By then, if we have not rehydrated, we are past the point the U.S. military warns about in its leaflets, past the point when we experience fatigue, headache, dry mouth, and dizziness. We can no longer walk, our tongues swell, we cannot swallow, and if we don't receive liquids intravenously, we dehydrate further. Our blood thickens, the circulation slows down. Our bodies overheat. According to the World Health Organization's Web site, "dehydration can kill a healthy adult in a matter of hours."

Hence, the CamelBak. The functional gadget contained enough

water to keep me hydrated for the rest of the afternoon. But it definitely did not carry enough to share the elemental life force with the small circle of women, children, and elderly men who were talking to me in the bush. And at that moment the CamelBak epitomized the role I play during most of my reporting from extremities: a transient witness only there long enough to document pain and privation; a professional intruder, mostly safe from the devastation I have arrived to write about. An inadequate outsider whose only response to terrible human condition and suffering is to take notes about it and then leave, taking my water with me to the relative safety and comfort of my hotel room, guesthouse, or tent, where more liquids—and food—usually await.

The child let go of the CamelBak straw. I bid farewell to the villagers, and left, numbed by my own helplessness.

In the United States in 2008, more than twelve million children did not have enough to eat, according to various antipoverty groups, and in Massachusetts, approximately one in ten children that year went to bed on an empty stomach. In the world, more than a billion people are starving, and every day, almost sixteen thousand children die from illnesses that could have been prevented had these children had access to enough nutrients. In the pediatric ward of Garissa Provincial Hospital in 2006, all fifty-six children in the charge of Dr. Khadija Abdalla were dying of starvation.

Humid air pressed down on the ward with a stifling heaviness that seemed never to bulge: not when the mothers slouching on sagging cots slowly flapped the loose ends of their tie-dyed head scarves over their absent-faced children; not when the fans churned uselessly above the cots and the plastic still lifes of water jugs and cheap, chipped bowls with unfinished baby formula. The heat poured in through the mosquito netting of open windows like syrup, clung to the perspiring white walls painted with garish balloons. Even the large, black-and-green flies did not lift themselves up in the air when Dr. Abdalla, the chief pediatrician at the hospital, made her afternoon rounds, but lazily crawled out of her path along the pale brown floor tiles that smelled of cheap disinfectant.

The drought that had forced the Woman with a Broken Jug out of the bush in search of water had killed the livestock and destroyed the crops of the parents, rendered barren the mothers' breasts, and wasted the children's bodies, eroding their limbs to the thickness of a grown-up's thumb. Assisted by six nurses, two per shift, who had time to do little more than deliver medicine and weigh the patients, the doctor was fighting to reverse the effects of malnutrition and treat the diseases that typically affect starved children everywhere close to the equator: tuberculosis, measles, malaria, cholera, dysentery, pneumonia.

Hypothermia, too, was a problem, despite the suffocating heat: "They have no fat," Dr. Abdalla explained, curtly.

There was no tenderness in the doctor's voice, no warmth in the way she touched her fragile patients. It was as though she was resisting becoming attached, as though she knew that these children would not be in her care for long, and was steeling herself. She may have been in charge of the main pediatric ward in the region, but ultimately, it was not up to her to determine whether the children made it through or succumbed to the famine that had put at least half a million Kenyan children at risk of starvation. The decision lay with the children's mothers—most of them barely adult themselves. Every day, as nurses in the pediatric ward weighed the children to see if the treatment was working, the children's mothers weighed the pros and cons of the treatment itself, doing the unsentimental arithmetic of famine: Who needs them more, the famished baby in their arms or the hungry family back in the bush? Which of their children gets to live, and which dies of starvation? More often than not, the mothers scooped up the wasted, weak children weeks or even months before the treatment was complete, crossed the disinfected tiles of the ward's courtyard, and disappeared in the thorny acacia bush as suddenly and without warning as they had arrived at the only hospital in the province of four hundred thousand people that could help nourish their children back to life.

Malyun, a two-year-old girl who weighed less than thirteen pounds when I met her, needed to remain at the hospital for six months to receive a daily dose of a special cocktail of protein and nutrients. But her mother, Ladhan, a slight twenty-year-old who would have had to administer the medication nine times a day, told me she and Malyun would leave as soon as the girl looked, to her, fit to survive the trek back to their home village on Garissa's outskirts.

Ladhan had made the decision to leave not because she could not afford the seventy cents a night the hospital charged for the bed—Dr. Abdalla was able to waive the fee so that the little girl, whose tiny neck and bony shoulders stuck out from an oversize yellow T-shirt like sprigs of some endangered wildflower, could receive treatment. Ladhan was leaving because of her son, the five-year-old Faisul, whom she had left with her sister and parents in order to bring Malyun to the hospital. Ladhan's husband had left for South Africa to become a day laborer when Ladhan was still pregnant with Malyun; she had not heard from him since. The woman did not trust her family to take good care of her son; she worried that Faisul, like Malyun, would wither from malnutrition in his mother's absence. Now, Ladhan explained as she watched her daughter pick bread crumbs out of a beat-up aluminum bowl, she needed to go back and take care of her son, who, as far as she knew, was still relatively healthy.

When I meet children during my trips, I imagine that my own children are there, too, in this very same situation. In Afghanistan, I pictured Fyodor dozing off next to Abdullah, Mahbuhbullah's selfless twelve-year-old boy who was my bodyguard for one night. In northern Iraq, I pretended that Alex was in the tiled Irbil patio when Afrah and her daughters were making dolma, squatting next to them and laughing at their jokes. In Israel, I imagined that it was me and the kids having lunch at the Sbarro pizza parlor in Jerusalem when the suicide bomber took Yokheved Shushan's life. It happens automatically. It takes no conscious effort for me to start calculating how much older Fyodor is than the children I meet, and try to remember what he was like when he was their age. I smile at the similarities. I step into the sense of pride of these children's mothers, and into their grief. I imagine that many mothers do that.

In Garissa, I sat down on Ladhan's hospital cot, next to her little girl. I, too, was a twenty-one-year-old mother once—scared, poor, headstrong, living on red beans, cigarettes, and the unpalatable fry bread my boyfriend, when sober, would concoct out of flour and salt. Ladhan and I glanced at each other. Then we both stared at the floor. I wanted to try on what it was like to be her, to imagine the dilemma she was facing, but my brain refused. It was too brutal.

In the room next door, Hadiwa lay on a crinkled white sheet covering a tarp-wrapped mattress and stared at the ceiling with unseeing eyes. Malaria, tuberculosis, and pneumonia were eating away at her nine-month-old body. Wrinkled skin hung loosely around the baby's angular pelvic bones; she weighed eight pounds, just over a pound more than when she was born. Two months of intensive feeding would assure that the girl recovered, at least temporarily. But, like Ladhan, Hadiwa's mother said she could not wait that long.

"There are a lot of things I need to attend to at home," said Habiba Mohammed, offering her emaciated child a breast that had not carried milk for months. Which things, Dr. Abdalla demanded. Did Habiba have other children in the bush who needed her to take care of them, to make sure they did not starve? Was there a jealous husband waiting for her, a man who, like many in the patriarchal society of northeastern Kenya, might have thought it was inappropriate for a woman to leave the house for so long?

"Some of them insist they must leave before the child reaches the target weight," Dr. Abdalla said, pursing her lips. "It's very frustrating, especially when you know that they're going to need to come back.

"See?" the doctor continued, lifting up Hadiwa from her mother's side. The sagging skin drooped around the child's skeletal thighs, like hand-me-down clothes too large for her. "Too much loose skin. She has no fat or muscle at all."

In this hospital full of despondent mothers, Khadija Abdalla was the ultimate parent, meting out drugs and discipline as she strode through the halls. A parent respected, but defied.

Habiba, age nineteen, avoided the doctor's stern eyes.

"I'm afraid thieves will steal our sleeping mats and utensils," the teenage mother said.

"She will gain one more kilo," she repeated quietly, "and then we'll leave."

The doctor knew she could not stop Habiba from leaving any more than she could squeeze rain out of the heavy, muggy air. Instead, Khadija Abdalla scanned the room with a scrutinizing gaze until she spotted a banana peel on a wooden stool near Hadiwa's cot.

Something she could control.

And she said:

"You've made this place a mess. It's unsanitary. You have to keep it clean."

A group of former nomadic herders had settled on top of a cauterized Kenyan hillock just north of the equator. Two miles away lay the Dagahaley refugee camp, where forty-seven thousand people, mostly migrants from Somalia, which has not had a stable government or peace since 1991, had been living for fifteen years in a settlement operated by the United Nations. The refugees were barely making ends meet, but to the sixteen hundred villagers on the hill the refugee camp was a shimmering green oasis that had everything their village did not: constant access to water, mud-brick houses with tin roofs, schools, basic food items, sleeping mats and kitchen utensils, all provided by international aid organizations. Herders who had lost their livestock first began to settle on the hill in 2004 and named their village Dagahaley, after the camp. By 2006, when I visited Dagahaley the village, a new family of former nomads arrived each day. By living in proximity to the camp, the herders reasoned, they would draw the attention of relief agencies that travel along the old, beat-up colonial roads but almost never venture into the roadless bush. The agencies would arrive in Dagahaley bearing aid handouts for the former nomads—even if this aid came at the cost of abandoning their traditional lifestyle forever.

Ninety percent of the people in northeast Kenya, like the mothers at the Garissa hospital or the Woman with a Broken Jug, were ethnic Somali herders. With each drought, they found themselves farther and farther removed from the nearest watering hole. By relief workers' own acknowledgment, the international campaign to help the millions of people worst hit by the drought was akin to offering a group of dehydrated villagers a couple of sips from a stranger's CamelBak, albeit on a much larger scale. Several workers told me that any aid at that point was contributing to the the creation of monumental dependence.

The aid workers appeared to have a clear idea about what needed to be done to really help the herders in the long run: keeping them updated on the true value of their meat so that they did not get ripped off by middlemen; building roads that would provide them with direct access to markets; teaching them to better manage their land and livestock. But, like journalists who can't do much about the suffering they witness, they could not find donations that would help generate long-term projects after cable-news images of starving babies and emaciated adults have faded from television screens, giving way to footage of the next disaster.

"Every time there is a humanitarian catastrophe, you hear the same promise: there will be a seamless transition from humanitarian assistance to developmental assistance," Marina Ottaway, an expert on political reconstruction at the Carnegie Endowment for International Peace in Washington, told me one time. "In the end it never happens, because these agencies have to go on to put out the next fire, and there is simply not enough funding."

I wrote a story about the Garissa hospital. It went on page one, along with Michael Macor's haunting photograph of a starving girl—her eyes big and tragic and wise, the eyes of some early Christian saint from the wall of an ancient monastery, her birdlike body shriveled and broken. The girl's name was Fatuma Hillow. She was two years old, and she was dying of tuberculosis, dehydration, malnutrition, and a recent heart attack. Over the several days that followed, more than a hundred people from the Bay Area wrote and called me, asking how they could send a check so that it reached the hospital. They wanted the girl in the picture to get well. Even for those people thousands of miles away, she was too beautiful, too precious. It was the best response that I could have hoped for. But Dr. Abdalla had told me: the little girl had only a few days to live. By the time those checks reached the hot, fly-infested malnutrition ward in Garissa, Fatuma Hillow was dead.

Many people have asked me if it is difficult to leave Fyodor and Alex for weeks, sometimes longer, while I travel. Some have asked if I feel guilty.

Some have told me I should feel guilty. Yes, I reply. I do. In return, I over-compensate by trying to cram all the parenting I have missed into the weeks that pass between my trips. Sometimes this parenting comes out too overwrought, too forceful. I feel guilty about that, too.

Three years after the trip to Garissa, I arrived at a crime scene: five or six meaty, orange, green, and crimson stems of Swiss chard, each about the length of the palm of my hand, discarded and withering on the freshly mown grass next to our house. The suspect: my stepson Alex, age thirteen, who was standing over the large wooden barrel in which I grow this variety of beet with kitchen scissors in one hand and a bunch of severed, colorful leaves in the other. The leaves were for his school lunch. The stems were supposed to have been for the salad I was making for dinner. The charges: wasting food. My verdict: guilty.

Retribution was swift.

"What the hell are you doing?" I roared, advancing across the patio at the startled teenager. "Since when are we throwing out food?"

I went off at the kid, letting fly a verbal barrage that sounded ill-ad-vised the moment it left my mouth. Do you know that I've seen people pick undigested maize kernels out of cow manure for lunch? Do you know that I've lived on red beans and tea for months? Do you know that I've seen babies who would have lived had they only had the nutrients you just tossed on the ground, and instead they died of hunger?

It is that dark, musty ingredient lurking in the back of the war re-porter's pantry: the war reporter's self-righteous cliché. You know: "I've been there, I've seen privation and suffering, and you haven't so you have to respect what I have to say."

Cue thousand-yard stare.

Alex gave me an apprehensive look of confusion and hurt. In his world, babies didn't die, a handful of greens did not constitute the dif-ference between nourishment and starvation, and, ideally, adults did not go berserk over some slightly metallic-tasting, crunchy, and difficult-to-wash stems of a leafy vegetable. I backed down. I felt remorseful about my outburst. Minutes later, I apologized for raising my voice and ex-plained, rather redundantly, that watching food go to waste makes me very upset. Alex, always on the quest for fairness and closure, apologized for throwing out the stalks and explained that he saw a slug crawling on one of the stems and thought it made all of them too gross to eat. (I tamped down the urge to describe impoverished collective-farm workers in Siberia picking slugs off cabbage to supplement their insufficient protein intake. In fact, I have never seen anyone scrounge for slugs, even though I am sure someone does it somewhere.) We hugged, and I set out to make the kids' dinner: pasta with homemade turkey Bolognese sauce, and a side of salad. With tomatoes, peppers, carrots, and what was left of the Swiss chard.

As I diced the vegetables, it occurred to me that I bear the main responsibility for the fact that these images of privation and famine are not indelibly etched in the minds of these children. Their innocence is the result of a parenting choice I myself made in 2001, when Fyodor was four years old and I called him from the outskirts of Kabul.

"Hi, son! I'm calling from Afghanistan!" I announced over a satellite phone connection so slow and distorted that adults on the other end of the line—editors, relatives, friends—typically responded to my greeting by immediately inquiring as to whether I was badly wounded or simply very drunk. The best way to engage Fyodor in a somewhat meaningful conversation using such a mangled signal, I had decided, was to go for some condescending and exaggeratedly cheerful adult-to-toddler talk.

"Afghanistan is a different country!" I chirped into the receiver. I had just filed a story about residents of a mountain village who had abandoned their infertile farms after yet another year of drought. The villagers—several hundred men, women, and children—were now living in lean-tos they had erected of burlap sacks and sticks so that they could become eligible for handouts of humanitarian rice, flour, tea leaves, and vegetable oil, which international relief agencies distributed to Afghans who had been displaced from their homes by war. It was fall; the rain, which had arrived too late to make a difference in the harvest, had soddened the clay soil underfoot. Children Fyodor's age with runny noses and horrible, dark, asthmatic coughs were getting stuck in ankle-deep glop. I felt like chain-smoking and crying, preferably at the same time, but I had promised to call home. So I continued: "It has really tall mountains with snow on top and really big deserts with real camels, foxes, and gerbils!"

Fyodor, who was staying in our Moscow apartment with his nanny (a former teacher with a master's degree in mathematics, whose monthly earnings as a babysitter were more than five times the pay she would have earned from the government of her native Uzbekistan teaching high school algebra and geometry in Tashkent), turned out to have been much more informed about where I was than I had expected.

"Be careful, mama," the four-year-old boy said. Somewhere over the Indian Ocean a satellite picked up his words and beamed them down to my Afghan mud-brick guesthouse. "I saw Afghanistan on TV and it has real tanks."

That was all it took for me to amend my theretofore unshakable belief in freedom of information and impose censorship in my own house. Good-bye, TV news. Radio: music only. If I had been a government, the Committee to Protect Journalists would have made room for me on its "Ten Most-Censored Countries" list, somewhere between North Korea and Belarus. If my kids have reached puberty with little or no knowledge about the events that were pivotal for my understanding and appreciation of food and waste, I had only myself to blame. Tomatoes, then peppers slid from my cutting board into the salad bowl and I wondered if the time had finally come for me to tell Alex the story about the Garissa Provincial Hospital, so that he doesn't assume it is not worth rinsing off and chopping into a salad a bit of food that has been slightly chewed on by a garden slug.

In our society, food is enjoyment—an opportunity for creativity, for expression, and for variety. Searching for just the right ingredient is part of the enjoyment, the thrill of the hunt. In many parts of the world, food is a necessity that is too rare for the hunt to be enjoyed. Sometimes, as the story of Mengchuqur has taught me, the hunt can become fatal for the hunters. But just because someone is hungry does not mean they are not going to feed their donkeys peanut butter; besides, in some societies, feeding your livestock is as much a matter of life and death as feeding yourself. Food choices range from the most inconsequential (do we eat Swiss chard or kale) and personal (do we indulge in lamb kebab or go vegan) to the profoundly, chillingly fundamental. And in the worst of cases, just because someone is hungry does not mean they get to eat, especially if someone else who has a better chance of living needs the food that is available. That was the harsh choice before the mothers at the pediatric ward in Garissa.

Try to explain this to a pubescent boy growing up in a moderately prosperous American suburb.

I may have tried to censor, as much as I could, war out of my children's lives—I am certain Alex and Fyodor have never heard of Meng-chuqur—but war keeps finding its way in. It rides into my pantry in grocery bags stuffed with ten pounds of dried chickpeas, "just in case." It sneaks into the kids' lunch boxes when I ply them with the lettuce and fruit that are supposed to ensure that they get their required vitamin intake. It erupts into small skirmishes in the patio and at the dining table over what gets eaten and what gets thrown out.

The morning after I go berserk over Swiss chard, I watch Fyodor, eyes mostly closed, pitching face-first toward the bowl of oatmeal on the table in front of him. It is instant oatmeal, with maple syrup and brown sugar already stirred in, and Fyodor has picked it out and prepared it himself—therefore, I decree, he must finish it. He has twenty minutes before the school bus comes to pick him up, and he will not have lunch until one in the afternoon, and I know that he will have trouble staying focused on his studies if he doesn't eat now. But it is seven in the morning and what he wants to do is sleep, not eat (and I cannot really blame him, for so do I). Fyodor opens his eyes and stares at the porridge as if it were something that has sneakily infiltrated his plate while he was innocently dozing off. I suspect that secretly he is waiting it out, hoping that if he snoozes at the table until it is time to go to school he will be allowed to not finish his food and slide it off his plate into the compost. His tea is untouched.

I hear my voice rising again.

I am about to pull out the starving in East Africa thing, the Meng-chuqur thing, anything. But what is he supposed to do? Eat all the food these people, half the way across the world, do not have? Drink all the water?

This is ridiculous. It makes no sense to me. And it most certainly is not going to make any sense to a boy who can barely keep his head from falling into his oatmeal.

Masala Chai Tea

Makes about 6 cups

Masala chai originated in India. It was probably brought to Kenya, which for centuries lay on the crossroads of global marine trade, by Indian merchants. Now it is a drink du jour in Kenya, where teatime is a holdover from British colonial times, and is consumed with breakfast, lunch, and dinner. Kenyans tend to use a lot of sugar with their tea; feel free to cut the amount in half or omit it entirely. Today many stores in the West sell "black chai tea" in tea bags, with the spices already mixed in, but that doesn't allow the flavor of the spices to fully blossom, the way the traditional method of brewing the spices does. So forget the prefab tea bags, and follow me.

3 cups milk
2 sticks cinnamon
6 whole green cardamom pods
4 whole cloves
12 black peppercorns
6 heaping teaspoons loose unflavored black tea or 9 tea bags
12 teaspoons sugar, 2 per cup (or to taste)

1. Combine the milk with 3 cups cold water in a large pot and bring to a boil. Add cinnamon, cardamom, cloves, and peppercorns, stir well, turn off the heat, cover the pot, and let the spices steep for about 10 minutes.

2. Add the tea leaves or tea bags and sugar and bring to a boil. Reduce the heat and simmer for 5 minutes, covered. Strain into a warm ceramic teapot. Serve immediately.

Note: To warm a teapot, bring 1 cup water to a boil in a separate pot. Pour it into the ceramic teapot, put the cover on, swirl the hot water inside the teapot, then pour it out. Cover the teapot with a tea cozy or a kitchen towel.

Ugali with Sukuma Wiki

Serves 4

Kenyan cuisine is as varied as the more than seventy ethnic groups that make up the country's population of 31 million people. Like the country's main spoken language, Swahili—which incorporates the tongues of the Arabic, German, and Portuguese merchants who have traveled to the Horn of Africa to trade their goods, and the British colonialists who once dominated the region—the food of Kenya has adopted and adapted cooking from the Arabian peninsula, Central and South Asia, Europe, and other parts of Africa.

But even in the years when their land is not battered by drought, most Kenyans live in extreme poverty and hunger. The average income is about one dollar a day. In some parts of the country, a quarter of all children are acutely malnourished, according to UNICEF reports. So the diet of most people commonly relies on basic staples that are cheap, more or less accessible, and can be cooked in bulk to last a large family a few days: *ugali,* made with cornmeal and water, and *sukuma wiki,* which translates as "to stretch a week"—sautéed collard greens or kale with (if they are available) garlic, pepper, and curry.

For the *ugali*:
3 cups cornmeal (the finer, the better)

For the *sukuma wiki*:
2 tablespoons vegetable cooking oil (any kind)
2 cloves garlic, crushed, optional
1 large onion, diced, optional
1 large bunch collard greens, kale, or—that's right—
    Swiss chard from your garden (or from your favorite
    grocery store or market)
1 large tomato, diced, or ½ cup tomato paste, optional
Pinch of salt
½ jalapeño pepper, diced, or ½ teaspoon cayenne pepper, optional
½ teaspoon curry powder, optional
1 lime or lemon cut into wedges, for serving

1. Make the *ugali:* Bring 3 cups water to a boil in a medium saucepan. With your hands, add the cornmeal in batches (don't add it all at once or it will be hard to mix—you should have five or six batches). Lower the heat

and simmer for 7 to 10 minutes, mixing periodically (especially in the beginning) so that it doesn't clump. *Ugali* is usually not made with salt, but feel free to add some. The *ugali* is done when it is the consistency of polenta and pulls easily from the sides of the saucepan. Turn the pot upside down over a flat plate until the *ugali* falls out; it should look like a white cake. Let it cool until it's not too hot to touch; it will be not just your bread, but also your spoon.

2. Make the *sukuma wiki:* Heat the oil in a large saucepan, pot, or pan. If you're cooking *sukuma wiki* with garlic and/or onion, sauté those while you're cutting the greens into very thin strips (the whole thing, leaves and stems). Add the collard greens, the tomato or tomato paste if you're using it, the rest of the seasonings, and 1 cup water. Bring to a boil, then reduce the heat and simmer for 30 minutes.

3. Serve the *sukuma wiki* on a plate with a wedge of lemon or lime. Cut the *ugali* into 8 slices (as you would with corn bread or polenta cake) and serve 2 slices with the greens. No cutlery is needed: simply tear off a piece of *ugali,* shape it with your fingers into something resembling a spoon or a scoop, and use it to scoop the greens into your mouth. Not comfortable? Fine, use a knife and fork.

❧

Nyama Choma

Serves 4 to 6

Nyama choma, or grilled meat, is the traditional dish for those in Kenya who can afford this expensive protein. It can be made with any kind of meat or even chicken, although in Garissa, those who can afford it typically make (or buy) goat *nyama choma.* But if you, dear reader, find the distinctive, earthy flavor of goat meat not to your taste, feel free to substitute pork or beef (those will also make it slightly less chewy). The catch, of course, is that you absolutely have to have a grill that works on wood or charcoal; gas simply won't translate into the smokiness that distinguishes the real *nyama choma.* You will need:

Juice of 2 lemons
2 cloves garlic, crushed
1 teaspoon curry powder
1 teaspoon ground turmeric

1 teaspoon ground coriander
1 teaspoon paprika
Salt and pepper, to taste
3 pounds goat ribs (or goat meat on the bone),
　　pork spare ribs, or beef short ribs

1. Combine the lemon juice and spices in a large, nonreactive bowl. Add the meat and mix well, so that the meat is completely coated in the spice mixture. Allow to marinate for at least 1 hour. Grill on one side over slow heat for 20 minutes (15 minutes for beef or pork), flip over, and grill on the other side for 20 minutes more. The meat should be very well done. Do not cover.

2. When the meat is done, cut it off the bones onto a large plate. *Nyama choma* is typically served as small, bite-size pieces that you can scoop up with your *ugali* or a piece of flatbread. Or, if you're more comfortable with silverware, go at it with a fork.

Ten

Lobster in Tikrit

American military bases in Iraq usually bore the names of fallen warriors (Forward Operating Base Speicher, named after navy pilot Michael Scott Speicher, whose F/A18 Hornet was shot down over Mesopotamia during the first Gulf War), desired outcomes (Camp Liberty), or famous battles of yore. The ascetic, gravel-strewn constellation of tents, guard towers, and metal living containers near a former airstrip outside Tikrit, where I spent several weeks on assignment for the *Chronicle* in 2005, was called Forward Operating Base Remagen, named after the famous March 1945 capture by American troops of the last standing bridge on the Rhine.

The significance of that conquest was not so much strategic (by then it was clear that the Nazis were losing the war) as it was symbolic: it boosted the morale of Allied forces and spelled another devastating blow for the retreating Wehrmacht. In 2003, the capture of Tikrit, Saddam Hussein's hometown, was also thought to be symbolic: The fall of the last stronghold of Saddam's military machine at the hands of American troops was expected to spell the unequivocal defeat of the dictatorship; the end of most military operations; and the dawning of a new, democratic Iraq.

Two and a half years after the invasion, Remagen, like other American military bases in Iraq, was an austere refuge from the untamed violence that had deluged the country. Most soldiers on the base were serving their second or third tours of duty in Iraq. Most could plainly see that the battle they were fighting was not yielding the victorious results they had been told to expect. To raise the spirit of troops deployed to the war zone for a year and sometimes longer, Remagen—and most forward operating bases—treated them to Friday dinner specials of steak and lobster.

These delicacies, like pretty much everything else on American bases in Iraq, arrived from the States to Kuwait in enormous freezers stored aboard giant cargo ships. From Kuwait, civilian contractors with military escorts drove the food into Iraq in long, apprehensive caravans of mammoth trucks. Such cavalcades became known, among the military, as "cheese convoys," although they transported through the blood-soaked desert many other extravagances than muenster, mozzarella, and shredded cheddar: they also carried avocados, for example, and shrimp. Once the trucks crossed the border from Kuwait, they became easy and obvious targets for ambushes and homemade bombs lurking along highway medians and shoulders. American taxpayers paid millions of dollars for the gourmet meals that were supposed to boost the troops' morale; the truck drivers and their escorts paid for these meals with their lives and limbs.

Most of the food did reach the bases, where it was served in chow halls: typically, giant tents or metal hangars fortified with sandbags on the outside and spruced up with pennants and banners of favorite NFL teams on the inside. On large bases, food selection in chow halls was astoundingly vast, if a bit bland, and somewhat made up for the stark settings.

(As a rule, the smaller the base, the less exciting the food; on some company-size outposts men survived mostly on ready-to-eat meals in thick, brown plastic bags and care packages mailed from home. Each package of the ready-to-eat meals, commonly known as MREs, contained enough proteins, vitamins, toothpicks, and tiny bottles of Tabasco sauce to last an average male a day. Each MRE also contained a book of matches, swamp green, inscribed with the following statement: "These matches are designed especially for damp climates but they will not light when wet, or after long exposure (several weeks) to very damp air." These must have been leftovers from Vietnam. The average annual humidity in Iraq is just above 40 percent.)

At those chow halls that served real food, steak and lobster were the highlights of the week, despite the fact that the meat and the shellfish were drastically overcooked, and that it was equally difficult to cut the steak or to extricate lobster tails from their shells because all cutlery in the chow halls was plastic. There were certainly no lobster crackers. On Remagen, Friday lobster followed Thursday stir-fries, corn chowder and fried chicken followed chicken noodle soup and jambalaya, and the dessert stand offered, every day, at least half a dozen puddings and pies, plus a variety of Baskin-Robbins ice-cream flavors, some of them kosher. All food in all chow halls was free.

On every large base I have visited, the troops liked to show off their chow halls, and Remagen was no exception. At the time, the base was home to the soldiers of the Third Infantry Division's Second Battalion, Seventh Infantry regiment—Two-Seven, as the troops called it. The soldiers' task was to eradicate insurgency in a swath of tribal farmland, pastures, and desert (home to a major oil refinery) that was the birthplace of Iraq's deposed dictator and home of his many rich, disaffected relatives. The way Two-Seven's soldiers bragged about their meals one would have thought the variety of food inside their heavily guarded base, and not the security outside, was the measure of military success.

Outside, Iraq was spiraling toward a civil war that already seemed inevitable, and American troops were losing ground to a relentless and infinitely adaptable Sunni rebellion. In Baghdad (where military cooks at the prematurely named Camp Victory served fresh guacamole in shiny, gallon-size, stainless-steel basins), religious militias were already remapping neighborhood boundaries along sectarian and political affiliations, turning flat rooftops into battlements, apartment blocks into fortresses, and streets into front lines. In western Iraq, the desert highways leading to Forward Operating Base al Qaim ("The best chow in the country," one marine officer there proudly assured me) were lined with al Qaeda billboards encouraging the locals to kill Americans and anyone who was perceived as collaborating with them, the same way that American highways are lined with billboards encouraging the locals to buy the latest hybrid SUVs.

Beyond the concrete-and-sandbag walls that enclosed the arid grid of Remagen's tents and hangars, along the fertile banks of the meandering Tigris River, Two-Seven's soldiers were battling a vicious insurgency. The war appeared determined to etch indelible images into the soldiers' memories: faces of comrades killed in the fight against a largely faceless enemy; charred remains of Iraqi civilians blown apart by mortars; children playing soccer next to roadside bombs rigged to detonate with wires colorful like Christmas tree ornaments. One moment the soldiers were sipping sweet tea at the mayor's office, and the next, they were staring down, slack-jawed, at two Iraqi policemen: almost limbless, still smoldering, contorted grotesquely in early rigor mortis, they lay on the pavement amid the mostly pulverized shreds of the man who had smashed a car packed with antitank shells into their cruiser. The suicide bomber's head was the largest fragment that was still somewhat held together, by the scalp; it had landed in front of a house a block away, where a middle-aged woman had been cooking okra for lunch. The head was flat, splayed in the dust. "Like an inside-out dog," a soldier spat.

Two hours later, the soldiers were back on the base, in time for chow. It was Monday. Monday was pizza day.

On afternoons like that one, familiar food was the only comfort amid the arbitrary violence. Monday pizzas, Friday steak and lobster—and the everyday supplies of shredded iceberg lettuce and cheddar cheese, cherry pie, ice cream, and fruit punch—represented a dependable ritual, a predictable end to a day that could have been anyone's last.

Few soldiers at Remagen embraced the monotony of chow hall meals as wholeheartedly as Two-Seven's commander, Lieutenant Colonel Todd Wood. He dined almost exclusively on corn dogs, burgers, French fries, and Jell-O, as though the reliability of these tastes, echoes of his childhood in the calm expanses of Iowa farmland, could somehow bring him relief from the randomness of the deaths of his soldiers and the Iraqi civilians around him.

———

By the spring of 2005, Western reporters in Iraq had become targets for kidnapping gangs and militias looking for a foreign trophy. American news organizations fortified their Baghdad bureaus with sandbags and bullet-resistant glass, and hired expensive security consultants doubling as bodyguards. Some reporters resorted to what they called "hotel journalism": interviewing sources at their hotel rooms or by phone, and using reporting by their bureaus' mobile and courageous Iraqi staff to put together stories without leaving their offices. A giant billboard advertising "certified armored cars from Germany" loomed over the luggage carousel at Amman International Airport, a common layover point on the way from the United States and Europe to Iraq. WHEN GOING TO IRAQ, MAKE SURE TO DRIVE ARMORED! the sign warned. Paying for such protection was beyond the *Chronicle*'s means, and I did not want to be cobbling together stories based on other people's reporting. The only affordable way for me to work in Iraq more or less safely—safety, of course, being in the eye of the beholder—was to "embed" with American troops.

Embedding with the troops meant that I would travel on military helicopters, Bradley fighting vehicles, and humvee trucks from one military base to another, spending a few days or weeks with different American military units that, hopefully, would take me along with them on patrols or raids. I was not thrilled with the prospect. Having a perpetual military escort would significantly cut into my ability to interview Iraqis—if I were ever allowed to do that at all. What I would be able to see and report would depend less on my qualities as a journalist than on the benevolence and understanding of the military commanders of the units that would take me in.

The first few days of my trip went remarkably badly. At the sprawling Camp Victory in Baghdad, I could hear massive explosions rumble outside the base and see plumes of dark smoke rise on the horizon. But my military minders didn't allow me to leave the base; instead, they invited me to report about a Bay Area dentist who fixed soldiers' teeth ("When people think of combat trauma, they think about wounds and medevac,* but have you ever cracked a tooth?" was how a colonel in charge of American military dentists in Iraq made the pitch). Out of desperation, I wrote five hundred words; thankfully, they never made it into the paper.

I briefly stayed on a base in Samarra, an ancient northern Iraqi city that at the time was home to about 150,000 mostly Sunni Arabs and one of the major hotbeds of anti-American insurgency. Seven months after my visit, the city became a watershed of the civil war after terrorists blew up al Askariya shrine, the mosque with a golden dome whose mirror-encrusted walls glowed with sunlight and made it appear to be floating in air, and which was one of the holiest sites for Iraq's Shias. The explosion sent a signal to twenty-five million Iraqis to start killing each other in earnest.

For a day in Samarra, I caught a glimpse of the war. It clung to the tip of the army-issue boot of Sergeant First Class Louis D'Angelo.

I met D'Angelo in the barely furnished house of a suspected insurgent named Jamal Faluh Jasem, who was not home when the sergeant and his men came looking. Jamal's female relatives and children were there. It was difficult to understand their level of kinship to Jamal; they were terrified and tight-lipped. Now the Americans were ransacking the house in search of weapons Jamal may have hidden between flower-patterned mattresses stacked atop creaky plywood shelves or in the threadbare clothes the soldiers had tossed out of the sole closet onto the poured-concrete floor. The closet looked like a disemboweled whale.

Stomping on the clothes, frying pans, and construction tools now strewn underfoot, D'Angelo stormed from room to room as a group of children clung, shivering, to women squatting and kneeling on the

---

*Medevac—stands for "medical evacuation." It refers to evacuation, usually from the battlefield (or from a war zone), of someone who is seriously ill or wounded.

house's sole carpet in their black *abayas*. So far, his soldiers had unearthed, amid clumps of dry clay in the family's backyard, several rounds of ammunition for Kalashnikov semiautomatic rifles; a pipe that may have been a homemade shoulder-mounted missile launcher (or a defunct bit of the sewage system); a coil of copper wire; and a simple electronic device, with wires, they said looked like a detonator for a homemade bomb (I couldn't tell). In a house next door, they found a rocket-propelled grenade. In the bedroom, D'Angelo spotted two clips for a Kalashnikov rifle. (Iraqis were allowed to keep one Kalashnikov per household.) Towering over the women, he held up the clips and bellowed:

"They don't have weapons? They don't have weapons?"

He turned to a private from his platoon:

"Go in the shitter there and check it out. Look in the washer."

Muttering in a voice raspy with rage—"We've been here since January. I had two people shot. My track guy was hit with a VBIED,* and we hit two land mines. With all that in consideration it gets more personal"—the sergeant marched into a closet where three burlap sacks sagged in a corner.

The sacks were stamped with the blue olive branches of the United Nations emblem: they were part of the monthly food ration that Iraqis were receiving from the world's foremost relief agency. Each parcel was supposed to contain six pounds of rice, four pounds of sugar, eighteen pounds of flour, and one liter of cooking oil per person, but the allocation of these staples was sporadic and unreliable because of widespread corruption among Iraqi officials in charge of the distribution, an imperfect rationing system, and violence that frequently targeted the market areas where the food was handed out. These sacks contained flour. They were the family's entire supply for that month. The only other food in the house, apart from a large aluminum bowl of ripe tomatoes on the kitchen floor, was a quarter-full burlap sack of sugar, and a grimy, deformed plastic bottle of vegetable cooking oil.

D'Angelo pulled out a serrated pocketknife and ripped the bags open.

---

*VBIED—the acronym stands for vehicle-borne improvised explosive device, a U.S. military term for a car bomb.

White flour spilled onto the dirty floor. Without hesitation, D'Angelo shoved his boot ankle deep into the finely ground powder, and spread it on the concrete with the Vibram sole of his tan suede boot.

In the Muslim Middle East, few insults are more offensive than shoving someone or something with the soles of your shoes. (Not that this gesture is a sign of affection in any culture I can think of, but in that part of the world it is particularly degrading.) Even showing someone the soles of your shoes is considered uncivil. On the day Saddam's government fell, April 9, 2003, joyous revelers threw shoes at his statues and whacked the ubiquitous murals and posters bearing the dictator's image with their sandals. Muntadher al Zaidi, the Iraqi television journalist, became a national hero for flinging his shoes at President George W. Bush at a press conference in Baghdad in 2008. The president, who adroitly dodged both shoes, was not the first Bush to interact with Iraqi footwear: after the first Gulf War, Saddam had ordered a mosaic portrait of George H. W. Bush installed on the ground floor of Baghdad's popular al Rasheed Hotel so that everyone who entered the lobby could tread upon Forty-one's face.

There was no question that D'Angelo knew about the symbolic significance of shoes. All American troops deploying to Iraq received what the military called "cultural sensitivity training," which discussed the shoe taboo, touching women, or bringing bomb-sniffing dogs into mosques. In a hasty act of anger and revenge, the sergeant desecrated the family's monthly food supply—a cruel punishment in a land where most people were eking out a living off food stamps.

"What are you doing?" I asked.

"Looking for weapons," he growled, giving the flour one final tap with his boot. "These people hide stuff everywhere."

After that glimpse of the war in Iraq came long days of waiting inside the base—for something, anything. I spent a lot of time watching Sergeant Saikichi Simram, a beautifully muscled tank commander, shoot hoops. I listened to another soldier, Specialist Mike Rauch—who said he was twenty-three but looked ancient, all crow's-feet and hollow eyes, like those teenage fighters in Afghanistan—tell stories about the insurgents' creative approach to homemade bombs: 105-millimeter shells sewed up inside dead dogs, loaded into donkey carts, inserted into the anus of a cow. Was it all true, seen firsthand? Was it the modern adaptation of the ancient lore of trench-side fear? It was hard to tell. There was a lot of chain-smoking. Battalion medics watched *Three Amigos!* on DVD and fed me defrosted buffalo wings. Time dragged. At one point the commander of Simram's armor battalion suggested that I spend an action-packed day riding around the perimeter of his base in circles in a tank.

What the hell was I doing? All I could see from the turret of the M1 Abrams was a pile of fishing boats that had once plied the Tigris River looking for carp, rusting by the side of the road; the snail-shell spiral of Samarra's twelve-hundred-year-old al Malwiya minaret jutting out of the flat horizon next to al Askariya's gilded dome; and, one day, farmers selling watermelons under a rest-stop sign that read: WELCOM. I could not stop the tank to talk to the farmers. I could not even talk to the tank gunner. The soldiers hadn't given me a radio headset, and the racket of the treads drowned out all other sounds, deeming any conversation impossible.

Inside the base, it was not much better. The military's traditional suspicion of journalists ran deep. After a brief introductory interview, best summarized as "the enemy wants to kill us but we're kicking their insurgent asses back to the Dark Ages," the battalion commander in Samarra—the man in charge of my itinerary there—avoided me. He was not the only one. The printout of an email tacked to the door of the battalion commander in al Qaim, where marines fought daily battles with al Qaeda fighters (when they weren't eating bacon and guacamole at "the best chow hall in the country"), warned the troops about the *real* threat: "the liberal media." (I suggested to that commander that if I were so dangerous, he probably should not have let me so perilously close to his office, and there was some uncomfortable cackling. I left the base a few days later; the printout stayed.) To get embedded in the first place, I had been required to email military press officers in Baghdad a sample of my clips, which they perused and evaluated. The resulting official judgment on my work pronounced me "mostly fair, slightly liberal." This evalua-

tion was then forwarded to all the units of my destination in lieu of introductions. Most commanders were wary of my slightly liberal presence
even before I arrived.

Usually, I was left to stumble around military bases trying to per-
suade the troops that my only agenda was to understand whether
there was a story to tell, what that story was, and how to tell it right,
in a fair, adequate, interesting way—all the while diligently trying to
get their rank insignia right. Picking through that thorny terrain was
frustrating. The suggestion that I circle the base in a tank reinforced
my worry that I would never get anywhere near understanding—or
explaining to my readers in the United States—what this war was like
for the troops, the insurgents, and the civilians caught in the crossfire.
After a week or so, my time in Samarra was over and I climbed into
a Black Hawk helicopter, my ride to my next stop, Tikrit. The rotors
whipped up hot desert air with deafening thumps: there would not
be any meaningful interviews onboard, either. The gunners spent the
flight intently scanning the ground and training their machine guns
on the flat rectangles of rice paddies and palm groves growing in shadowy grids caked with sand from years and years of sandstorms. From
the air, central Iraq—the desert, the orchards, the villages, the cities,
everything except for the Tigris and the Euphrates, which ran metallic
green and brown and sometimes turquoise blue—was all dun, like a
bas-relief sculpted out of mud.

I looked past the gunners' backs at the tiny ocher figures tending their
ocher crops below and wondered whether that sight would be the extent
of my human interaction for the trip.

Later that day, I met Todd Wood.

————

The colonel was a slight, wiry man. He compensated for his compact
build with an authoritative posture befitting somebody tasked with representing Washington's policy in Iraq's tribal heartland. His job was to
appease tribal leaders and ordinary civilians, train Iraqi police and army,
hunt down insurgents, and act as a peacemaker among feuding neighbors whose grudges over plots of sandy soil went back generations. At

the same time, he served as a father figure to nine hundred young, fatigued soldiers, whom he had to encourage to keep fighting even as their comrades were killed and wounded before their eyes, and the support for their war dwindled at home.

Colonel Wood and I would talk until late, usually outside his sandbag-choked battalion headquarters. I usually spent the evenings out there, filing my stories via a portable satellite modem beneath concrete blast walls, which still gave off the heat they had absorbed during the day. Once, Wood gallantly suggested that I sit in an armored humvee to protect myself from the occasional mortar round that would land inside the base: the insurgents' way of announcing that they were out there, fighting the occupation. (You couldn't really hear the incoming mortar rounds until they bit into the ground because of the constant, loud din of generators that powered the military bases. The 82- and 105-millimeter projectiles suddenly detonating inside the base was a reality most troops in Iraq faced and accepted as a nuisance—sort of like the intense summer heat, which sometimes rose to 130 degrees, albeit more deadly. The explosions unnerved me, but I had to be outside to get satellite reception.) The colonel would emerge into the evening haze carrying two Styrofoam cups of Starbucks coffee—one for him and one for me—brewed in the back room of his tactical operations center (off-limits to me, a civilian with no security clearance) with a stash he and his officers faithfully replenished from care packages mailed from the States.

Wood spoke mostly candidly about the war he was supposed to fight. During the invasion of Iraq, his men had been among the first American soldiers to roll up the Mesopotamian peninsula. They had deployed to Tikrit a year and a half later, expecting a battlefield. The colonel—an infantry officer and an army ranger—had trained for his entire life to lead troops into battle.

"I have come here with a very myopic focus," he told me once, "that success equals the defeat of the bad guys through shooting bullets. I thought all we needed to do was come here and kill enough terrorists."

Instead, he and his soldiers found themselves in a different kind of war: one in which they sat in a provincial Iraqi town jump-starting the local government; acted as judicious mediators between warring Iraqi factions; played sheriff in a town where the locals despised them and harbored insurgents who packed taxicabs with explosives and detonated them in streets crowded with civilians. One afternoon the colonel would be line-dancing at the wedding of a local sheikh, and several hours later, in a stealthy predawn raid, he would be kicking down the metal gates of a sleeping compound of suspected rebels. What happened between one all-American, corn-dog–burger dinner combo on Wood's plate and the next was anybody's guess. It was difficult to predict how any of Wood's decisions would reverberate among the local Sunni tribes. On the fertile Mesopotamian plane, any small misstep quickly blossoms into a tragedy. As an American proconsul, the colonel found himself responsible for all of them.

It was during these conversations with the colonel—as much as during the tortured visits to widows and orphans, raids that roused sleepy families from their rooftop cots on moonless nights, and long tea parties with Iraqi sheikhs in parlors gray with cigarette smoke and mistrust— that I finally saw: there was no cut-and-dried narrative of American troops battling Sunni insurgency. The story, instead, was about the maddening lack of clarity for the mission of an American unit deployed to Iraq. It was about the excruciating dilemmas the troops faced as they scanned jade fields of winter wheat through the scope of their M16s; about the decisions they made each day as they tried to root out a mostly invisible enemy in this hostile land full of defenseless people eking out a living in the middle of a war; about the moments of elation over the right choices and the prolonged grief over the wrong ones.

One October morning Todd Wood sat in a beige plastic chair in the middle of the small, walled-in patio of Nebras Khalid Nasser. Nasser's wife had recently been killed by American soldiers. The colonel shifted his feet uneasily; the patio tiles were sticky with spilled soda and the Vibram soles of his combat boots clung unpleasantly to the surface. To his right stood Omar Elmenshawi, his translator. To his left sat Captain Ramon "Ray" Osorio. The captain held a plain white envelope in his right hand. Inside the envelope were twenty-five hundred dollars. Wood had come to give the cash to Nasser, who stood wiping tears with the collar of his gray *dishdasha**shirt and holding a baby boy in the crook of his arm.

They were called "condolence visits." According to a military regulation for Iraq, the money was somehow supposed to compensate the man for his loss and settle the Iraqi-American score opened each time a soldier accidentally killed a civilian. American officers found the regulation macabre, but no one could think of a better way to provide restitution for human lives in the land of Hammurabi, where tribal justice often reverted to the most famous provision of the Babylonian king's code of law: "an eye for an eye, a tooth for a tooth." The accidental shootings of civilians, Wood explained, led one sheikh to "threaten to increase attacks against us."

Several days earlier, Nasser had decided to move his family from Beiji, an insurgent stronghold north of Tikrit, to Tikrit, which was considered a safer town. He had helped his wife, Zahoya, and their year-old son into his brother's beat-up Toyota sedan. They had just started driving south when an American military convoy approached. The car in front of Nasser sped up suddenly. The Americans did not like that. A single shot rang out. Blood poured from Zahoya's head. The American convoy kept going. The convoy was from a different unit, not part of Todd Wood's command.

Nasser was weeping quietly. He could barely speak.

"She was pregnant," was all the widower could repeat. "She died right away."

Five feet separated the two men. It may as well have been five thousand miles. The colonel avoided looking at Nasser. He, too, was saying the same thing over and over.

"I am sorry. It was not intentional," he kept saying, and Omar translated in a quiet voice. The colonel told the bereaved Iraqi man that the soldiers who fired at his car had not meant to kill his wife. Nasser kept crying.

---

*Dishdasha—a long shirt worn by many men in the Middle East and North Africa. Depending on the country, a *dishdasha* can go down to the wearer's knees or ankles, or all the way down to the ground. American troops in Iraq, not your paragons of sensitivity, usually refer to *dishdashas* as "man dresses."

The day Zahoya was killed, Wood had stood beneath the bleachers in a large gym at a military base in Beiji, where some of his soldiers were stationed. Behind him, on a small makeshift stage hammered together with pine two-by-fours, dog tags dangled over the pair of tattered tan suede boots of Specialist Joshua Kynoch. The twenty-three-year old soldier had been killed when the Bradley fighting vehicle he had been driving had struck a bomb fashioned from a land mine wired to several 155-millimeter antitank rounds. The mangled, jagged remains of the Bradley were parked in the lot outside the gym, like a horrible, ghoulish monument.

"Remember, now there's another one looking down on you," the colonel had told Kynoch's friends at the somber memorial service, rummaging for words to help the men carry on with their deployment. "This mission is for their memory, and to protect the men to your left and right."

The specialist was the eighth soldier the battalion had lost during that year in Iraq; in a few days his framed portrait would join the others lining the hallway of the command center, marking the toll of war along with unanswered roll calls, unoccupied cots, untold jokes. The absence of the dead was so palpable it became a presence of its own when soldiers reminisced in the clipped, almost monosyllabic sentences they reserved for the friends who were no longer with them.

Each death crushed Wood, whose oldest son was just a couple of years younger than some of the soldiers he had lost.

"Gut-wrenching" was how he described these memorial services to me. "I hate them."

Wood had a hard enough time explaining the randomness and the suddenness of the death of his own soldiers. And now he was somehow supposed to explain, through a translator, the indiscriminate reach of war to an Iraqi widower whose wife had died at the hands of soldiers the colonel did not know and who had been aiming at someone else. The colonel searched for words to comfort the grief-stricken man and found none. He lifted the soles of his feet again, feeling the pull of the sticky courtyard tiles. He had paid condolence visits a dozen times, but each time hurt anew. Nasser never looked the colonel in the eye.

"She was pregnant," the Iraqi man kept saying. He had stopped wiping his face. The stubble on his cheeks was wet with tears. "She died right away."

Why did Wood let me see this? Not just the moments of relative glory (like the time when the colonel led his men in a meticulously orchestrated, predawn joint raid with Iraqi soldiers that netted two terrorist suspects and a pile of assault rifles), or the almost comedic episodes (like the night I met Wood, when the colonel took a small group of his soldiers to play pool against Iraqi teenagers in a barely lit Tikriti dive; the Americans lost miserably, likely because the Iraqis were using several cue balls at once)—but also the times when his soldiers, at that nightmarish site of the suicide car bombing that killed two police officers, mistakenly shot and killed the driver of an Iraqi fire engine who had arrived to collect the shattered, smoldering bodies of the victims? Or the time when one of Two-Seven's men, a young lieutenant from upstate New York, threatened to maim an Iraqi teenager because the kid refused to talk about the whereabouts of a suspected insurgent? Or the times when it was clear that Wood would have given almost anything to be anywhere in the world but there, like the agonizing visit to Nasser's patio?

Every day, I would email Wood and every soldier I had written about a copy of that morning's story. The stories were rarely glorious or anything the soldiers should have been proud of: midnight searches that turned up no suspects, distraught Iraqis blaming Americans for their myriad misfortunes, soldiers worn out by the exasperating hunt for elusive guerrilla fighters. Some soldiers refused to speak to me afterward. One soldier's parents wrote me indignant emails and wished horrible things upon my children. The colonel would emerge from his spartan, windowless cell in the cinderblock battalion headquarters holding a cup of coffee too strong for anyone else to drink, and announce:

"Read your story this morning, Anna."

"And?" I would ask, prepared to defend every word.

He would spit a black wad of chewing tobacco into a clear plastic bottle. Nod.

Then, he would say:

"It happened."

There was almost a hint of satisfaction in his voice, as though the only certainty in the ever-changing landscape of his war—apart from a chow hall serving corn dogs and burgers—were the events that had already taken place.

As far as food went, my favorite days in Tikrit were when I got to accompany Two-Seven to the local Iraqi army headquarters at the sarcophagus-shaped granite palace on Saddam Boulevard. The architectural monstrosity had once belonged to Saddam Hussein, who had owned dozens of oddly designed palaces across the country; the Americans had dubbed this one "the Birthday Palace," after the famous photograph of the Iraqi dictator firing a shotgun, one-armed, from the building's balcony during a military parade honoring his birthday. Whenever Wood and his entourage of a dozen or so men showed up at the Birthday Palace, the Iraqi officers would always insist that they stay for lunch.

Lunch was served in an echo-filled hall at the end of the palace's left wing. Everyone sat at a long table according to rank: the Iraqi army leaders next to Wood at one end, the Iraqi lieutenants and specialists from Wood's crew at the other (in keeping with the local tradition of mistreating the common grunt, Iraqi enlisted men were not allowed at the officers' table). Each meal resembled a wedding feast. There was the blackened *masgouf,* the famous fish splayed between two metal nets and grilled over open fire. There were two or three different kinds of chicken. There was lamb. There were the neat cylinders of dolma. There were rainbow-colored platters of pickled red cabbage, garlic, cucumbers, purple turnips, and carrots. There were mounds of white and yellow rice; bowls of okra stewed with tomato sauce and beans; boiled potatoes; and fresh vegetables. We ladled food onto pewter plates, Iraqi busboys served hot tea in small glasses, and by the time bite-size desserts, oozing honey and rolled in crushed pistachios, were served on a separate table I was usually too full to move.

After lunch, the soldiers would cordially thank their hosts and file out into the sunlit plaza in front of the palace. There, the colonel would stretch, squint at the sun, put on his body armor, and announce:

"Well, I'm hungry."

If it wasn't burgers and corn dogs, it wasn't food enough.

I visited Two-Seven three times during their deployment to Tikrit. The last time, I left Remagen just days before the unit was scheduled to return home, to the longleaf pine forests of Fort Stewart, Georgia. The soldiers were tired and restless; conversations during patrols inevitably veered toward all the bars and restaurants the men would patronize when they got home.

"When we get back, Anna's taking us all out to Denny's," daydreamed Sergeant Derrick Stephens as he watched the white smoke of shepherds' fires rise from the silvery orchards on the Tigris shores one sweltering afternoon.

"Nah, we're gonna go out to IHOP," drawled his friend, Sergeant Darrell Foster. (When we did meet in the States, Darrell took me to a bar inside a former cotton exchange on Savannah's redbrick waterfront, and we reminisced about our Tikrit days over a pitcher of Bud Light.) Foster and I usually sat in the back of the humvee the guys had christened Old Betsy; Stephens sat directly in front of me, in the navigator's seat next to the driver. With colored markers he charted his version of the history of the Two-Seven's deployment in neat handwriting on the armored windshield of his truck.

"Green KIA VBIED," read one inscription, in black marker, followed by coordinates for the spot where a car bomb had taken an Iraqi soldier's life.

"Pos. IED w/bag pos. 155," read another, in orange, commemorating the curb into which insurgents had stuck a bomb fashioned from a 155-millimeter round.

"B. bag w/wires," read another, in green. "Explosion."

On some, better-stocked bases, Burger King, Taco Bell, KFC, and Pizza Hut had set up kiosks selling the troops' favorite fast food. Service was slow, demand was high, and on some days at lunchtime you had to wait in line twenty minutes before you could order a double Whopper or a slice of pepperoni with olives. And still, the troops did it, so intoxicating was the allure of homegrown fast food.

Remagen was not one of those. The nearest Pizza Hut was at Forward Operating Base Speicher, a perilous twenty-minute ride up a highway that often blew up under the tires of the soldiers' trucks. (B. bag w/wires was here.) Whenever soldiers from Remagen had business at Speicher, they would take orders and return bearing cardboard boxes with the familiar red-roof logo. Often, the colonel would pay for the whole batch.

"Why would anyone spend money on burgers and pizza when you can get them at the chow hall for free?" ranted young army Captain Brett Walker, whom I met during one of my visits to Baghdad. (Walker, whose job as an infantry officer somehow involved working as a public relations liaison, limited his diet almost exclusively to meat products. "My favorite vegetable is salami," he liked to say.)

I don't know, Brett. Perhaps because to these young guys, raised on food from America's chain restaurants, there was comfort in the familiar brand names. For a brief moment, when they chowed down on their Popcorn Chicken, Whoppers, or tacos beneath their favorite logos, they could forget that they were standing in forty pounds of body armor in grassless patios shaded with camouflage-mesh canopies in the middle of a war zone—even if most Whoppers came without lettuce and the Taco Supremes didn't always have sour cream.

At night, Todd Wood passed the hours watching bootleg episodes of *Deadwood* on the laptop in his room, or summoned his officers to the battalion's tactical operations room for endless reruns of *The Big Lebowski* on a giant flat-screen TV. In the seven weeks I spent with the colonel over the spring, summer, fall, and winter of 2005, I watched the Coen brothers' cult classic half a dozen times. By the time Two-Seven was packing up to go home that December, the officers could lip-synch all of John Goodman's lines.

Their combat tour was finally over, but the implacable violence and the loss of nine of their comrades shadowed the joy of anticipation. The sense of pride over helping build a more or less functional provincial government mixed with the lingering shock of having walked through too many scenes of carnage. Patrols kept drawing fire in the same streets they had when Two-Seven had first arrived in Tikrit a year earlier. Some officers were wondering out loud about whether their deployment had made any difference at all.

If Wood had doubts, he never shared them with his men.

"I can't have them go home feeling 'I just lost a year of my life,'" he told me. He knew that his soldiers were reading my stories, and he was cautious about expressing his thoughts on the course the war was taking with me, as well.

A couple of weeks before he returned home, the colonel came the closest to questioning his mission in my presence. He had invited me on a helicopter ride over the section of Iraq where Two-Seven had killed and bled.

From the air, Wood pointed out the farmland in Mukshifa, where a bomb hiding in a clay road goopy with rain had killed one of his soldiers. He squinted at the palm groves of Qadisiyah, where another of his soldiers had died: the soldier had been handing out toys to village children when a suicide bomber had detonated a car packed with explosives. He took in the sand-caked tank berms and crumbling, charred buildings of Saddam Hussein's former Republican Guard* training complex, where his soldiers had often found caches of weapons that insurgents used to make bombs.

"Did our presence prevent Saddam from killing thousands of Iraqis, as opposed to the thirty thousand Iraqis killed since we've been here?" he wondered out loud, looking down on Iraq from his aerial vantage point. We were talking over the Black Hawk's internal radio, the kind that required us to hold a switch whenever we spoke so that our words would carry over radio headsets—the only way to have a conversation in a thunderously loud helicopter. I waited for the colonel to continue his thought. But after Wood uttered his question, he let go of the switch. For a while, we flew in silence.

---

* Republican Guard—under Saddam Hussein, the military force responsible for protecting members of the Iraqi government and official buildings.

The intense heat of the afternoon sun made the courtyard of Nebras Khalid Nasser feel like a bread oven. The colonel rose from his beige plastic chair at last.

"These fucking patrols that drive around and shoot people have been a thorn in everybody's side all year," he cursed under his breath. Captain Osorio handed Wood the envelope with the twenty-five hundred dollars. Wood stuffed the money awkwardly into the widower's hand. Nasser said nothing.

We walked back to the humvees. Wood spoke.

"They either yell and scream at me, or they react like that," he said. "I'd rather have them yell and scream at me."

A couple of hours later, the colonel stopped by my table in the Remagen mess hall. It was Wednesday, but for some reason, the cooks had served lobster tails that day, probably to mix it up a little. Determined to eat my taxes' worth of chow hall food, I was stabbing the rubbery crustacean with a dull plastic fork in a feeble effort to pierce its tough red shell. It kept slipping off my flimsy polystyrene plate and onto my brown serving tray. In front of me, Omar Elmenshawi, the soft-spoken army translator from Florida, was very neatly eating chicken and shrimp jambalaya. I was embarrassed.

"What's good today?" Wood asked in an upbeat, chatty voice.

"Jambalaya, sir," Omar replied. "It's really good, sir. You should try it."

The battalion commander studied Omar's tray.

"Looks good!" He nodded, and took off to get his food. He was back in a couple of minutes, and placed his tray next to Omar's. On it were a corn dog; a burger; some French fries; and a jiggly, translucent cube of orange Jell-O.

❧

The World's Best Burgers

Serves about 8

I visited Todd Wood twice after Remagen: first in Savannah, when the colonel was still Two-Seven's commander, and, a year later, with my entire family, in a Washington suburb, during his stint at the Pentagon. (The colonel complained about feeling claustrophobic at his desk job, but his wife, Diane, and his three teenage sons looked relieved that he was out of harm's way.) Both times, Todd grilled steak and burgers; his steaks were nothing at all like the hard, leatherlike meat they served at Remagen. They were juicy, and so large they hung off our plates. The burgers were a particular hit with Fyodor, the family meat eater. The adults washed down the food with sweaty Michelob Ultras. There were no corndogs; that gives me an excuse not to write a corndog recipe. You can look that up online (it involves inordinate amounts of cooking oil, heavy batter, precooked franks, and little imagination).

The colonel's burgers were no-frills, store-bought beef patties he threw on the grill (meat-eating, fox-hunting gunmen of northern Afghanistan: you would have enjoyed this). I like vegetables even in my meat, so I have adapted for the grill the recipe of *kotlety,* or minced meat cutlets, that my grandma used to make when I was growing up in the Soviet Union. Use your favorite steak sauce.

I know most American grillers use gas or charcoal, but humor me: these burgers taste even better over hickory or birch coals. A coating of fine Iraqi dust is optional.

> 7 pounds ground beef, 80 percent lean
> 2 large onions, diced
> 1 cup bread crumbs, flavored or plain
> 1 cup minced cilantro
> 2 eggs
> 1 tablespoon Worcestershire sauce
> 1 tablespoon minced thyme or rosemary, or both, preferably fresh
> Salt, to taste

1. At least 1 hour before you start grilling, arrange wax paper on a flat surface in your kitchen. Combine all the ingredients. Slowly add about

1 cup water—you want to make sure the mixture is moist but not runny. It should be firm and peel off your fingers pretty easily, but not crumble. Shape the mixture into large, flat, round patties, 4 to 5 inches in diameter and ½ inch thick, moving them at the end from one hand to another several times, and place them on the waxed paper. You can stack the patties on top of one another; they won't stick. Leave them to marinate like that for at least an hour.

2. You can grill these burgers on aluminum foil, but they will most likely stick to the surface. If your grill grate is pretty small, you can throw the burgers directly onto it; if not, use an extra cooking grate. To find out when the burgers are ready, stick a knife into them: if the juices run clear, the burgers are done medium-well.

❧

Boiled Lobster

One lobster serves 1 to 4, depending on your appetite, wallet, and willingness to share

The first time I decided to prepare lobster (at the request of Alex and Fyodor), I brought the crustacean back from the supermarket, boiled some water, and was about to stick the lobster into the pot when I had the brilliant idea of having the kids watch. Wouldn't they love to see the lobster turn from gray to red? The boys were outside, and I stepped into the yard and yelled out their names, but they didn't hear me. I decided not to wait.

That was a good thing.

The lobster didn't like being stuck headfirst into boiling water at all. It clawed at the sides of the pot, beat its tail, and writhed and thrashed even after I put the lid on. It was a heartbreaking sight. The kids, I'm sure, would have been traumatized for life. Instead, they were pretty happy when dinner was served. My suggestion for the softhearted chef: Remember that if it were you at the bottom of the ocean, the crustacean would have no qualms about picking you clean off your bones. Then steel yourself.

One 1½-pound lobster
2 tablespoons salt, optional
8 tablespoons (1 stick) butter
1 clove garlic, optional
1 lemon, cut into wedges

For each 1½-pound lobster, use about 3 quarts water. Some people put salt in the water or even use seawater to boil the lobster (for what? to fool the beast into thinking it's going on vacation in Hawaii?), but in my experience it doesn't really affect the way the lobster tastes. The trick is not to overcook it. Use this simple chart:

1 to 1¼ pounds	cooks for 10 to 12 minutes
1½ to 2 pounds	cooks for 15 to 18 minutes
2½ to 5 pounds	cooks for 20 to 25 minutes

1. Do not remove the rubber bands from the lobster's claws. Bring the water to a boil. When the water is boiling, decisively plunge the lobster headfirst into the pot (I recommend wearing an oven mitt and an apron—you may get splashed) and cover it with a lid.

2. In the meantime, melt the butter and press the garlic into it. Prepare a large plate or tray on which you will serve the lobster.

3. When the lobster is ready, take it out of the water (use tongs or spatulas), put it on the tray, and break free the claws, the tail, and the head. Remove the stomach and the intestinal vein, but serve the head: some people like to pick at the tender bits inside. If the lobster is female and has roe (it's called coral because of its color), definitely keep that: it's delicious. It also freezes well. Serve lobster hot with melted butter, lemon wedges, lobster crackers for the claws, and small forks or other implements to reach into the narrow parts of the shell. Don't forget plenty of Wet-Naps, or, for a classier event, cloth napkins dampened with lemon-infused water, for the diners to wipe their hands.

～

The Birthday Palace Combo

*T*wo easy Iraqi side dishes to serve with your all-American main course.

Salat Hummus

Salad with Chickpeas

Serves 4 to 6

Two 15-ounce cans of chickpeas, rinsed and drained
3 large ripe tomatoes, diced
2 large or 6 small cucumbers, diced, not peeled
2 large bell peppers, any color, diced
1 medium onion, diced
½ cup chopped parsley
3 tablespoons olive oil
Juice of 1 lemon
Salt and pepper, to taste

Combine the chickpeas, tomatoes, cucumbers, bell peppers, onion, and parsley in a large bowl or on a large tray. Dress with the olive oil, lemon juice, salt, and pepper. Serve right away.

Tabouleh

Serves 4 to 6

1 cup medium bulgur
2 large bunches very fresh parsley, chopped
½ cup pitted kalamata olives, whole or halved
¼ cup olive oil
Juice of 1 lemon

Soak the bulgur in 2 cups hot water for about 15 minutes, or until all the water is absorbed. Combine with the parsley and olives. Dress with the olive oil and lemon juice. Serve right away.

Eleven

Shopping for Bread in a Bradley

The inside of a typical Soviet convenience store looked like an installation Andy Warhol might have thought up after a weeklong vodka binge: shelf upon shelf of expired cans of herring or prune juice stacked in neat pyramids, interspersed with an occasional glass jar of lard. In this obscene deprivation our corner bakery stood out, with its hot, round loaves of fresh pumpernickel, the bread's thick crust craggy like a miniature model of the Hindu Kush; dark, moist bricks of *Borodinsky khleb,* sprinkled with halved coriander seeds and raisins; squat white baguettes; and sundials of bagels generously adorned with poppy seeds. When I was a little girl in Leningrad, my favorite chore was to be sent to the bakery with a handful of copper change.

The bakery was a large, L-shaped mezzanine with a marble floor worn down by many generations of shoppers into gentle slopes. These fell as the floor approached the bread counters and rose closer to the little station where a portly woman in a stained white apron served sweetened, watery coffee with milk and chicory out of an aluminum barrel the size of a small child.

The shop sat behind an art nouveau wood-and-glass door cut into a regal, nineteenth-century edifice on the corner of the city's main avenue, Nevsky Prospekt, and the elegant neoclassical facades of Tolmachyov Street. Tolmachyov originally had been called Karavannaya (back when Leningrad was called St. Petersburg, and then, briefly, Petrograd) for its historic role as the final leg in the route of caravans of elephants and camels traveling from exotic lands to the imperial circus, which presides over the street to this day like a giant pink-and-white cream pie. Soviet leaders, who liked to leave their stamp on everything, had renamed the street after a little-known revolutionary from Siberia who had shot himself to avoid being captured by tsarist troops.

After the Soviet Union collapsed, and the city became St. Petersburg again, the new government, in an apparent bout of monarchic nostalgia, indiscriminately reinstated the pre-Soviet names of all the old streets. Tolmachyov got tossed out, poor bastard; so, several blocks away, did the writer Nikolai Gogol, one of the fathers of Russian realism and the master of the run-on sentence, leaving his fans to wonder what this nineteenth-century scathing critic of tacky and corrupt provincialism had ever done to disgrace himself before the new regime.

Our sixth-floor apartment snuggled halfway between the circus and the bakery, overlooking a paved courtyard completely surrounded by the pale-yellow walls of our building and devoid of vegetation apart from a couple of miserable-looking bushes that grew, despite a complete lack of direct sunlight, between someone's Lada sedan and a large metal dumpster dominated by unhealthy looking kittens. I was seven or eight years old when I was deemed old enough to shop for bread on my own, and I would get scared whenever I passed Tolmachyov's gaping, dark entryways on the way home from the bakery. For safety, I would clutch the bread to my chest and run home, slowing down only to tear off a piece of the warm crust. Just this one little bit, I would promise myself each time. By the time I arrived home, a quarter of the loaf would be blissfully missing. My parents never seemed to mind.

All Soviet children were taught that bread was the most important of all foods. School posters depicting a looming, slightly creepy loaf of rye, with bulging eyes and a fatherly smile, extolled: BREAD IS THE HEAD OF EVERYTHING. Teachers and kindergarten workers endlessly reminded us: "Respect the bread." The bristling wheat stalks on the Soviet coat of arms ingrained in us the same reverence for bread as for Grandpa Lenin.

In some Soviet lore, bread and Lenin even appeared together, as brave and cunning co-conspirators against the tyranny of the tsars. A popular children's tale told how the revolutionary leader, imprisoned yet again by the tsarist regime, would fashion an ink pot from a piece of fresh rye bread, pour milk into it (the presence of lactose in his diet suggested that the tsar treated his political prisoners way better than the Soviets later did theirs; the Soviet political prisoners only got bread and water), and, dipping his stylus into the milk, pen invisible letters to his comrades. The milk writing between the lines only became visible when Lenin's friends heated his letters over a candle; the tsarist censors saw only the seemingly innocuous regular ink inscriptions on the paper. Whenever a prison guard would check in and ask whether Lenin was writing something, the story went, the future founder of the world's first Communist country, in his best James Bond mode, would pop the milk-filled bread ink pot into his mouth and shrug in mock surprise, as if to suggest that the guard must have been hallucinating after last night's vodka party, old boy. Of all the stories about Lenin I had to read as a child, the Lenin as Bread Bond one was my favorite.

While most of us 1970s kids eventually discovered the tragic flaws of Lenin's ideology, the cult of bread remained unchallenged. No meal ever went without bread; at my school cafeteria, slices of rye were served as a side dish with mac-n-cheese. For Leningraders bread had a particularly grave historical meaning. In Soviet ideology, revolution and war were religion. Lenin was God, the defeat of Hitler's Germany was the New Testament, the nine-hundred-day siege of Leningrad by the Nazis was the Passion, and the legendary four-ounce daily bread ratios during the siege became the Holy Host. There it was, a shriveled, hard, brown crust behind the glass of a World War II museum we visited with our class each year: much smaller than the pieces of crust I would vandalize from the loaves I bought at the corner bakery on Tolmachyov Street. Only after I had begun to write about conflict and privation was I able to imagine what it really was like to have just that one piece of bread to eat in a whole day.

As if its monumental role in my childhood needed to be cemented any further, bread also served as my introduction to Judaism: most years around Passover, which my ethnically-Jewish-but-absolutely-secular father never celebrated, my mostly-non-Jewish mother would buy a couple of pounds of brittle squares of matzo bread at the only place that sold it, Leningrad's sole operating synagogue. (Mom also taught me to color eggs for Easter. In the Soviet Union, where all religion was practically prohibited and anti-Semitism was sanctioned by the state, dyeing eggs was only slightly less daring than buying matzo, which is why, I suspect, my nonconformist mother rebelliously did both.)

One year, when I was twelve or thirteen, she took me along to get the matzo. Whether by accident or by design, no public transport stopped near the Jewish temple, so we walked. It was snowing. Opulent squares that Europe's most celebrated architects of the age of enlightenment had designed for the tsars gave way to bare brick factory towers spewing soot over a granite embankment. Then came Sennaya Square, a panoptic of flea-market stalls and haphazardly built beer kiosks, followed by the nineteenth-century slums where Rodion Raskolnikov, the college dropout in Fyodor Dostoyevsky's *Crime and Punishment,* had famously slaughtered an old pawnbroker with an ax. More than a century later, this section of the city was still crippled by the Dostoyevskian physical and spiritual decay. Narrow streets ran at strange angles between zigzagging canals. Low archways led to damp, interconnected courtyards. Sagging apartment buildings leaned toward one another like tired old whores. Old women spied on local drunks from behind the yellowing lace curtains of the communal apartments they shared with twelve other families and innumerable cockroaches.

That was where the Grand Choral Synagogue towered over a poorly lit street. When, in 1869, Tsar Alexander II finally granted permission to build a synagogue—having let some of Russia's Jews, who had been banished to the Pale of Settlement outside major cities, into the country's capital—he stipulated that it not be near any Christian church, or on a road the tsar and his family would ever want to use.

I think I had expected the synagogue to provide us—if not its congregants, then at least its paying customers—with some sort of shelter from the general air of foreboding that accompanied our trip. I had anticipated an invitation to step inside, warm up, and look around; or, at the very least, a kind word. None came. The temple's looming, terra-cotta building behind a granite-and-wrought-iron fence seemed to be exhaling darkness. Women were not allowed on the main floor. We picked up the matzo bread from a small side door, and slogged back home.

Twenty years later I stood in front of a bakery in the wreckage of the

Baghdad neighborhood of Risala, and not much felt different. After the *Chronicle* could no longer afford to continue sending me overseas (the newspaper was among the first to succumb to the unfortunate overhaul of American news outlets that has botched much of the international press coverage), and a nine-month stint covering local news for the Boston *Globe* left me with a severe case of wanderlust, I returned to Iraq as a freelance reporter. The most brazen sectarian fighting was over, but Baghdad was still bleeding, the anti-American insurgency—which now included not only Sunni but also Shia militias—continued to brutalize the occupying forces, and most Iraqis blamed the Americans for the violence that gripped their country.

Why had I harbored a misguided, giddy expectation that I would be welcomed, celebrated even, for showing up in the company of several American soldiers to purchase some bread in one of the most war-wrecked parts of the Iraqi capital? The boat-shaped, pitalike loaves of *samun* were so hot they melted the flimsy plastic of the striped, lavender-and-white bags into which the baker was furiously stuffing the bread, ignoring my attempts at small talk about the wonderful fragrance of his freshly baked dough.

It was as though the bread, too, was sizzling with the baker's poorly disguised hatred. To him, the soldiers and I were not long-awaited customers. We were invaders whose disproportionate aggression had unleashed the inexorable violence that had gutted his land. And now we were encroaching on his very bakery in our flak jackets and Kevlar* helmets, some of us armed with rifles, and riding in a Bradley fighting vehicle that trained its cannon down his street.

———

A Bradley is twenty-one feet long, ten feet wide, weighs twenty-five tons, can pivot three hundred and sixty degrees, and moves, with a deafening rattle, on caterpillar tracks at the speed of up to forty-five miles per hour. It has a crew of three (a driver up front and a gunner and a commander

———

*Kevlar—a synthetic fiber that is several times stronger than steel. It is typically used in body armor and bullet-resistant face masks. A bullet-resistant helmet, the kind American troops wear in war zones, can also be called "Kevlar," as in, "Why aren't you wearing your Kevlar?"

in the two-man turret), and fits, very uncomfortably, six passengers, who climb onto two slightly padded benches through a back hatch, which opens out and down to create a gangplank into the vehicle and shuts with a sinister metallic clang. Designed during the Cold War to carry infantry into combat and to fight alongside M1 Abrams tanks against the Soviet Union in the forests of Eastern Europe, the tracked vehicle is sheathed in armor that can withstand thirty-millimeter rounds, and carries a twenty-five-millimeter chain-fed cannon called "the Bushmaster," which has a range of more than a mile and can fire two hundred rounds per minute. A Bradley is also equipped with an M240C machine gun, which fires 7.62-millimeter bullets, and TOW antitank missiles, which are capable of disabling, within the range of almost two and a half miles, any armored vehicle in existence today. It costs about three million dollars.

For the first year or so following the invasion of Iraq, the Bradley's heavily armored, heavily armed shell was considered largely redundant: most American troops rode around in canvas-top humvees, often with the tops down. That changed quickly. There would be a loud crack on the road—from inside a humvee, a roadside bomb explosion sounds not like a deafening boom, but a surprisingly short, high-pitched clap, shallow and flat, almost anticlimactic—and a black pillar of smoke would shoot out into the air. If the humvee was not right on top of the bomb, then shrapnel would ping off the steel cladding of the truck, and hot dirt and chunks of asphalt would rain from the sky into the turret. But many bombs went off directly underneath the trucks. Some hit fuel tanks. I have seen humvee cemeteries on some large military bases in Iraq: the singed remains of the trucks looked contorted, like fried crickets. Such bombs left no survivors.

Five years after the invasion, patrolling certain parts of the country in a humvee—which by then had acquired about two thousand pounds of extra armor to protect its passengers from hand grenades, shrapnel, small-arms fire, and bombs fashioned from mortars or antitank shells or even cut-up surface-to-air missiles poached from some defunct, prewar Iraqi army base—was seen as the equivalent of marching into a firefight armed with a slingshot. The Bradley became the warhorse of the Iraq war.

In response, Iraqi guerrillas came up with many effective ways to defeat the Bradley. Powerful homemade bombs ripped through the vehicle's armored underside, turning the Bradley's own armor into hot shrapnel dispatched by the force of the explosion into the crew and the passengers. Carefully aimed rocket-propelled grenades and discreetly placed explosives disabled caterpillar tracks, making the vehicles easy to ambush. Between March and May 2008, the American army battalion with which I was staying that spring in southern Baghdad—the Fourth Armor Battalion, Sixty-fourth Regiment of the Third Infantry Division's Fourth Brigade—had lost five men in two separate incidents when insurgents attacked its Bradleys with remotely operated, homemade shaped charges. (The charges are concave disks fired out of tubes with such force that they become slugs capable of penetrating armor and then setting the diesel-soaked insides on fire.) After one of the attacks, the charred bodies of four soldiers were found pressed against the hatch in the back of their Bradley. The fire from the explosion had melted the mechanism that allowed the hatch to open into the hull of the vehicle, trapping the men inside. They were burned alive.

To adapt to the constantly evolving threat of the insurgents' increasingly sophisticated arsenal, the U.S. military asked for, and received, a new vehicle to take the troops on missions and patrols: a ballistic steel behemoth known as MRAP (pronounced "emm-rap"), which stands for "mine resistant, ambush protected." An MRAP is an SUV on a cocktail of steroids and human growth hormone: its colossal, V-shaped hull sits high off the ground to deflect explosions and protect the passengers and crew from roadside bombs and mines, and its thick armor withstands rocket-propelled grenades and small-arms fire. The hitch: in addition to being so top heavy they frequently tipped over, the MRAPs were too unwieldy to maneuver in the narrow mazes of Iraq's ancient residential neighborhoods, and their high antennae routinely got tangled in the low-slung power lines. As the military analyst Loren Thompson once remarked: "Nobody builds a city with the idea that there will be MRAPs driving around there."

Ripping up power lines with trucks that look like the evil Deceptions from the *Transformers* movie series was counterintuitive to the Americans' flailing effort to endear themselves to the locals. By 2008, the chronic lack of electricity was one of the besieged Iraqis' biggest concerns, second only to the lack of security. Most of Baghdad got only two to four hours of power a day. The massive tracks of the Bradleys did destroy curbs, churn up pavement, and trample flowers Iraqi homemakers defiantly planted on medians, but they only occasionally knocked down an electric pole, and, therefore, were more power line friendly. The soldiers of the Four-Sixty-Four Armor preferred to ride around in Bradleys, and it was with them that I rode in one for the first time.

Before I climbed in, a young sergeant named Justin Lee explained how the ride was going to work. Surrounded by his squad in a field of ankle-deep gravel that served as the Bradleys' parking lot (ankle-deep gravel was the pavement of choice on most American military bases in Iraq; the gravel, which the troops lovingly called "ankle breakers," was supposed to tamp down the dust during the dry season and prevent people from sinking in the muck during winter rains), Sergeant Lee barked out these concise instructions:

"You squash up against Travis, I squash up against you, and you squash up against Anna. And you," he told me, "squash up against that fucking thing up there."

That fucking thing was the fire extinguisher and the first-aid kit in an olive green metal box on the far end of a bench. After the hatch of the Bradley snapped shut, Sergeant Lee closed his eyes and silently mouthed a prayer. Then his eyes opened and he yelled over the roar of the engine at the soldier sitting across the aisle: "Did you pray?"

The idea of battle-hardened soldiers asking for divine protection before a ride in a vehicle that was built to safeguard its passengers was unnerving. I wanted protection, too, so I held on to the fire extinguisher.

The inside of the Bradley is dark regardless of what time of day it is outside, because very little light seeps in through the three tinted periscopes, each the size of a Coke bottle, that serve as windows for the passengers in the back. The periscopes are too high for passengers to understand what is really going on outside; all I could see was the dun road dust with hints of some erstwhile pavement, destroyed by tank and Bradley tracks in the course of the war. I tried deducing our direction from the pitch of the track. When my teeth nearly collided with the rifle of the soldier across the aisle, I guessed a left; when my helmet crashed against the wall behind me, a right. The Bradley jerked and my cheek squeezed against the nozzle of the fire extinguisher: we had stopped moving. The men around me gripped their rifles.

Soldiers traveling in a humvee typically are able to assess the level of danger outside before they dismount, by looking through the armored glass of the truck's windows. When a Bradley pulls to a stop, the troops in the back can't really see which hazards await outside its armored hide, so they have to be ready for the worst. Be it a midnight raid on a suspected insurgent hideout, a noon rendezvous with an Iraqi police squad, or a dinner visit to a friendly sheikh's mansion, as soon as a Bradley's hatch drops open, soldiers pour out of the intimidating monster of a vehicle in an impressive show of force, holding their M4s against their chests, prepared to fire. That was how they charged out into a dark street on the edge of a putrid marsh in Risala that night.

It was one of those raids that by 2008 had become routine in Iraq. Acting on a tip from a local informant, American soldiers ran out of their Bradleys, and sprinted, single file, to a house behind an iron gate. A black flag, a symbol of Shia Islam, flew from a wooden pole perched on the flat-tiled rooftop. A man and three boys selling soft drinks and cigarettes from a little lean-to clapped together with rusted car doors and illuminated by one dim yellow bulb stared at the troops. A burst of machine-gun fire rang out about a mile away. Invisible frogs croaked.

Clutching M4 rifles to their chests, American soldiers shouldered their way through the gate, painted pale blue to ward off evil spirits. They swung open the front door and stomped into the house. The mud caked to their suede boots fell in clumps onto the cheap jute rug covering the cement floor of a tiny, crowded living room, where a young man, two women, and three children were sitting cross-legged around a tomato, eggplant, and bell pepper frittata in a cast-iron pan. An Egyptian soap opera blared from a small TV. Two army interrogators gestured for the young man, apparently the only male in the house, to follow them into a bedroom and then shut the door. The soldiers ushered the women and children into a dark master bedroom; the women pleaded with the Americans in sorrowful Arabic, but one of the translators had gone with the interrogators and the other had not yet entered the house, so no one understood a word. A baby wailed. One of the soldiers stood guard by the master-bedroom door; the rest proceeded to search the house for weapons, tossing clothes and extra blankets out of closets and overturning mattresses.

Tripping in my dirty shoes over a row of slippers the family had left by the doorway, I followed the soldiers around. The kitchen smelled like pie, and the teakettle on the gas stove was beginning to boil.

Maybe the family had somehow angered their neighbors, who had told the Americans that they were terrorists. Maybe the young man behind the closed bedroom door was a militant plotting to kill someone, possibly even me. Maybe he already was responsible for the deaths of American soldiers, men barely out of their teens who had left behind widows who were too young to be widows and children who were too young to remember their fathers. I jotted down what I saw: the women in black *abayas*; the unfinished frittata getting cold on the floor. The water in the teakettle was boiling now. I asked the soldier guarding the women if it was okay for me to turn off the gas burner.

The women—were they would-be suicide bombers? spies for Shia militias? unfortunate bystanders stuck in the middle of a fratricidal war?—stood just inside the bedroom's doorway and stared at me. I said *"Salaam aleikum,"* and they responded with a torrent of Arabic implorations. I smiled and shrugged, to show that I could not understand them. Embedded journalists who, like me, don't speak Arabic fluently depend on military interpreters for translation, but both of the interpreters who had come on the raid that night were busy: one was still helping interrogate the young man behind the closed door of a small bedroom, and the other was now helping rifle through the house for weapons.

A small girl with a thick, long braid came up to me. In my limited Arabic, I told her that I liked her hair. A young woman—her mother, I guessed—thanked me, and asked me if I had children. I took out my cell phone and showed her a picture of David, Fyodor, and Alex reading a book about dinosaurs at our dining table in Plymouth.

"Zauj, walid, walid," I said: "husband, son, son."

The older woman, apparently the family matriarch, reached into the folds of her *abaya* and pulled out her own phone. On the screen was the photograph of a stocky man with a graying stubble and receding hair in front of a wall painted with pink and white roses:

"Zauj."

Her hands trembled. She brought her right hand to her neck and flicked her wrist. What was she telling me? She made a fist, extended the index finger and thumb, and pointed this imaginary pistol to her chest, then to her head. Bang! Bang!

"Maku zauj." No husband.

It was time to borrow one of the army translators.

The woman's name was Nadir Hamid Shamkhi, and she had not stepped outside for two months, since she had retrieved her murdered husband's maimed body from a Baghdad morgue, buried him, and fled to her son's house in Risala, a Shiite slum in southwestern Baghdad. A Sunni Muslim, she was observing the traditional mourning period, four months and ten days for widows. There was also another reason she never went outside: as long as she was indoors, she hoped the Shiite flag flying from her son's roof would protect her from the Shiite militants who had kidnapped and killed her husband, Naman Jabar, a car mechanic, because they had suspected him of collaborating with the Americans.

One day in March 2008, she recounted, Naman had been chatting with his neighbors in the street when a car pulled up. Armed men in black masks grabbed him, and forced him into the backseat of the car. Then, they went to Nadir's house, pulled her into the street, handcuffed her, gagged her with tape, put another strip of tape across her eyes, stuffed her in the trunk, and drove off.

The gunmen held Nadir for three days. They explained that they were punishing her because her husband was an American informer. They slapped her face. They ripped off her clothes. They did something else, Nadir told me, wrapping her *abaya* tightly around herself, something that she "cannot repeat."

"It is shameful," she whispered. "I am an old woman."

Two days after Nadir's captors released her—blindfolding and gagging her again, binding her hands, stuffing her in a car, and dumping her, trussed, on the side of a highway in southern Baghdad—she received a call from a city morgue. The body of her husband had been found. There were bullet holes in his chest and head. His eyes had been gouged out. Morgue officials wanted Nadir to identify the remains.

"He didn't do anything wrong. He was not rich, but he made me happy." Nadir looked at the picture on the screen of her phone. She was crying now, the way war widows cry: only tears streaming down the wrinkled cheeks, without a sound. "We were in love, even though we are old."

Nadir craned to see what was going on in the rest of the house. On the second-floor landing, old black-and-white wedding pictures, dirty sweatpants, and white cotton bras lay in a pile on the floor.

"The soldiers are messing up my house," she sighed. If her husband had been alive, he would have reasoned with the soldiers. He would have explained to them that there were no insurgents here. He would have made her feel safer.

The soldiers told me that Nadir's tragedy did not automatically mean that her son could not have had a connection to the militants. Often, they explained, militias terrorize civilians into collaborating.

It was past midnight, but the stagnant heat of May clung to Baghdad even at night. I asked for a glass of water. The little girl, the one with the thick braid, motioned for me to follow her to the kitchen. She opened the fridge. It was empty apart from a bag of prescription medicine and several plastic jugs of filtered, cold water. I picked up a clean-looking glass coffee cup from a rack near the sink and poured. Two soldiers materialized next to me; they poured some water for themselves, too. They had found nothing incriminating in the house, and let Nadir's son go. They shook hands with him, told him to call if he notices anything suspicious. Routine speech. Someone lit a cigarette; the soldiers were going to take a short break before moving on to the next house on their list. It was safer to smoke inside the house than out in the street. The scene was preposterous: we had turned Nadir's house inside out, terrorized her family, reopened the wound of her most private pain, and now, in lieu of an apology, we were lounging in her kitchen, drinking her chilled water out of her coffee cups, and flicking cigarette ash on her floor.

Then it was time to go. I told Nadir Shamkhi that I was sorry about her loss. We embraced and exchanged three kisses on the cheek, the way women in Iraq do when they say good-bye. Then I stepped out of her kitchen into the stuffy darkness of nighttime Baghdad. In the fenced-in yard, I put my helmet back on, with my name and my blood type written on the black Kevlar rim in silver Magic Marker, in case something goes wrong. I tightened the Velcro closure on the front of my Interceptor Multi-Threat Body Armor flak jacket, the seventeen pounds of Kevlar and boron carbide ceramic designed to stop a 7.62-millimeter round with a muzzle velocity of 2,750 feet per second, as well as some shrapnel. Someone opened the gate. I tried to imitate the soldiers' stealthy movements, never venturing out of the shadows of the stucco fences that rose along the poorly lit road, always scanning the flat rooftops for movement other than the slight flutter of religious flags or drying laundry, or for the dim shimmer reflecting in the scope of a sniper's rifle. I climbed into the Bradley. Five soldiers climbed in with me. The door clanged shut.

In the little house with a black flag on the edge of a Baghdad marsh, Nadir was left to collect her clothes and mementos of her butchered marriage strewn on the dirty floor, wipe her kitchen of our cigarette ash, and wash the dirty water cups we had piled in her sink.

Later that week, I was back in the Bradley. Our small caravan of two Abrams tanks and the Bradley had screeched to a halt on an awakening market street, after a moonless night had yielded the bullet-lashed city blocks of southern Baghdad to the gritty yellow haze of a spring sandstorm.

The street lay in Baghdad's troubled Risala neighborhood, which Shiite militias had carved out as their sphere of influence. The militias intimidated residents into providing a safe haven for fighters and their weapons, and used the area to stage mortar and rocket attacks against nearby American military bases and the so-called Green Zone, the fortress-like home of the Iraqi government and most foreign embassies on the west bank of the Tigris River. Sean Chase, the melancholy army captain whose company patrolled Risala, bluntly referred to the neighborhood in his charge as "a shithole." To patrol it in anything less armored than a Bradley was unthinkable.

The Bradley's hatch crashed open onto the potholed road with a loud whack, and passers-by quickly shuffled closer to the walls of crumbling stucco and brick and ducked for cover into shops. A couple of women in black *abayas* huddled together, clutching their plastic grocery bags to their chests like shields; a butcher froze with his knife in midair over a freshly slaughtered sheep. Several American soldiers in body armor, Kevlar helmets, and mirrored ballistic goggles ran down the ramp with M4s at the ready. They walked briskly toward a small shop where four young men in short-sleeved T-shirts coated with flour were feeding *samun* loaves into a large wood oven with an enormous wooden spatula. A translator and I followed. Two of the soldiers turned their backs on the shop, scanning the street for anyone who to them looked like a terrorist; in the Bradley, the gunner was standing up in the turret, doing the same. A sergeant reached through the metal bars on the shop's small window, handed the men inside a crumpled twenty-dollar bill, and asked, through a translator, for some bread.

———

Before Risala, like the rest of Baghdad, had succumbed to a spate of block-by-block religious violence in 2006, the neighborhood was home to both Sunni and Shia Muslims and some Christians. By the middle of 2008, the sectarian cleansing was mostly over, and Risala effectively had become a segregated community: Sunnis had moved to the northern part of the neighborhood, Shiites had moved to the south, Christians had fled and gunfights and executions had given way to quiet and chilling mistrust. In return for a handsome monthly paycheck, some former Sunni militants had agreed to cooperate with the American forces and now manned checkpoints in their section of the neighborhood, keeping insurgents—and terrified Shiites—away. In southern Risala, Shiite militias continued to fight the Americans and operated like the Mafia. They levied taxes on the few businesses that dared stay open; barred the municipal government from bringing to the area the most basic services such as garbage disposal or sewage maintenance; and threatened or killed the contractors American forces hired to pave roads or fix power lines. Black flags adorned minarets and the flat roofs of people's homes; it was not clear whether residents flew them out of loyalty or, like Nadir, out of fear of being singled out by armed gangs. Captain Chase told me of a Sunni man who was afraid to check on a sick relative in southern Risala because he believed he would be executed at the hospital run by Shiites.

The American forces patrolling Risala were members of a single company, a hundred or so soldiers stationed at an abandoned schoolhouse they had christened Combat Outpost Guerrero, after army Specialist Marieo Guerrero, killed in Baghdad in 2007. Guerrero died when his Bradley hit a powerful roadside bomb, a chilling testimony to the insurgents' ever-improving methods. The school's stucco walls had been defaced in battles fought between Iraqi militias and American soldiers for the outpost's control months earlier. The troops were using the abandoned classrooms as a barracks, the administrative offices as a tactical operations center, and the fly-plagued patio as a makeshift gym.

In the back of the school, there was a small, air-conditioned room with a small window that was permanently shuttered and concrete walls that were painted black and white, like the insides of a cheap coffin. The room was furnished with some chairs, desks with five military-issue laptops hooked up to the Internet, several extra Ethernet lines dangling from the walls, and two phones from which soldiers could call home for free. The official name of this room was Morale and Recreation Facility. Some called it the Room of Broken Hearts.

"Now, about those other male friends," a young soldier growled into the phone one evening. "I am shocked and awed to hear . . . ," and his voice turned to a whisper. Everyone else in the room—four other soldiers, plus me—hunched lower over our screens, not wanting to hear the rest. The men would hear it all anyway, later, in the classrooms they shared at night, in the shaded school hallways where they bummed Marlboro Lights off each other, in their Bradley after a long patrol.

"In September she tells me we should have another baby and in December she tells me she wants a divorce!" a soldier bellowed inside a curlicue of concrete blast walls that dead-ended in a narrow area where the men smoked.

"Second deployment, second divorce," summed up another, stubbing out a cigarette. A military study in 2008 showed that nearly a third of enlisted men and more than a fifth of married noncommissioned officers were planning to get a divorce by the end of their fifteen-month deployments to Iraq and Afghanistan.

The schoolyard at Guerrero had been partitioned into sections as well. In the gravel parking lot behind two massive generators that supplied the outpost's power, the company kept its Bradleys and tanks. Separated from the parking lot by a fifteen-foot concrete wall stood several wooden outhouses, known as the burn shitters, so called because each morning a detail of soldiers was assigned to pull out the metal barrels, mix the contents with diesel fuel, and burn them along with whatever trash had accumulated over the past twenty-four hours. The process—typically relegated to "the fuckup du jour," one former marine explained to me—sent plumes of acrid, black smoke in the air.

Next to the burn shitters was a white air-conditioned metal container with showers, but it was off-limits to me, the only woman on the outpost. I was instructed to use the outpost's one indoor washroom. It was, conveniently, across the hallway from the former storage room where I was allowed to bunk, adjacent to what probably had been the principal's office, where Captain Chase now lived. Chase also used the washroom, which had no lock, so the soldiers fashioned for me a paper sign to tape to the door when I was in the shower. It said: DO NOT ENTER, FEMALE INSIDE. I wanted to change it to DANGER: FEMALE INSIDE but didn't, out of fear of jeopardizing my showering privileges.

On top of some concrete blocks near the Bradley parking lot sat a small, dark shipping container that served as the company's field kitchen. Soldiers assigned to kitchen duty worked hard to spice up the bland provisions, frozen or in cans, that arrived at the outpost from Kuwait via a larger base: burgers, red beans and rice, pasta, breakfast grits, eggs, and, of course, Friday steak and lobster tails. The troops picked up their food at the kitchen and carried it on brown polypropylene trays to a dining room inside the school, where they ate in front of a large, flat-screen TV that always seemed to be showing either old American sitcom reruns or cartoons. The dining room was stacked with cereal boxes, Pop-Tarts, and long-life variations on coffee cake; two refrigerators stored water, milk, Gatorade, juice, and fruit punch. A cardboard box with individually packaged ketchup, mustard, salt, and pepper sat on a desk, but, ultimately, one can add only so much flavor to powdered eggs and reheated canned peas. Any food beyond the army-issue provisions—care packages from home, or Pizza Hut pies soldiers would occasionally bring in from larger army bases in the Iraqi capital—disappeared quickly.

By May 2008, some parts of Baghdad were beginning to recover from two years of the ferocious sectarian fighting that had pitted Sunni and Shia militias against each other. Gun battles had abated, and the city was tentatively coming back to what passed for life. Residents were venturing gingerly out of their cordoned-off streets to see if they could get food. Doctors were checking the extent of damage to their offices to see if they could resume practice. Day laborers stood in line outside neighborhood councils to see if they could find work. Shop owners were not exactly rushing to take back the streets where a few months earlier stray dogs had feasted on corpses, but some businesses were reopening amid the rubble of gutted mansions and shuttered convenience stores.

In Dora, a southern Baghdad neighborhood where al Qaeda had for a time run an ultrafundamentalist micro-state, slaughtering barbers for shaving men's beards and executing women for appearing in public without head scarves, American soldiers who patrolled the market now sometimes stopped at a bazaar to buy falafel sandwiches and freshly grilled kebab. Soldiers in Saidiyah, a neighborhood next to Risala, felt safe enough to walk out of their outpost occasionally and stroll about a quarter of a mile to Sun City Foods, a two-story, glorified *shwarma* joint decorated with bright plastic flowers, a large fish tank, and black and mirrored wall tiles. Had it not been for the soldiers' elaborate body armor, rifles, and the structured formation in which they walked down the street, always keeping an eye on overgrown yards behind the fences pockmarked with shrapnel, one could have called those outings laid back. Occasionally, Sun City Foods delivered lamb burgers to the gate of the base.

Risala was nothing like that. There was a sense—felt most acutely at night, when firefights between Iraqi gangs clashing over this street or that punctured the dust-filled darkness just beyond the walls of the outpost—that the men of Bravo Company were holed up, rather than stationed, at Guerrero, the way Todd Wood's men had been holed up at Remagen three years earlier. Children did not run out of pale blue gates to wave at their Bradleys, and most adults stared at their patrols with revulsion and fear. There were no laissez-faire forays for falafel or beef burgers, which in Baghdad usually came heavily spiced with thyme and had French fries packed inside the bun. There were no friendly neighborhood cookouts in honor of the Americans, no restaurants delivering *shwarma* to the sandbagged walls of their outpost.

Then, one morning, Sean Chase made the executive decision to get some *samun* for his soldiers.

The captain's Bradley and two M1 Abrams tanks had been standing on a deserted intersection in Risala since five in the morning. They were there to watch civilian contractors deliver several blocks of fortified concrete. The concrete would be arranged into a checkpoint for the Iraqi police, which, the Americans hoped, would help bring the neighborhood to some semblance of order.

Ideally, the police would have been building their own checkpoint, or, at the very least, sitting in the street before dawn, waiting for the contractors to arrive. But, five years and twenty billion dollars after the United States had first begun to train Iraqi security forces, Baghdad's finest were terrified of the nefarious Risala militias they were expected to help subdue. The Americans hoped that if they set up a fortified roadblock to hide behind, they could lure the police to patrol the intersection. If you build it, the thinking went, they will come.

Baghdad's power was off, and so were the neighborhood's generators.

I thought of all the terrible stories I had heard about attacks on Bradleys. In the middle of the street we were sitting ducks. What if there was
an ambush? I listened for shots outside our armored hull. Nothing. I
strained my neck to see through one of the periscope windows, but the
city outside the Bradley was as dark as the vehicle's insides. One of the
soldiers lit a small flashlight with a red-tinted lens (red light is less visible
from afar than white, and therefore attracts less attention; it also does not
disrupt our natural but limited ability to see in the dark as much as any
other color), and I could see that across the aisle from me the Iraqi translator had dozed off. The translator's name tag read: XZIBIT.

Most Iraqi interpreters used nicknames to protect themselves and
their families from militants who took revenge on anyone they found collaborating with the American occupation. Some were given nicknames
by the first American military unit they had worked with, others picked
their own. Xzibit, an aspiring rapper ("Most of the people like ghosts
and zombies/Fucking Saddam was holding guns to innocent bodies/
They were Iraqis"), had picked the name of his favorite West Coast artist
("You ain't really real, I can tell when I look at you/So ease off the trigga
talk, you ain't killin' shit"). The evening before, I saw him pumping iron
with the soldiers in the patio gym, swearing in English and laughing and
smoking cigarettes. Now, with his eyes closed, he looked like the nine-
teen-year-old kid he was: too young to shave, and full of dreams. He reminded me of Abdullah, my young bodyguard in the Afghan village of
Dasht-e-Qal'eh. Seven years had passed since I watched Abdullah sleep.
I calculated that he was nineteen now, too, like Xzibit.

Minutes passed. Outside the Bradley, the night had begun to pale
and the street filled with noise. I stood on the bench on my knees to look
through the window again at the broken capital. If you were willing to
disregard the buildings crippled and charred by bombings; the stagnant
pools of sewage that had leaked into the streets where underground sewage pipes had burst from years of disrepair, and which now collected in
craters left by roadside bombs; and the mounds of trash that choked the
neighborhood, the Shiite militant stronghold looked like a lot of cities
waking up to an early weekday morning. A woman in a knee-length

skirt was talking on her cell phone as she got into a minibus. A group of willowy teenage girls in form-fitting jeans and turtlenecks, with bright scarves on their heads, were stepping around muck-filled craters as they hurried to school with books under their arms. A stocky fellow in a striped polo shirt was settling in on the side of the road to sell petrol from age-yellowed plastic canisters: a wartime gas station.

It was now six thirty, an hour and a half after we had pulled up to the intersection. Xzibit woke up, groggy and disoriented. Soldiers moved their rifles from one hand to the other, shifting their weight slightly to help blood circulation. It became clear that there was not going to be an ambush after all. It also became clear that there were not going to be any contractors bearing concrete blocks, either, at least not this morning.

"Infantry officers are taught to take the hill, and, when it comes to security, they take the hill," one civil affairs officer in Baghdad told me. When it came to working with Iraqi contractors, however, storming the hill was not always the right approach. Perhaps it was foolish of the soldiers to expect Iraqi drivers to show up before dawn in a neighborhood where armed gangs routinely preyed on contractors. Or maybe there had been some other misunderstanding. Either way, like so many American-led projects in Iraq, dropping off a bunch of concrete blocks in the middle of the street was going to be more complicated than it sounded.

The United States had been trying to build things in Iraq pretty much since the war began, and the war had made American combat troops double-task as county sheriffs, police officers, and civil engineers. But more often than not, they were unsuccessful in these pursuits. By 2008, the reconstruction of the beleaguered country had become an insatiable vortex into which billions of dollars had disappeared, for one reason or another. At first, the troops blamed insurgents and "Saddam sympathizers" for sabotaging their work. Then they blamed sectarian violence. But privately, American commanders blamed a culture gap between the Americans proposing the projects and the Iraqis who were supposed to carry them out, maintain them, and benefit from them. Many Iraqi tribal and local leaders, mistrustful of the Americans' intentions and also wary of being seen as collaborating with the occupying forces, preferred to keep their distance from projects sponsored by the occupiers. One defense contractor, a Canadian of Iraqi origin who supervised some reconstruction projects in the Sunni tribal heartland of Iraq's Anbar province, told me that sheikhs often gleefully reacted to failed reconstruction projects in his area.

"They would point to a wall that fell, or a pipe that leaked, and say: 'See? Americans don't care about the Iraqi people,'" said the contractor.

To get the Iraqis committed to the United States' idea of reconstruction, soldiers sometimes hired local middlemen, whose ways of ensuring success were just as unorthodox from the American point of view as they were traditional from the point of view of Iraqis. One such middleman I met was a middle-aged Iraqi who introduced himself to me, in flawless English, as "Dr. Phil." Dr. Phil was a hustler; at the time, his job was to enable the installation of an American-purchased, 500-kilowatt generator that would provide streetlights and electricity for about two hundred shops on a market street in Saidiyah. To do that, Dr. Phil arranged for a ritual slaughter of four sheep on a busy thoroughfare.

A squat man named Bassam the Butcher slit the throats of the sheep, collected the scarlet arterial blood into a plastic bag, and let neighborhood boys (children of an influential local sheikh, I later found out) dip their hands in the sacrificial blood and press their palms against the canary yellow walls of the new generator, fuel tank, and transformer. Americans lowered their weapons and, giggling, snapped pictures of the event with their digital cameras. However strange the consecration ceremony may have seemed to them, it made local residents feel invested in the project. When the power finally went on, the entire neighborhood converged on the newly illuminated street to celebrate. Arab pop tunes streamed from speakers and the owner of Sun City Foods handed out free cans of 7-Up.

By seven o'clock, sweltering in their armored vehicles on the Risala intersection, Bravo Company soldiers did not need a cultural adviser to tell them that waiting any longer was pointless. From the turret of his Bradley, Captain Chase ordered his driver and the two tanks to pull forward a few hundred feet and stop by the bakery.

Few things smell as good as fresh *samun* bread with a sprinkle of sesame seeds, especially after the diesel fumes of a Bradley. I stood as close to the bakeshop's window as I could and just inhaled. It was the yeasty smell of home, of the corner bakery with uneven marble floors, of being seven years old and running past the creepy, dark entryways of Tolmachyov Street. It was all I could do to keep myself from tearing off a piece of fresh, hot bread and popping it into my mouth.

The *samun* was eight loaves for a dollar. The soldiers bought a hundred and four loaves, each the size of a paperback book. The baker took the twenty-dollar bill and demonstrably, gravely counted out seven dollars in soiled Iraqi dinar, disregarding the soldiers' suggestion that he keep the change. Was he trying to show that he wouldn't take a penny from the occupiers? As soon as he had handed the soldiers their change, the baker turned his back to us and disappeared in the white flour mist of his shop.

We pulled into Guerrero's parking lot, kicking up clouds of grimy dust, just in time for breakfast. Since Xzibit and I were not carrying rifles, the soldiers asked us to take the bread to the kitchen, where men on kitchen duty poured the loaves onto a large tray next to a deep stainless-steel basin of breakfast pork sausage. I grabbed a piece of *samun* and a Styrofoam cup of weak coffee and walked into the shade of the school building. Captain Chase was standing in the doorway of his room, already chewing on his own piece of Iraqi bread. We nodded at each other, and made small talk about how neither of us had ever gone shopping for bread with that much force protection before. Then the captain went back to his room to plan his company's new day in Risala, and I took refuge from the heat in the air-conditioned dining hall, where the TV was, as expected, showing cartoons. In the dry, 130-degree weather the crust of the bread had gone a little crisp, but the spongy crumb was still soft and just as fragrant as it had been inside the bakery.

❧

Samun Bread

Makes 10 loaves

I confess: I find bread very complicated to make. The recipe for a very tasty whole wheat loaf I once tried at a friend's house, for example, required the cook to start making the dough 48 hours before it was supposed to be served, and the two days in between were to be spent turning and flattening and poking. Not for me. Then there are prefab bread mixes that allow you to make bread quicker; if that's the direction you decide to go, I highly recommend Swedish Rye Bread from IKEA. It comes in a container that looks like an orange juice carton, and all the recipe requires of the cook is to add water to the powdered mix, shake well, pour into a pan, and bake the thing for 40 minutes. Add some raisins to the batter and sprinkle it with smashed coriander seeds before sticking it in the oven, and your loaf will taste very much like the *Borodinsky khleb* of my childhood.

But *samun* is worth it. And it is ready in only a few hours.

3 tablespoons dry yeast
1 tablespoon sugar
9 cups white bread flour
1 tablespoon salt
2 cups milk
¼ cup olive or other vegetable oil

1. Dissolve the yeast and sugar in ½ cup warm water, but don't stir too much. Set aside for at least 5 minutes.
2. Combine the flour and salt. Make a well in the middle. Add the yeast-sugar mixture to the flour. Add the milk. Stir with a wooden spoon, then oil your hands and knead for 5 minutes. Oil the dough, cover it with a linen towel, and set aside someplace warm (but not hot). Wait until it doubles in size, which can take 2 or 3 hours.
3. Oil a baking sheet. Punch down the dough and divide it into 10 portions. Roll a piece between your palms until it becomes a 7- to 8-inch-long sausage. Lay it flat on the baking sheet, then flatten to broaden the middle of the sausage. It should look like a rhombus. Repeat with the remaining 9 portions of the dough. With a very sharp knife, make a long slash in the

middle of each rhombus. Cover with a linen towel and allow the dough to rise again for about 30 minutes. In the meantime, preheat the oven to 450°F.

4. Put the bread in the oven. Quickly spray the bread, the oven door, and the inside of the oven with water, then shut the oven to keep in the moisture. Spray again in 5 minutes. Bake for a total of 15 to 20 minutes, until the bread is golden. If you don't want the bread very crisp, let it cool in a bag lined with a linen towel.

~

Zataar Twists

Serves about 8

*I*f you don't have time to make bread from scratch, try this recipe. It is ready in 20 minutes and will bring the flavor of the Middle East into your home (although not as much as good *samun* would).

   1 cup *zataar* mix (see Note)
   ½ cup olive oil
   2 tablespoons coarse salt
   One 17.3-ounce box puff pastry dough, defrosted

1. Preheat the oven to 375°F. Lightly oil a baking sheet.

2. Combine the *zataar* with the olive oil and salt and let soak for a few minutes.

3. Unfold the puff pastry dough and cut it into strips 2 inches by about 3 or 4 inches. Using a teaspoon, place some *zataar* paste on each strip and roll the strip lengthwise, pressing it down lightly so it keeps its shape in the oven. Place the rolled-up pieces of dough on the baking sheet and bake for 10 to 15 minutes, or until the strips are puffy and golden-brown. Serve hot or cold.

Note: *Zataar* is a spice mix that's sold in most Middle Eastern groceries, but you can also make your own. Combine 1 cup crushed dried oregano leaves, ½ cup crushed dried thyme leaves, 3 teaspoons ground sumac, and ½ teaspoon ground allspice.

Twelve

Spice Girls

There once lived a beautiful and worldly Sunni woman from a middle-class Iraqi family who collected antiques and wore lip gloss and sweet perfume; and a fiercely independent Shia woman with three master's degrees, who could talk for hours about art history and Baghdad architecture. Shatha, the Sunni woman, and Thanaa, the Shia, were best friends. In the cosmopolitan and mostly secular art world of pre-war Baghdad, they had found the much-coveted unity and harmony of common interests and passions: a shelter from the forbidding reality of a country constrained by religious barriers, terrorized by Saddam Hussein's dictatorship, inhibited by international sanctions, and bled by ubiquitous corruption. In the spring, summer, and fall of 2003, Shatha and

Thanaa took turns working as my interpreter. We were approximately the same age, and shared a love of art and good food. In the middle of a war, we found rapture in arabesque scrolls. Our bond was instant.

Freed of Saddam's regime, occupied by Western troops, and anarchy, Iraq had metamorphosed from the restricted society in which the two women had grown up into a land without rules and limits. The bedlam at once heralded violence, promised momentous change, and granted seemingly unlimited access to knowledge hitherto forbidden not only to foreigners like me, but also to Iraqis like my friends. Suddenly, everyone in Iraq was a stranger in a new land. The three of us were on a journey to discover this new country together, with all of its delights, incongruities, and heartbreaks.

One May morning, Thanaa, the photojournalist Thorne Anderson, and I drove twelve miles south of Baghdad, strolled through a set of unguarded metal gates, and walked into the concrete guts of Tuwaitha Nuclear Research Center, the heart of Iraq's nuclear program. This was one of the sites that, according to politicians in Washington, may have been used for the production of weapons of mass destruction and therefore made Iraq worth invading. Now the complex of concrete buildings and sand-covered bunkers masquerading as suspiciously identical dunes was nominally—and barely—watched over by a small unit of infinitely bored and demoralized American soldiers, who had been promised they would go home weeks ago and who saw our visit as a rare opportunity to bum some cigarettes and call their families on my satellite phone. Most of them had not spoken to their loved ones since the invasion had begun in March. I gladly let them run down my phone battery in exchange for allowing us to wander, unobstructed, around this momentous slice of the Axis of Evil.

We found no weapons of mass destruction (neither, of course, did the American troops—since there had been none to begin with). What we did find was a group of local villagers who had pilfered radioactive materials from Tuwaitha, looking for an opportunity to make a quick buck or simply augment their households with freebies. The villagers had carried off dozens of barrels filled with toxic waste, particularly yellowcake, a uranium derivative that is used in the preparation of fuel for nuclear reactors and is highly poisonous when ingested. They had dumped the hazardous contents onto the parched desert soil, and then had either sold the contaminated drums or used them in their own homes to store water, flour, and milk. Now, scores of people in the area were complaining of symptoms typical of radiation poisoning—nausea, nosebleeds, head-aches, fatigue, skin rash, and hair loss.

When local religious leaders figured out why everyone was getting sick, they called on the villagers to get rid of their dangerous loot by dumping it in the hallway of a local high school for girls. Then the clerics cordoned off the hallway with sheets of plywood: to keep radiation from spreading into the classrooms, they explained. Thanaa, one of whose de-grees was in medicine, shook her head as she translated my conversa-tion with a thirteen-year-old girl who had been vomiting and bleeding from her nose ever since her mother had started using the refrigerator a relative had dragged home from Tuwaitha to store the family's food, and had fashioned a cooking pot cover from a NO PARKING sign stolen from the research center.

Looters were not unique to Tuwaitha. In Baghdad, police officers guided Thanaa and me through the remains of their downtown police station. The front door was gone. So were the locks on the jail cells in the back. So were all the weapons, window glass, furniture, overhead lights, ceiling fans, pictures from the walls. Even the nails on which the pictures had once hung had been wrested out of their sockets. At al Yarmuk Hos-pital, most of the medicine, gauze, syringes, and all anesthetics had been stolen. The emergency room was overflowing with patients who had stab and gunshot wounds, victims of robbers and looters who were prey-ing on anything of value and anyone with money. Thorne and I stayed in the emergency room for hours one day as more and more patients ar-rived, dripping blood onto the murky concrete floor tiles, the hospital staff unable to ease their pain—or even to find room for them on the few hospital cots the looters had left behind. Doctors in bloodied latex gloves laid the younger patients two or three to a cot; at times, the ward looked like a grotesque, monstrous mockery of a game of musical-chairs as weeping parents dashed from one occupied bed to another with half-naked children in their arms. "There are no nurses, no casts, just this!"

one enraged doctor yelled at me, pulling out a roll of medical tape from his pocket.

Despite her background in medicine, Thanaa could not bear to watch. She left after the first hour, and waited for us in the hospital courtyard.

But she was there when volunteers in bulldozers unearthed the killing fields in the dried-out marshlands south of Baghdad: the mass graves of the men, women, and children Saddam Hussein's henchmen had executed in retaliation for the 1991 Shiite uprising that followed the first Gulf War. The Shiites, encouraged by the United States, had taken over major cities and towns in southern Iraq—but then had received none of the military backing Washington and its allies had promised. When it became clear that the rebels were on their own, Iraqi forces had easily overwhelmed the lightly armed guerrillas, firing at them from tanks, strafing them from helicopter gunships, and rounding up real and suspected insurgents to shoot them and dump their remains into shallow pits dug in highway medians, prison yards, playgrounds and parks. In a field outside Babylon, Thanaa and I watched hundreds of quiet mourners pick, ghostlike, through brittle fragments of bone, decayed identification cards, and scraps of rotten clothes, searching for their relatives. From time to time, a woman's shriek, like the call of a wounded marsh bird, would sound; everyone would flinch and stop moving for just a second. Then the field would fall silent again, and the search would resume. A watch. A femur. A decayed checkered shirt. One woman tried to calculate how old her two sons would have been that day, twelve years after they had been killed. She closed her fingers into a fist, then opened them. Then she collapsed onto a pile of bones of someone else's murdered children. Her neighbor looked on: he had found nine of his relatives in that field already. He breathed in her grief tranquilly, without a word. He had no sorrow left to spare.

Later, the three of us sat in front of Shatha's new computer. Owning that desktop would have been illegal when Saddam was in power; the computer was one of the first purchases Shatha's family had made after the regime had fallen. Now we watched, on its screen, poorly recorded footage showing an execution of dissidents by Hussein's elite Republican Guard.

We had picked up the DVD from a vendor in Bab al Sharji Market, a giant Baghdad clearinghouse for almost anything that wasn't food—roller skates, Tupperware containers, handguns, Mickey Mouse watches, old coins—most of it looted. The vendor who sold us the disc was doing a brisk sale in porn videos and bootleg copies of Hollywood blockbusters, but the execution videos were also in great demand. The footage, jerky and not very clear, showed half a dozen officers of the Republican Guard in a dry field, or a desert. Then it showed several men in civilian clothes kneeling on the ground. The hands of the civilians were bound behind their backs. The officers laughed as they beat and kicked the men.

There was a glitch in the recording. Then the screen showed soldiers tying dynamite to the chests of their prisoners and blowing them up, one by one.

Even after the trip to the killing fields in Babylon, watching the grisly video made my stomach grab. In the armchair next to me, Shatha gripped the handles, staring at the screen, her large eyes black with grief. No one in her family—at least no one she knew of—had perished in Saddam's prisons. Her middle-class, Sunni parents, aunts, and uncles had quietly hated the regime, but they also knew that criticizing the Iraqi president or his Baath Party was a crime punishable by death, and avoided discussing politics, even at home. Shatha had never imagined the scope of the brutality. The combination of the unsparing security apparatus, the fear of reprisals, and the efficient government propaganda had sufficiently concealed from most Iraqis the blood-chilling truth that their government had executed hundreds of thousands, perhaps even millions, of its subjects, and had destined many more to prison and torture.

"You just suddenly realize that you didn't know what was happening. I feel deceived," Shatha told me. She said she had heard a theory that Saddam was an agent of the CIA. She found the theory somewhat plausible.

"Because why would a true Iraqi want to kill his own people?" she said.

Thanaa, who had lived for more than thirty years in a totalitarian state that oppressed members of her religious sect, said that she had not heard a whole lot about the brutal executions of tens of thousands of Shiites after the first Gulf War, either.

"Have you heard about Halabja?" I tried, naming the site of the March 16 and 17, 1998, chemical attack on the Iraqi Kurds. About five thousand people had perished, poisoned, on those two days. Photos of the massacre depicted hundreds of people hugging the ground, as though they suddenly had been overpowered by an irresistible desire to take a nap in the middle of the street: a man with a baby, two children in knit winter hats. Everyone outside Iraq who followed world events knew.

"I've heard of it, but I'm not sure," Thanaa replied. She hesitated. "I think—did Saddam kill some people there?"

After we watched the video, I spoke to Peter Bouckaert, a researcher for Human Rights Watch, who in 2003 was documenting abuses in Iraq. I asked him about the avalanche of reports, videos, and personal accounts detailing the crimes the deposed Iraqi government had committed against its people. For years, all information about the killings had been off-limits to anyone outside Saddam's security apparatus. Now Iraqis spent days poring over police files, many of them marked TOP SECRET, looking for word about their relatives.

"A lot of Iraqis believed the propaganda of this government," Peter told me. "It's very important now that people come to grips with Iraqi history, with their own history."

So that's what they call it. As Thanaa, Shatha, and I interviewed mothers sifting through mass graves filled with broken bones for the remains of their sons, and shuddered at the grainy video of prisoner executions, the three of us were coming to grips with Iraq's history, past and present.

I was staying at a place not far from Baghdad University called al Hamra Hotel and Suites. The twelve-story hotel towered conspicuously over Baghdad's skyline of Soviet-style apartment blocks, most of them five or six floors high. At the time, al Hamra seemed to be less of a terrorist target than the eighteen-story Palestine Hotel on Firdos Square—the same grassy circle where on April 9, 2003, American marines had famously helped topple a giant statue of Saddam Hussein. (Both hotels eventually were attacked, more than once.) At one point during that first post-Saddam summer, al Hamra's owners, flush with the cash spent by the hundreds of journalists who had stayed in their rooms, and misguidedly convinced that the worst of the fighting was over, painted the building a daring white and highlighted the balconies with scarlet. ("*Al Hamra*" means "the Red" in Arabic.) Reporters have a habit of making light of our worst fears, and we liked to joke that instead of the scarlet rectangles the hotel management should have painted concentric circles on the façade, making the hotel swimming pool—in those early weeks of the war, the favorite evening hangout spot for many journalists—the bull's-eye.

Each day of reporting in the new Iraq carried a new warning that the hotel owners' serenity was premature. In Fallujah, men at a gun market that operated out of the back door of a large, stucco mosque stopped my car, shaking fistfuls of rocket-propelled grenade launchers at the windshield. Tracer bullets lit up the night, like fireflies, around al Hamra. One Sunday afternoon, two white sedans—a Toyota Corolla and a Peugeot—packed with dismantled antitank bombs swerved toward the Baghdad Hotel, the residence of some Western military contractors, and drove at full speed past a security checkpoint. The cars detonated almost simultaneously, a few feet apart. The twin explosions killed at least ten people, most of them Iraqis. I was standing in the large crowd outside—I had just interviewed a bank clerk bleeding through the bandage that girdled his forehead—when a boy came up to me and put a seven-inch knife to my diaphragm.

The wide blade tapered to a curved, serrated end. The steel reflected a cerulean sliver of the sky.

He looked up at me, this kid no older than ten—skinny, stunted by malnutrition, just a couple of inches taller than Fyodor was at the time, dressed in brown gym shorts, plastic sandals, and a dirty T-shirt emblazoned with the picture of a soccer ball—and asked:

"Okay?"

By then I knew that it was usually best to agree with armed men. (Just a week before the Baghdad Hotel bombing I had given a thumbs-up to the weapons traders at that Fallujah mosque gun market, and flashed them my most charming smile. They had smiled back and waved me through.) But unlike the Pashtun robber bodyguards on the Grand Trunk Road, this boy did not want my money. Nor did he want to fool around, like the teenage gunmen outside Shibirghan Prison. The cold expression on his face told me he meant business: he saw me, a Western woman, as an envoy of the occupiers, an enemy. His was the blade of a killer. I couldn't help but smile at his power. It was the raw, untamed power of a new country, a country without direction: *bilattijah*.

When my friend Ahmad Shawkat was picking a name for his magazine, did he envision this boy who now was holding a knife to my stomach?

"Okay," I said.

The crowd of onlookers around us was pulsating, swelling with men and women pushing toward the hotel entrance to see up close the wreckage from the bombing. Anguished people were weeping, screaming out the names of their relatives, yelling out questions about survivors, calling out for friends lost somewhere in the crowd. American soldiers were shouting, in English, for people to move back as they unfurled rolls of razor wire around the craters left by the explosions. Iraqi police officers were shouting, in Arabic, for people to come closer to help with the wounded. No one noticed the Iraqi boy and the Western woman who stood still in the middle of the street, held together by a knifepoint.

Then the kid looked me in the eye, and smiled back:

"Okay, okay!"

He must have been feeling generous. He sheathed his blade and walked away.

———

I filed my stories from one of al Hamra's red, eighth-floor balconies, where I could get decent reception for my satellite phone. Every morning a man in blue overalls would arrive to wash away the fine yellow dust that would accumulate in twenty-four hours on the tiled balcony floor. Carrying a bucket and a mop, he would slide open the balcony door in an aluminum frame, splash some water from the bucket onto the tiles, and, with his mop, push the dirty wash over the side. The water would spout from a hole in the concrete, occasionally streaking the white hotel walls with brown smudges as the muddy stream cascaded, like a string of dark yarn, eight stories down into the heart of Baghdad's upscale Jadriyah neighborhood. Across the street, on the low balconies of an economy, six-story hotel called the Flowersland, a woman in a dark blouse with rolled-up sleeves repeated the ritual, and sometimes it appeared as though the two were performing a meticulously choreographed modern dance. The water pooled beneath at the hedges, which had been immaculately trimmed to spell out, in Arabic, the name of the hotel, as though there had been no war.

I sometimes forgot about the war, as well. With Shatha and Thanaa, we talked about boyfriends, dating, marriage, love, premarital sex, overbearing parents, newborn children—secrets and gossip women share everywhere in the world. The discrepancy between the extraordinary violence and tragedy we were observing during our working hours and the most ordinary conversations we were enjoying after work was striking. These mundane exchanges, and the women's intimate knowledge of Iraq's art and history that preceded the fallen dictatorship, became for me an oasis of sanity and beauty in the hailstorm of the havoc, power struggles, and revenge that was sweeping through the country.

After I filed, my friends would whisk me out of the hotel and take me on hours-long excursions into the carved and cavernous limestone depths of ancient Baghdad, with the shadowy galleries, exquisitely proportioned arches, and domed cupolas of *A Thousand and One Nights*.

Together, Shatha, Thanaa, and I explored the museums and spice shops of Baghdad, scoured the antique dealerships in the oldest parts of the city for etched copper serving plates, and picked out pieces of calligraphy at the book market on Mutanabbi Street, the intellectual heart of the city where every Friday vendors piled their books—the translated works of Shakespeare, erotic verses by the eighth-century Arab poet Abu Nuwas, the Koran, Fyodor Dostoyevsky—on oilcloths spread directly on the pavement. A popular Arab saying goes: "Cairo writes, Beirut publishes, Baghdad reads." On Fridays, slow processions of Baghdad's readers flocked to Mutanabbi Street—the street itself bears the name of a tenth-century Iraqi poet—like sedges of herons: necks craned, fingers brushing pensively against cardboard and leather bindings, eyes squinting, searching out the printed word to satisfy their habit.

Here you could still feel the ancient breath of the city that had been the Eastern Hemisphere's center of learning during the five centuries of the Abbasid rule, when Baghdad had drawn Muslim scholars to its libraries, hospitals, mosques, and schools. In the tenth century, one hundred book dealers traded here. Wealthy patrons invited poets to entertain their guests. While Europe festered in the Dark Ages, Baghdad studied Aristotle, translated Persian texts, and gave the world algebra.

The clatter of our footsteps echoed off the tiered archways of Qasr al Musannat, known in most guidebooks as the Abbasid Palace: the twelfth-century residence of Abbasid Caliph al Nasir Lidin Illah. Beneath the muqarnas corbels that dripped down like man-made stalactites, Thanaa explained how Abu Jaafar al Mansour had built Baghdad in 762 A.D., surrounding it with a wall and carving four gates at ninety-degree angles—and erecting a library where interpreters translated into Arabic and preserved works in Persian, Greek, Sanskrit, and Syriac on astrology, mathematics, agriculture, medicine, and philosophy.

A short walk from Qasr al Musannat, a tracery of ewans and ornamented galleries shaded the courtyard of the thirteenth-century Mustansiriya School, one of the oldest Islamic universities in the world. The building had long been a museum, and a modern university in a different part of Baghdad now bore the school's name. But once, almost a millennium ago, the school had held a library of more than eighty thousand titles and displayed, in the patio, a famous clock that, in addition to telling the hours, also specified the position of the sun and the moon. When Shatha and Thanaa took Thorne and me there in May 2003, the museum was open for tourists, but we were the only visitors. The veiled woman running a little souvenir shop in one corner of the courtyard was as surprised to see us as we were to find her store open. I bought a large, annotated book of photographs, *Iraq: The Land of the New River,* published in the Netherlands in 1980. On the first page there was an ode to Iraq's coveted oil reserves: "May those great fires that have sprung from the bowels of Iraq continue rising to the sky!"

The school was built less than a quarter of a century before the Mongol invasion ransacked the Abbasid empire, marking the beginning of Baghdad's decline. Some accounts say that after the Mongols plundered Baghdad, in 1258, the lethargic waters of the Tigris River, usually bottle green, ran red with the blood of scholars. Other accounts say the waters ran black, dyed with the ink of the thousands of priceless manuscripts that the invaders had flung into the river. Whether either of those accounts is true, that invasion, like the many others to come—by the Anatolian Turks, the Persians, the Ottomans, the British, the United States—crushed Baghdad's intellectual standing in the world. Seven and a half centuries later, the blood of Iraqi writers and chroniclers, and the ink and ashes of their work, continued to imbue Iraqi soil.

We climbed up the narrow and steep stairs of the school and ran across the giant, flat rooftop like children, laughing at our own lighthearted foolishness. There were some gunshots in the dim streets below. The war lapped at our feet.

Every hotel room at al Hamra had a small kitchenette with an electric stove, and I used mine to boil water for the tea and ramen noodles I would purchase—along with some Basrawi dates, cucumbers, tomatoes, eggs, and bread—at a Western-style supermarket on the busy Haifa Street. I also often went out to eat. In 2003, there was no shortage of excellent restaurants in Baghdad—there was even a rather good pizzeria, whose owner had lived in Italy at one point and served red table wine out of a clay jug to his customers—and almost every street corner had a kiosk selling freshly squeezed fruit juices. Just around the block from the hotel there was a shop selling *shwarma* sandwiches. In Baghdad, *shwarma* was served with salad, mayonnaise, and French fries packed into fresh baguettes together with the long, juicy shreds of grilled lamb or chicken. I usually asked the owner to hold the French fries. After a couple of visits, he remembered me. Standing at a tall counter, dripping spicy mayonnaise out of my *shwarma* onto a sheet of butcher paper, I missed sitting down to a home-cooked meal, trading stories and jokes, and helping clean up afterward.

In October, Shatha invited me to join her family for dinner. She lived with her parents, siblings, and her brother's wife and toddler son, Hamza. Their large house in a quiet, middle-class Baghdad neighborhood was drowned in the watercolors of the herb and flower garden that Shatha and her mother tended; the living room was ashimmer with tasteful pieces of *baghdadiyat** that Shatha had collected over the years: Persian tapestries, old Damascus trunks, etched silver and copper vases salvaged from beneath layers of grime in Baghdad's many antique shops.

Being proper Iraqi hosts, the women in Shatha's house had begun cooking our meal hours before dinner was scheduled to start. I arrived in time to help carry the bowls, trays, and plates from the kitchen crowded with aluminum and cast-iron pots into the spacious living room. The women, their quick hands full of pans and cutting boards laden with vegetables and poultry, bumped into each other, lost and caught their balance, spilled and wiped away water, and laughed, and the kitchen was full of warmth.

It took us twenty minutes to move all the food. Of course, there was not enough room on the table for everything Shatha's family had prepared—of course. I had been invited for dolma, but there was also biryani rice, endless salads and sauces, and an event of a dish that was introduced to me as "Shatha's special chicken." The chicken's brown and crispy skin was taut and twice the size of a regular bird's thanks to the spiced rice Shatha had stuffed into its skin before sticking the thing in the oven. When Shatha slashed across the cooked chicken's breast with a sharp carving knife, the rice spilled out onto a large tray, releasing an aroma of cinnamon, allspice, and cumin that made me swoon. The rice was like nothing I had ever tasted before: ambrosial.

We filled our plates and sat on couches and chairs around a low, glass-top coffee table in the living room and talked about Iraq's past, present, and future. Shatha's mother and siblings worried out loud about the mayhem that was wracking the country, and her uncle and father talked about how the censorship, the political persecution, and the secret police

---

Baghdadiyat—pieces of Iraqi and Middle Eastern art and antiques, such as decorative plates, vases, and tapestries, often collected by Baghdad's intelligentsia.

were gone—but so were reliable electricity, phone lines, medicine, and thousands-year-old artifacts from museums vandalized after the Saddam government collapsed.

It was the conversation I was hearing at many middle-class Iraqi homes in those early months of the war. Old Baghdad families watched their country turn almost overnight into a lawless land without a government, jobs, and police; terrorized by Iraqi criminals; overrun by foreign tanks—a land where nothing was certain and nowhere was safe. The opportunities that they had hoped would follow the fall of Hussein's regime—freedom of expression, freedom of movement, the freedom of doing business unimpeded by the punitive international sanctions the United Nations had imposed on Iraq after the first Gulf War—were getting lost in the mix.

"We have more day-to-day problems now than under Saddam," grumbled Farouk al Safi, the owner of a firm that serviced equipment at cigarette factories. Farouk's company was at a standstill because Baghdad's two tobacco factories, like most businesses, had not reopened after the invasion. An air conditioner hummed to life in the living room, briefly sending a wave of cool air into the midafternoon heat. Then the humming died, mimicking the erratic pattern of Baghdad's postwar power supply.

"This is not true," his son, Othman, corrected him softly. "Saddam was a murderer. But the Americans must change the situation. They must give people jobs as soon as possible. They must do something about security."

If they did not, Othman warned, the United States would lose its credibility in Iraq and allow anti-American religious political groups to fill the void that the ouster of Saddam's regime had created. Iraq had been hungering for change for decades, he said. It had no patience for a power vacuum.

Such political groups already had begun rapidly gaining support among Iraq's largely underprivileged Shiites. One of them was led by Moqtada al Sadr, the hitherto little-known son and nephew of immensely popular Shiite clerics murdered by Hussein's regime. Sadr was young and stared menacingly through small eyes set close beneath low eyebrows; his bloodline and his recklessness galvanized more than two million followers into becoming one of the major anti-American fighting and political forces in the years to come. Other, less influential groups, many led by Iraqi clerics freshly returned from exile in Iran, were also creating their own private armies of zealots.

By late May, the post-invasion chaos was crystallizing into two clashing insurgencies. In the Shiite ghetto of Saddam City (hastily renamed Sadr City to honor the slain brothers) and in Shiite towns and villages south of Baghdad a powerful, quasi-political alliance of senior Shiite Muslim clerics called the Hawza, following the example of Hamas in Gaza and understanding that at a time of crisis, food is synonymous with control, had taken over the provision of flour, rice, and cooking oil. Hawza was also distributing propane, handing out cash to the neediest, and organizing neighborhood militias to patrol the streets. I went to one propane distribution point, where a long, black line of veiled women weaved silently past a defunct gas station. I had to leave quickly. A group of boys pelted me with chunks of broken brick.

In the Sunni tribal land to the west of Baghdad, small and highly mobile groups of insurgents had begun to stage regular attacks with mortars and rockets on American troops. One insurgent told me over a glass of cool orange soda outside the restive Sunni city of Ramadi: "They occupied our country" and, by doing so, "became our enemy." As the summer went on, attacks on civilian Western targets—hotels where military contractors liked to stay, embassies, the United Nations offices—also became more frequent.

For my two friends, these changes promised to spell new restrictions, the likes of which they never had experienced before, not even when Saddam was in power. Bizarrely, with the fall of the dictatorship, the room in Iraq for freedom-loving, independent-minded women was rapidly shrinking, eroding the few personal liberties women there had enjoyed.

Saddam Hussein's secular regime had allowed women to wear what they wanted, travel wherever they wanted without the company of male relatives, study at universities, and serve in the armed forces alongside men—freedoms almost unparalleled in the Arab world. Thanaa, who had a job as a curator at an art gallery, could wear jeans and a sleeveless T-shirt to work. Now Saddam was gone, and the clerics who began to take charge of the country called for Iraq to become an Islamic state.

"I worry a lot about my future and my freedom in this new country," Thanaa told me one day. We were visiting a formerly government-run orphanage, home to twenty-six boys and twenty-six girls, which was now operated by the Hawza. In the name of security, the new managers had confined the girls to one of the orphanage's four wings. They built a brick wall separating the girls' wing from the rest of the building, and forbade them from going outside, into the courtyard, except for two hours in the evening. The boys were allowed to play on the squeaky jungle gym in the courtyard the rest of the day. The girls spent most of their time lying or sitting on mattresses arranged on a grid on the cement floor of their two rooms. Sometimes they played, indoors, with a large rubber ball—the only toy left after the looters had swept through. They read the Koran. The wing smelled sour, like stale sweat.

"This is the only way we can control the girls in an Islamic fashion," the new director explained.

What did the girls think about this?

"The most important thing for us is to be protected; the Hawza gives us that," explained Sahat, a tall teenager in an oversize brown dress. At fourteen, she was the oldest of the group. She had heard the firefights that rolled through the suburbs outside the orphanage's walls each night. She also may have heard the stories of teenage girls kidnapped from the streets and raped by gangs rampaging through Baghdad virtually unchecked. Khadija, Wahid's sister, came to mind: her confinement to her mother's house in Kabul may have been initiated by her oldest brother, but by the time we met, it also seemed self-imposed, a choice, almost a comfort. It occurred to me that perhaps behind her burqa, she, too, was looking for safety from marauding militias.

Not Thanaa. She wore her bell-bottom jeans and a tight-fitting T-shirt to the orphanage; she did not wear a scarf. The director shook his head. Women should cover their hair and arms, he told her sternly. She responded angrily, that her outfit was none of his business.

"I am Shia, but I don't want to wear a scarf on my head," she told me later. "And I want to be able to work and travel unrestrained. If I can't do it in post-Saddam Iraq, I will have to leave the country."

———

The third chapter of the famous cookbook *Kitab al Tabikh,* one of the oldest known culinary documents from the Middle Ages, first published in Iraq in the tenth century, is all about spices. It is titled "Spices and aromatics used to perfume the cooking pot," and comes right after "What causes the cooked food to spoil, have greasy odors, or vitiate," and "Utensils used in cooking, making desserts, and baking bread."

"I am doing this here for fear the cooks should overlook any of these," the cookbook's author, Ibn Sayyar al Warraq, explains.

So that I did not overlook any of the spices required to re-create her spectacular chicken-skin rice at home, Shatha personally took me to al Shorja, Baghdad's oldest market. Charlie Radin, a *Boston Globe* reporter who was at the time the chief of the newspaper's bureau in Tel Aviv, tagged along.

The cabbie dropped us off on a side street in downtown Baghdad so crowded with humans and farm animals—alive and dead and in the process of being slaughtered—it felt as though we were wading through a Hieronymus Bosch painting. Was this really a city at war? We pushed our way past tea vendors peddling drinks from their sidewalk tables, past antique shops glittering from the cool caves of semiunderground basements, past newspaper boys, past beggars sitting beneath fly-swarmed sheep carcasses hanging upside down from meat hooks; we turned a corner, another and another, and plunged into the dim guts of the centuries-old bazaar.

I never will be able to find my way through those pungent, stuffy alleyways on my own. For one, I am terrible with street names. I remember the names of the streets in St. Petersburg because I grew up there—some streets, some names, because, like the city itself, the streets were renamed, some more than once, during the seventy years of Communism, and then renamed back at different times during the last two decades (remember poor Tolmachyov?). Moscow, by comparison, is a blur of names and circular streets and crooked hills studded, in no particular order, with medieval churches and modern glass high-rises and gray slabs of Soviet apartment blocks (Moscow is a blur of a city). In Dasht-e-Qal'eh I navigated by cemetery and by asking people for Mahbuhbullah the Merchant's house; in Kabul Valley, where orchards drip down from the mountains like the blood of the fratricides that soak their roots, I sloshed about like tea leaves in a cup. Jenin was a bomb-blasted square of the besieged, booby-trapped camp rotting in the center of the city like gangrene. Jerusalem was a city of borders so rigid, and so numerous, it was hard to breathe without someone demanding their air back. But much of my geography is made up of numberless, nameless villages with blue and green metal gates—those I only remember by face, by story, by tears and jokes and meals. Al Shorja I will always remember by scent.

Like many markets in the Middle East, al Shorja was a sprawling labyrinth of passages barely wide enough for two people to pass, composed of shops flanked with stalls that sold, it seemed, any product you could possibly need. Toilet brushes hung on clothespins above a stall selling plastic tableware imported from Syria; mannequins dressed in Turkish tracksuits teetered over stacks of microwavable china; transparent plastic bags of luminous honey shone from clotheslines strung between a kiosk selling cheap makeup and a stall piled with ground chickpeas. All of this seemed held together not so much by the physical boundaries of the streets that girdled the market as by the blanket of fragrance emanating from spice stands like the one our small procession had arrived here to patronize: batteries of burlap sacks open at the top to reveal curls of cinnamon bark; hard, pale shells of nutmeg; black, stringy vanilla beans; peppercorns of at least four different colors; zesty crimson droplets of dried barberries; black ball bearings of allspice; green powdery leaves of thyme; and dozens of condiments I could not recognize.

Shatha asked the owner of the stand to grind up and blend several spice mixes for me.

"This is for rice, this is for fish, this is for lamb, this is for chicken rice."

She explained to me the purpose of each combination so rapidly that I knew right then I would never get them straight. I was bound to season my raisin pudding with the flavoring for fish, but it did not matter. The fragrance was heavenly. I wanted the vendor to take his time grinding just so that I could stand there and inhale. Soon, flecks of ground spices began to dance in the beams of light that cut through the dirty glass ceiling, gently bathing the wonderful cacophony of taste, smell, and color below.

Suddenly, Charlie reached behind his back and grabbed the wrist of a boy of about nine or ten. The boy's fingers were still inside Charlie's backpack, which my colleague had carelessly slung over his shoulder. The kid tried to thrash free, but Charlie's grip was steely. He pulled the boy's hand out of the backpack. Clenched in the boy's fingers were Charlie's passport and well-worn leather wallet.

Immediately, a small crowd formed around us. Great! I thought. We had just created an international incident, and were giving the Iraqis another reason to hate Americans: grabbing a little pickpocket, possibly hurting his wrist. But the crowd, it turned out, was not there to attack us. Someone dragged the boy out of sight. Someone inquired, in polite English, whether Charlie was all right. Someone else told me I should check my pockets right away. A woman scolded Shatha for bringing us to the market: "Don't you think that it is a dangerous place for foreigners?" Four or five people formed a semicircle around us, their backs toward us, facing the market and the rest of the shoppers. On the Grand Trunk Road, a group of unnamed Tajik fighters had come to my rescue. In al Shorja, it was a group of benevolent shoppers, armed with grocery bags.

"You are safe now," one woman, a heavyset matron of about fifty, explained over her shoulder. "We'll watch out for you."

"I am so deeply sorry for what happened," said a younger woman. She looked about my age. "I don't want you to think that people in Baghdad are not hospitable to their guests."

And so it goes: firefights will lash the streets and bombs will churn up the pavements, and in the middle of it all, a shopper at a market will worry that her nation not be judged bad-mannered.

For a long time, in a glass jar in my kitchen, I kept a little bit of the chicken-rice spice blend I had bought that day. I used the last of it six years later, preparing dolma for a friend.

The trip to al Shorja was my last real outing in Iraq for years. Soon after that walk, I left the country. A week later, Michael Goldfarb wrote in an email that Ahmad Shawkat had been killed.

David wrote an obituary for the *Globe*. Michael wrote an obituary for the *Guardian*. I could not write. I sat in Moscow, in front of my laptop, with an undone heart.

Friendships in war zones: it is an oxymoron. Friends are the people for whom you buy medicine when they catch the flu; the people you call when you need help moving furniture; the people with whom you share your holiday meals and your darkest fears. Ahmad's murder reminded me that in war zones, none of this is possible.

In Afghanistan in 2001 and 2002, Wahid was with me through the best of times and the worst of times. We crouched behind the same battlements, stared down the same gunmen (my bad), slept side by side on the same earthen floors, ate from the same plate, drank from the same whiskey bottle (my bad, again). But I never saw him move into the house he had hoped to buy with the money he earned translating for me. I don't even know whether he bought the house.

Mahbuhbullah, the tomb raider and vodka smuggler, gave me shelter and food in the northern Afghan village of Dasht-e-Qal'eh in 2001 and 2002. Once, he gave me his twelve-year-old son, Abdullah, to use as a bodyguard. But I never found books in Persian to help Abdullah learn to read. I do not know what has become of the boy.

Najibullah, the troubled, beautiful, finger-dancing, hashish-smoking, Valium-popping unemployed fighter who rode shotgun in my car near Osama bin Laden's supposed hideout in Tora Bora in 2001: I should have taken you to a psychotherapist in Kabul, someone who works with posttraumatic stress disorder and drug addiction. I never did. I am sorry. I want to believe you are well, and your pinkies are intact.

I fell out of touch with Ghulam Sahib, the unflappable Chicken Killer, King of the Roads, who drove me through (or around) Afghan mountains, dry riverbeds, and minefields in 2001. A year later, I heard that he had become a military commander—a warlord!—in his home village up north. But I don't know the name of the village. And I never did attend his wedding to the Faizabad girl whose beauty had derailed our travels for a day.

I have been talking, sporadically, with Todd Wood, whom I met when he was a lieutenant colonel commanding an infantry battalion in Tikrit in 2005. Four years later, Wood, by then a full colonel, took command of the First Stryker Brigade Combat Team of the Twenty-fifth Infantry Division, based in Fairbanks, Alaska. His two young sergeants, Derrick Stephens and Darrell Foster, email from time to time; the last I heard, they were both serving as instructors on different army bases in the American South.

I also receive an occasional note from Alan Cullison. When I was writing this book, he was a reporter for the *Wall Street Journal* and lived in Moscow. I read, online, that after leaving the *Financial Times* for a stint with the *Economist,* Robert Cottrell moved to Latvia, where he became the editor of the *Browser,* an online digest of English-language journalism, and operated a secondhand bookshop. No word on the two colonels of the Russian border guard who detained us and forced us to drink vodka at gunpoint in Tajikistan in 2001. The way they guzzled hard liquor, I'd worry about their livers.

I have returned to Amman a few times since the death of Bassam Shream, a Jordanian tour guide and driver, a devoted friend, and, once, a wannabe Palestinian terrorist. But I did not know where to look for his grave. Instead, I had *mansaf* at al Quds. And one day, I went to watch the sun set over the Jordan River. Like that evening in 2002, when we faced west from Mount Nebo, it was hazy, and I could barely make out the lights of Jericho coruscating on the horizon.

After I read Michael Goldfarb's email about Ahmad, I sat in front of my laptop and cried. I mourned Ahmad, but I also mourned all the other friendships I had ever forged in a war zone, relationships that never would become as intimate and as continuous as I wished them to be. And yet, during the time we spent together, these people became my adopted brothers and sisters, mothers and fathers, my family. Our closeness inspired me, enlightened and elated me, and taught me, over and over, that there was much more to war than wreckage and loss.

An obituary, an epitaph, would never do justice to these friendships. They call for a paean.

This is it.

———

In 2004, Thanaa met a businessman from Bahrain, fell in love, and married him. She settled in Manama, gave birth to a daughter she named Enana (after the Sumerian goddess of love, fertility, and war), and opened a gallery that displays and sells modern Iraqi art.

David and I left Moscow and moved to a Massachusetts suburb. Good-bye, vodka-swilling government minders, cold-hearted bureaucrats, and hot borsch. We bought a house in the woods, with a garden large enough for me to grow Swiss chard.

I stayed out of Iraq for more than a year, and when I returned, in 2005, the only affordable and relatively safe way for me to travel around the country was as an embedded reporter with American troops. Bombs detonated daily, shattering government offices, mosques, markets, and tens of thousands of lives. Western reporters were getting kidnapped. In November 2005, a van and a water tanker packed with explosives detonated in front of al Hamra, killing at least eight Iraqis and blowing out all the glass windows in the hotel.

Traveling with the military meant I had to be tethered to a certain unit and was not allowed to leave its base except when I accompanied the troops on patrol or during a raid. That was when I went to Tikrit and met Todd Wood. Although Shatha still lived in Baghdad and Thanaa sometimes returned there to visit her family, they rarely saw each other. As for the three of us taking another trip to the echo chambers of the Mustansiriya School together, or even meeting for dinner, such frivolities had become out of the question. The way the war was reshaping Iraq made it difficult to believe that I would ever see either of them again.

Between August 2006 and March 2007, al Shorja market, where Shatha and I had gone shopping for spices, was attacked six times. On February 12, 2007, a homemade roadside bomb, a car, and a truck bearing explosives detonated within seconds of each other just after noon, setting ablaze a nearby seven-story shopping center. Clothing, oil, shoddy wiring, and hollow, plastic mannequins burned like kindling, trapping scores of people inside the market as the fire spread to stalls and cars parked outside. At least seventy-eight people were killed, and nearly two hundred were wounded.

In downtown Baghdad, religious militias executed women they caught wearing clothes the gunmen considered immodest. Over the phone, Shatha told me that not far from her house one woman was killed for driving a car.

In emails to me, Thanaa compared her country to a "sick lion" that was being picked apart by vultures, and wondered whether the war that had toppled Saddam Hussein had been worth it.

"I have a conflict with myself about what happened to us Iraqis," Thanaa wrote me after one of her infrequent visits to her parents in Baghdad. "Do you think this is better for us?"

Our friendship had taken an on elusive quality. Months, then years after we had met and worked and laughed and cried together, we were still in touch through quick and rare telephone calls and occasional email messages. That set our relationship apart from the friendships I had made in most other conflict zones, where the absence of cell phones or reliable Internet access or mail precluded any attempts to maintain a connection. But we never saw each other—except once, in 2005, when I saw Thanaa in Jordan. She was traveling to Bahrain after visiting her relatives in Iraq and I was traveling to Iraq from the United States. We met at the hotel where I was staying, but, because she had left her baby daughter with some relatives in a different part of town, she could not stay very long.

Shatha remained in Baghdad with her new husband, a strapping, tall businessman she had begun dating when we were working together. Soon she, too, gave birth to a daughter, whom she named Deema, which in Arabic means both "rain cloud" and "long, tranquil rain." She emailed me photographs of herself and her baby girl. I emailed her photographs of my kids and of the garden in my new American home. It was not as pretty as the garden she tended in Baghdad. For a while, Shatha continued to work for American newspapers, earning a prestigious journalism prize—an award she could not collect, she said, because the news organization for which she was working could not afford to bring her to the United States.

"I know it is sad. I was hoping to see you guys, have tea in your garden, and cook together," she wrote.

She and her husband were living in their own spacious house in her old Baghdad neighborhood, next door to her parents' home and her old garden. Most of their neighbors had fled, strangers had moved into abandoned houses, and Iraqi forces had set up checkpoints in the street. Shatha felt the war encroaching. She and her husband applied for refugee status in Canada.

"I cannot stand it here anymore, it doesn't feel like the Iraq I love anymore, everything good has left here. For the past two days the Iraqi forces closed all the streets in my neighborhood by concrete barricades and only left one point of exit and entrance, it made us feel like we are in a large prison," she wrote me. "I am counting the days to leave here."

The application was denied.

In November 2007, a car bomb blew up in Shatha's street, shattering every window in her house. A twenty-four-hour curfew left the family without bread. There were gunfights and rocket attacks. For a while, the men of her family took turns guarding the house with the weapons American troops allowed Iraqis: one Kalashnikov rifle and one pistol per household. Finally, after rival militias clashed in an hours-long pitched battle for her street one night, Shatha, her husband, and daughter fled their house, leaving behind Shatha's beautiful herb and flower garden and all of her painstakingly collected artwork.

They tried to leave Iraq legally, but most countries would not accept Iraqi refugees. They tried to sneak into Sweden, where many Iraqis were emigrating, but did not make it past the Czech Republic, where they were detained for weeks and then deported to Baghdad.

"Yes, *habibti,*"—she called me "my darling" in Arabic, a form of endearment close female friends or sisters bestow upon each other—"it was quite an adventure. Do not worry about us, we are now at home and not leaving it."

They stayed in Baghdad for several weeks before they realized that home still was not a safe place to be. They fled again, to Irbil, the Kurdish capital of northern Iraq. Shatha, an Arab, felt unwelcome in the quasi-autonomous region. Tens of thousands of Kurds had lost their loved ones during Saddam's ethnic cleansing campaign, al Anfal; although Thanaa and Shatha had heard nothing of Halabja in 2003, no Kurd—not even those who were born after the chemical attack—could ever forget it. Arabs in Kurdistan were disliked and mistrusted.

But Shatha believed she had no other place to go.

"I tried so hard to go [abroad] but I couldn't, it is very difficult for an Iraqi to get a visa anywhere," she wrote about the move. "We are not thinking about the future right now, we are thinking about survival . . . We are being treated here like foreigners. Our new house is small and has no garden, I really miss our old house and garden."

In a follow-up email, Shatha sent me a photograph from the Textiles Museum in Irbil. In it, she beamed at the camera, and next to her, tapestries of burgundy, indigo, and gold told stories of bird migrations and spring waterfalls and summer flowers: stories of Iraq in peacetime.

"I loved every piece. I felt I was in heaven and wanted to steal and run . . . I wish we can do all this [sightseeing] together," she wrote.

About a year later, her second daughter, Leila, was born. Iraqi president Nouri al Maliki pronounced Iraq safe and urged all refugees to return to their homes. Some heeded his call, despite the warning by the United Nations that Iraq was still lacking proper security. Shatha remained in Irbil. She made occasional trips to visit relatives in Baghdad, but she thought it would be a while before it was safe for her to live there again. She and her husband applied for refugee status in the United States.

"Now we can't return to Baghdad, not for a long time," Shatha wrote "We can't go to any other country, no one will grant a visa to an Iraqi passport holder, so this looks like our only option for now. Most Iraqis suffer the same dilemma but have no options."

In the United States, Barack Obama became president and pledged to pull most of American troops out of Iraq. On the surface at least, it seemed as though sectarian violence was a thing of the past. But Shatha and many other Iraqis saw it differently. Baghdad's exhausted scenery revealed to them more than shrapnel-scarred streets with a broken power grid, leaking sewage pipes, a damaged water supply, and barely functioning garbage-removal service. Gone were the mixed Sunni-Shia neighborhoods, the friendly public discussions about art, the carefree handshakes across the invisible ethnic or sectarian lines. Gone was the neighborly trust that once had allowed Sunnis and Shias to share the same street, the same city block. Jaded Iraqis offered grim projections of how long it would take to heal the deep emotional wounds caused by the civil war: fifty years, maybe more.

I imagine that in a way, Shatha's and Thanaa's self-imposed exiles preserved their friendship, which they had retailored to fit their now brief telephone calls and email conversations. Who knows what would have happened to the relationship between the two women—one Shia, one Sunni—if both of them had remained in post–civil war Baghdad?

In late March 2009, I returned to Iraq on assignment for *Ms.* magazine to report about rape, that secret war against women that always accompanies a shooting war between men. I was going to write about a clandestine network of shelters for rape victims operated by a small group of Iraqi women's rights advocates.

The photojournalist Mimi Chakarova and I subletted a suite at al Hamra, my old haunts.

The hotel had the feel of a besieged castle all but abandoned by its sovereign. The in-your-face scarlet balconies were a thing of the past; the hotel management had repainted all outside walls the dull ocher of a spring sandstorm. The glass in the windows and balcony doors had been replaced with fortified plastic, to prevent shattering in case a bomb detonated nearby. Blast walls circumscribed the hotel like a set of enormous domino blocks arranged there by a giant, obstructing all approaches, and a succession of uniformed security guards thoroughly searched anyone who requested entrance, by car or on foot. Just outside the concrete walls, rectangular boxes of affordable housing stood charred and blistered by the massive truck bomb that had detonated there four years earlier.

More security guards sat inside the hotel, checking the bags of guests and visitors beneath peeling wall paint and ceiling stained with leaks: at the time of war, who cares about such trivia? The display case of the souvenir shop next to the foyer appeared to hold the same silver earrings and knives inlaid with mother-of-pearl and turquoise it had been selling six years ago. The layer of dust on the jewelry was thicker.

A man in blue overalls appeared at my hotel room the day after I arrived. I could not tell whether he was the same janitor who had washed the balconies in 2003. He nodded at me, slid open the balcony door, splashed some water from a bucket onto the tiles, and, with his mop, pushed the dirty water over the side. The brown wash fell to the ground, where the former topiary now grew wild and abandoned. I glanced at the Flowersland hotel across the street. No woman stepped out onto a balcony there to carry out her part of the ritual.

(In January 2010, a sedan carrying armed men drove up to the checkpoint in front of al Hamra. The men rolled down the windows and opened fire at the checkpoint guards. While the guards were shooting back, a white Kia minivan sped past the blast-proof barriers they had been guarding. The minivan was packed with explosives. It detonated about fifty feet from the hotel. The blast ripped through an apartment building across the street, killing at least sixteen people. The explosion left a crater six feet deep. Leila Fadel, a *Washington Post* reporter who was staying at the hotel, wrote that day that blood—of the victims? of the suicide bomber who drove the minivan?—smeared the balconies of the Flowersland. After the explosion, journalists moved out of al Hamra.)

Reporting, too, felt different than it had when I worked in Baghdad for the first time. Even behind the walls of people's homes and inside the fortified offices of women's rights advocates, I did not find the sense of openness that had once allowed Thanaa and me to interview Shiite mothers sifting the dust of mass graves for their sons' bones. Iraqis were grieving in private now. My witness was unwanted.

A year earlier, Amnesty International had written in its report about Iraq that rape was being committed by "members of Islamist armed groups, militias, Iraqi government forces, foreign soldiers within the U.S.-led Multinational Force, and staff of foreign private military security contractors." But not even Meisun, the soft-spoken graduate student of English literature at Baghdad University who was our translator, wanted to talk about it. The subject was too embarrassing, too stigmatized. Meisun's voice would trail off whenever rape came up, which was often. Most of my questions, and most of the answers, got lost in translation.

It was clear that there would be no climbing the walls of the Mustansiriya School, no strolling through the Friday book market. I would have to get my fill of Baghdad's sights—miles and miles of blast walls; infinite checkpoints; collapsing, strafed shells of buildings—from the backseat of a taxi, and from the balcony of my room at al Hamra. The women I interviewed instructed me to stay as low key as possible, to wear a black *abaya* and cover my hair whenever I went outside. Meisun told Mimi and me to be very quiet whenever we were in public, lest we be discovered as foreigners. Friendly Iraqis were trying to protect me again, the way they had years ago at the al Shorja spice kiosk, but their hospitality now had taken on a more urgent tone.

"Cover up, cover up," women said to me whenever I was about to go outside. "You shouldn't let your hair show from underneath your scarf. You should look more Iraqi."

Such warnings would make me think of Thanaa, cutting through Baghdad streets six years earlier in her T-shirt and jeans. I would imagine how enraged my friend, who so worshipped Iraq's history and art, would have been if anyone had told her that she was not Iraqi enough because of her clothes. I would hear her deep voice in my mind: bellowing, swearing, rebelling, refusing to back down, ever, for anyone.

Then I would rewrap my scarf, making sure no hair showed from underneath, and step into the streets of Baghdad.

The morning Shatha arrived at al Hamra I was stumbling down the rickety stairs of the hotel suite, toward the living room mirror, twisting the long, narrow head scarf round and round my head. It was almost time for me to leave for another day of frustrating near-interviews, equivocations, half-spoken horrors, and I needed to make sure that the scarf, my ultimate urban camouflage, looked proper and nondescript.

"Hi, Anna," called a voice behind me.

I turned around and there she stood, holding baby Leila in her arms. She told me she could not stay long, she had come to Baghdad for only a short visit, just so that she could see me. She told me she was staying with her uncle, that she had left her older daughter, Deema, there, and that she would have to return there in a few minutes. She laughed. I cried. We embraced. She wore lip gloss and sweet perfume. Her beautiful dark eyes shone. She hadn't changed a bit.

War dissolves most man-made societal boundaries. Suddenly, everything is starkly public: the death of a suicide bomber and his victims, the disease of a starving toddler, the grief of a war widow. In this extremity, there is never an hour after which it is improper to knock on someone's gate. Very often there is no gate behind which to shut yourself from the rest of the world. Even the funeral of a teenage failed terrorist becomes a street celebration to which everyone is invited.

Such lack of privacy and pretense crystallizes our feelings and actions into absolutes. Pure loathing guides the arm of the killer. Pure love takes over most everything else. Shatha had driven south for seven hours from her safe haven into a city too dangerous for her to live in— just to see me. She did this not because our friendship had survived the war, but because it had grown stronger amid the fighting and the separation. In life's most punishing situations humanity reasserts itself with doubled force.

Smiling, Shatha wiped my tears with her hand. (Often, war also strips you of the acquired skill of hiding your emotions.)

"We should call Thanaa!" she said. She strode onto the balcony, pulled a cell phone out of her stylish leather purse, and dialed a number.

"Thanaa!" Shatha cupped the cell phone with her hand, trying to outshout the grind of street generators, Baghdad's wartime cicadas. "I am with Anna—Anna, talk to Thanaa!"

She thrust the phone at me, and I heard Thanaa's throaty contralto laughing in my ear:

"How are you, Anna? Are you in Baghdad?"

I worried about wasting the precious call. I worried about wasting my precious time with Shatha. I felt dysfunctional, unable to express myself.

"Thanaa! I am in Baghdad!" I yelled back into the phone, redundantly.

"Anna? I can't hear you," Thanaa's disembodied voice said. Then the cell phone battery died and the line went silent. Thanaa was gone.

All around us, Baghdad lay tourniquetted with blast walls and roadblocks. In the hazy distance, beyond the semipermanent traffic jam clogging the busy Jadriyah Street, neglected palm groves ringed a cluster of bombed-out palaces left over from Saddam's neo-baroque opulence. Directly beneath the balcony, the narrow side street with overgrown hedges glittered with chunks of concrete, mortar fragments, and bullet casings—the debris of the war that had brought the three of us together and had broken us apart.

~

Shatha's Special Chicken

Tbeet

Serves 6 to 8

*F*or years I had wondered whether "Shatha's special chicken" had a different name. Imagine my surprise when I found it online—and discovered that the dish my Sunni friend serves on special occasions is, in fact, a Shabbat dish called *tbeet,* and that it is unique to Mesopotamian Jews. Jews once had lived side by side with Muslims in Iraq, but most of them had fled when Israel was created, and by 2003 only a handful of Jews remained in Baghdad. It is somehow heartwarming to think that their culinary tradition survives in Iraq, even if much of the rest of their culture is lost.

I emailed Shatha about my discovery. My friend, ever the connoisseur of Iraqi history, responded immediately with a message oozing with excitement.

"Great information," she wrote. "I didn't know about the stuffed chicken, it's just something I learnt from mum which her mum made, and definitely it didn't matter in their days if you were Jewish, Christian or Muslim, they were just Baghdadi women exchanging recipes."

We all miss those days.

Now I am sharing my adaptation of Shatha's recipe with you. Remember, "spices and aromatics used to perfume the cooking pot" are key.

1 large 4–5 pound whole chicken (giblets and head removed)
2 cups long-grain rice, preferably basmati
1 teaspoon ground cardamom
1 tablespoon ground cinnamon
1 tablespoon ground cumin
1 teaspoon ground allspice
1 teaspoon ground cloves
Salt and pepper, for rubbing the chicken
Olive oil

1. Preheat the oven to 400°F.

2. You can slip your hand fairly easily between the skin of the chicken and its meat, but in parts of the chicken where it is attached to the meat—for example, down the back or around the thighs—carefully cut the thin connectors with a small paring knife to detach it. Combine the rice, spices, and 1 tablespoon salt and carefully, with your hands, push the rice between the skin and the body of the chicken. Stuff around the thighs, too. Fill the skin loosely, because the rice will expand significantly during cooking. You can "sew" the openings closed with small metal skewers (do not use a thread, because it will burn in the oven). Or you can leave the openings as they are: rice is sticky by nature, and most of it will not spill out. Rub the outside of the chicken with salt, pepper, and a bit of olive oil.

3. Place the chicken in a lightly oiled heavy-bottomed pan and put it in the oven for about 15 minutes. Be careful not to make the skin too crispy too soon, or else it will burst. After the skin is browned, reduce the oven temperature to 325°F. Cook until the chicken is done (the juices should run clear, not pink, when you pierce the meat between the thigh and leg), about 2½ hours, basting occasionally with the juices from the bottom of the pan. Add a few tablespoons of water if needed.

4. When the chicken is cooked, carefully move it to a very large platter: when you cut open the skin, rice will spill onto the platter. Cut the chicken (in front of your guests) into large chunks and serve the chicken, rice, and skin on the same platter.

Note: Shatha served her chicken with yogurt sauce she made with mint from her garden.

"I use fresh mint with yogurt. I chop it and add some crushed garlic, olive oil, salt, and black pepper," she wrote. For 2 cups yogurt, you will need about ½ cup chopped fresh mint, 2 cloves garlic, and 2 tablespoons olive oil. Serve the sauce on the side.

Epilogue

Here are some things that happened to me in war zones:

A man I barely knew gave me stewed pumpkin. Then he gave me his preteen son to protect my life.

A grieving father invited me, a complete stranger, into his funeral tent and fed me lamb and rice.

A hardened infantryman offered me his Starbucks coffee, his sorrow, and the shelter of his armored truck.

A dissident's wife slaved over the stove for hours to treat me to the perfect dolma while American planes dropped five-hundred-pound bombs on the city where her daughters and grandchildren were living.

The Polish journalist Ryszard Kapuściński wrote about his visit to Nagorno-Karabakh during the genocidal war there between Azeris and Armenians: "The table should always be set with whatever one has, with whatever is at hand, just so that it is not bare, for a table's nakedness alienates people, freezes conversation." But in the wars I have witnessed, a set table—or a *dastarkhan,* or a plate, or simply a palm holding forth some morsels—was always more than a prop, more than a backdrop denoting goodwill. Dining in war zones was an act of defiance against depravity. It was a celebration of the verity that war can kill our friends and decimate our towns, but it cannot kill our inherent decency, generosity, and kindness: that which makes us human.

All the meals in this book were such celebrations.

When I started writing about war, I sometimes carried my own food to conflict zones, and rather than sit down for a meal I would nosh during some torturously long drive or while typing, to save time. But over the years I have learned to accept the invitation to eat together with the people I write about whenever I can, even if the meal is no more than a fistful of dust-caked, green raisins. In extremity, an offer to break bread is more than an invitation to hear someone's story. It is a chance to link that person's life and yours.

All the people in this book are family.

In April 2010, Anna Badkhen returned to Afghanistan on assignment for Foreign Policy *magazine. For a month, she sent the magazine editors dispatches every day, chronicling her impressions, thoughts, and adventures and describing how the country had changed. These dispatches were collected and published as an ebook in July 2010. The text appears here in its entirety for the first time in a printed book.*

WAITING FOR
THE TALIBAN

A Journey Through Northern Afghanistan

ANNA BADKHEN

Introduction

When I first came to Afghanistan as a war correspondent, in October 2001, I went to the north. For three years that followed, I traveled through the region a lot—both during the fratricidal war between Taliban government troops and the U.S.-backed rebels of the anti-Taliban Northern Alliance, and after the strict Islamic regime collapsed. I witnessed human tragedy of a magnitude I theretofore never had thought possible—and the astounding generosity with which the people caught in the crossfire shared both their grief and their bread. Afghanistan was the first conflict I had covered. In a strange way, I suppose, it was like the first kiss: shocking, mesmerizing, heart-rending.

I made friends then: with Mahbuhbullah, my host in Takhar province who made a living smuggling vodka from Tajikistan and fencing 2,300-year-old artifacts from a town Alexander the Great had built a mile from his house; with his beautiful wife, Nargiz, who was pregnant the last time I saw her; with Ghulam Sahib, the intrepid driver who drove me around minefields (or through; all I know is that we survived them). And I fell in love: with the sedulous farmers who tenaciously carve their fields out of the infertile, salt desert in the punishing sun; with the ancient dirt roads that remember the footfalls of invaders who for millennia had tried—and failed—to conquer Afghanistan's contumacious people; with the perseverance of a nation that, despite wars, cataclysms, and disease, ekes out a grueling life beneath the portentous shadow of the Hindu Kush.

Between 2001 and 2004, after U.S. air strikes had banished the Taliban from Northern Afghanistan, villagers clenched by poverty still died of hunger and diseases, the literacy percentage among women remained in single digits, children as young as six still joined the workforce, and landmines and cluster bombs continued to kill and maim hundreds of people each year. But the land seemed full of hope. The plains of Kunduz and Balkh provinces appeared to exhale in relief, with the expectation that after a quarter century of bloodshed things were going to turn for the better. Even the massifs of Baghlan province seemed to have relaxed their Cretaceous frowns.

It may not have looked so then, but those were happy times for Northern Afghanistan. The region was considered the safest section of the country. You could hail down a taxi in Mazar-e-Sharif to drive to Kabul; you could stop for a lamb kebab at a roadside café; and if you decided to stay at a *chaikhana* for $15 a night you worried about bedbugs, not kidnappers. NATO forces and most international donors focused their attention on southern Afghanistan, where the Taliban had retained a stronghold. Most U.S. media outlets—including the newspaper for which I was working at the time, the *San Francisco Chronicle*—focused their attention on other troubled regions of the world. After 2004, I stopped going to Afghanistan.

To an extent, the generally accepted notion that the Taliban posed no threat in Northern Afghanistan spelled the region's undoing. While the world was distracted, the Taliban quietly returned to the north.

Now it levies taxes on farmers and robs and kidnaps travelers in Baghlan, which is bisected by the north-south highway NATO uses as a supply route. It operates courts that dole out swift and severe Shariah justice. It controls virtually all of Kunduz, where the highway crosses the Pyandzh River into Tajikistan, the staging point for many European troops headed into Afghanistan. Afghan forces periodically exchange fire with Taliban rebels in Takhar, a province that before the American-led invasion in 2001 largely had been an anti-Taliban stronghold. The Taliban has forged a tenuous alliance with the insurgent militia of Gulbuddin

Hekmatyar, the famously egomaniacal Islamist warlord who gained prominence as an anti-Soviet rebel commander in the 1980s, and who has opposed every Afghan government since then.

How was it possible for the insurgency to sweep to power in the part of the country where the militia was so loathed, where it does not have a lot of ethnic ties (Northern Afghanistan is populated mostly by ethnic Uzbeks and Tajiks, who have traditionally opposed the Taliban, with only a few pockets of Pashtuns, the largest ethnic group in Afghanistan, who make up the core of the Islamist militia)—an area that is cordoned off from the Taliban's southern hotbed by a mountain range whose lowest pass soars at a vertiginous 8,777 feet? What happened to the people I saw celebrate the Taliban's downfall in 2001: families who had returned from years of exile, brothers who had reunited after fighting each other, farmers who had reclaimed the fields the Taliban and the Northern Alliance had used as battlegrounds. What happened to Mahbuhbullah? And, the bigger question for the United States and NATO forces as they struggle to reassert control over the whole country: Is it possible to actually secure any territory in Afghanistan, even the seemingly most peaceable, for a significant length of time?

In April 2010, I returned to Afghanistan on a month-long assignment for *Foreign Policy* magazine to find out.

I brought along old newspaper clips, my notes from my previous trips to the region, and the photographs of my Afghan friends, with whom I had not spoken for years. When we had met, there had been no electricity in Afghanistan, no Internet, no cell phones, no way to keep in touch. I hoped the photos would help me track them down, to see them again.

I found some of them. I also found, to my sorrow, that despite the promises of international aid and prosperity, the region had changed devastatingly little since I had last seen it—and that the people who in 2001 had embraced the U.S.- led war are now wondering whether the Taliban's puritanical and cruel governance may be a better option than the anarchy, corruption, and abandonment that followed the militia's ouster.

Each leg of my journey brought new stories of woe, each stop along the road heralded new heartache. Each night, I sat down in front of my laptop and wrote a dispatch for *Foreign Policy* about what I had seen that day. The dispatches were part diary entries, part love letters from a land that nine years ago stole my heart. With very minor edits, they are collected here.

—Anna Badkhen, July 2010

Day 1. **Kabul**

He said that anyway it was not so much a question of a correct
map but of any map at all. He said that in that country were fires
and earthquakes and floods and that one needed to know the
country itself and not simply the landmarks therein.

—Cormac McCarthy, *The Crossing*

The 2009 edition of Nelles' map of Afghanistan marks the country's imposing mountain ridges, its life-giving rivers, some historical landmarks, and all of its major and many of its minor roads, some
just well-worn stretches of desert or parallel ruts hollowed out in steep
mountainsides by generations of motorists.

But when I show an Afghan aid worker in Kabul the road I want to
take, one that humps over the Hindu Kush and descends into Afghanistan's northern plains, he shakes his head: This road is off limits. He
knows what the map does not show—that every ridge along the way
can be a firing line; every gorge, an ambush; every valley, the backdrop
for a massacre.

Today, I am trying to plot out my route. The road from Baghlan to
Kunduz, I am told, is a no-go zone. I ask a security advisor for a Western relief agency about the highway from Mazar-e-Sharif, the capital
of Balkh, to Kunduz. He responds:

"Don't even dare travel on that road."

A political map of the country in his Kabul office shows Afghanistan's 34 provinces. According to a recent article by Kim Barker, a fel-

low at the Council on Foreign Relations, the Taliban has set up its own court system in 33 of them. The borders between the provinces are not important; what matters are the borders between territory controlled by the Afghan government (most of the provincial capitals and most of Kabul province, including Kabul) and by the insurgents (most of the rest of the country). These frontiers are not marked on any map I have seen, because they shift constantly.

I have been looking at a lot of maps. Each seems to reflect only a fraction of reality. A map with its own very particular reality hangs outside Kabul's Intercontinental Hotel, where I went a couple of times to poach free wireless Internet. This map is euphemistic. Instead of Bamyan, the province where the Taliban had famously destroyed the world's two largest statues of standing Buddha (and, less famously, raped and massacred thousands of ethnic Hazara Shiites), the map is labeled: BUDDHA. Instead of Kandahar: SPIRIT OF FREE. It is possible that the creator was Afghanistan's own Pangloss: He must have seen almond orchards where there are minefields; souvenir stands where there are checkpoints; shady, cool parks on residential street corners where putrid heaps of trash decompose in the sun.

But I prefer to think of the map's understatement as satire.

Northern Afghanistan is marked: ADVENTURE.

Day 2. **Kabul**

Night falls over Afghanistan's capital in waves. The tallest snow-streaked vertebrae of the Hindu Kush are the first to retire into the dusk, growing opaque and flat and then disappearing. Then kitchen lights go on beneath the myriad flat rooftops, erasing the city's subtle, montane geometries and dividing Kabul into small coruscations of light and blotches of darkness. From kitchen balconies the scents of cooking emerge—okra in tomato sauce, spinach with garlic puréed in ghee, lamb and potatoes stewed in pressure cookers—and commingle in the streets. They mix with the muezzins', calls to evening prayer and waft in and out of living-room windows, telling Kabulis what their neighbors are having for dinner.

For four nights I have been staying in one such living room in the house of a shoe salesman in Khair Khana, a middle-class neighborhood in northwestern Kabul. The unfaltering rhythm of life there—the teenage spinach vendor who pushed his wooden cart up my unpaved street at 6 a.m.; the tinsmiths who began their rumba at 6:30; the roofers who started laying beams across the street by 7 a.m.—could almost make it seem as though there were no war.

But then a B-52 bomber would lift off heavily from Bagram airport to the east, scythe the smoggy sky over the capital, and straighten out on a southward route, toward Kandahar and Helmand, where U.S. troops are fighting for control of the Taliban heartland.

Kabul to Mazar-e-Sharif

The ancient Boeing 737, operated by a small Afghan airline called Pamir Airways, makes a full circle above Kabul as it gains altitude. Khair Khana is a miniature dun basrelief sculpted into the valley floor. We cross the glaucous orchards and vineyards of Shomali Valley, the birthplace of the grape, and head north over the sawtooth spine of the Hindu Kush.

For tens of millions of years the Eurasian plate and the Gondwanaland supercontinent kept smashing against each other, thrusting and kneading rock like dough to make these mountains. The story of Afghanistan imitates the violent history of its geology: tribes and empires conquering and being vanquished, seizing territory and losing it—year after year, century after century.

Perhaps as a coping mechanism, Afghanistan seems to have developed a kind of a multiple personality disorder. Sandaled men with fruit knives lounge around cucumber stands in Kabul while 60 miles to the north, in Baghlan province, sandaled men with Kalashnikov assault rifles clash over who gets to levy taxes on farmers and set up illegal checkpoints to rob travelers—and 60 miles to the south, in Khost, sandaled men are planting roadside bombs that kill U.S. and Afghan troops. On the way to dine at an upscale restaurant in Kabul, a colleague and I pass women shopping for candy with their toddlers—and then we pass three cordons of armed guards (at least one guard is carrying an M-16 rifle) patrolling the entrance to the eatery. Some restaurant patrons arrive in flak jackets.

From the airplane window I see hairlines where the snowmelt gathers in the mountain creases into rivulets, streams, then gains momentum and flows north, draining into the Amu Darya, the river that marks Afghanistan's northern frontier. This is ancient Bactria. Alexander the Great had spent three years trying to vanquish this land, about which he said this: "Every foot of the ground is like a well of steel, confronting my soldier."

The plane descends over alluvial fans dusted with soft spring grass, over round pockmarks of bomb craters that deface the yarn of dirt roads, and lands smoothly on the airstrip of Mazar-e-Sharif.

A couple of hours later, I drag my duffel bag up the stairs to a second-floor room I have rented for $20 a night in a private house. The courtyard beneath my window is taken up entirely by a neighbor's milch cow. On hot afternoons, the cow sends wafts of hot, wholesome farm smell into my room. At night, it sighs meaningfully in its sleep.

Day 3. Wuima Ut

Have you heard of the flood that laid waste to the village of Wuima Ut? A day of heavy spring rain eased giant sheets of icy crust off the Hindu Kush. The snowmelt ran downhill and funneled into the canal that irrigates the fields and orchards of this small hamlet of a hundred or so sharecroppers and their families. Soon, the turbid water could no longer fit inside the narrow waterway. It pulsated and throbbed, like the heart of an enormous, adrenalized beast. Between 2:30 and 3 p.m., it rose 15 feet and rushed through the grove of pomegranate trees behind Badalsho's house, surged along the concrete walls of his crowded compound, found the gate, and gushed inside.

"There were 10 of us trying to close that gate, 10 grown men," says Badalsho. A lifetime of tending tomato fields has crumpled the skin on his neck and planted sand in the deep furrows behind his gray beard.

"Ten grown men could not stop that water from coming into my house."

Two days before the flood Badalsho had sown his tomato seeds in a field upstream from the village: all gone now. Some of the seeds may be buried in the half-foot of sludge the flood deposited on the floor of his living room, or in the knee-high coat of mud that rings the walls of his bedroom. Maybe Badalsho's tomatoes will unexpectedly sprout from the kitchen walls of Mohammad Nasir, a pomegranate farmer who lives downstream and whose family of eight spent the first two nights after the flood sleeping on soggy mattresses piled over ankle-deep puddles left after the water receded.

Maybe a few tomatoes will grow in what is left of the house of Sayed Hamayun, an unemployed car mechanic with a shy smile. The flood licked away Hamayun's house the way high tide licks away a sand castle on the beach. All that remains are three stumps of former walls and a heap of mud cascading onto what once was the front porch. Twenty families—a fifth of the village—lost their homes in the flood. The rest are not sure their houses will survive. Their walls are made with clay and straw. Scrape them with your fingertip through the muck left by the floodwaters and they give way easily, like frosting. In a few weeks, the villagers said, they may wobble, then crack, then crumble down like cake.

To people who live here, the devastation is biblical. But who cares about sharecroppers living hand to mouth 30 miles east of Mazar-e-Sharif when there is a war on? The Afghan government offered them recovery assistance amounting to a one-time distribution of 190 loaves of bread. In a land where the Taliban is getting stronger by the day, the miniature catastrophe in Wuima Ut, and hundreds like it, go unnoticed by the news cycle.

In Mohammad Nasir's waterlogged bedroom, men discuss their plan for digging out. Who will send their sons to clear the narrow unpaved streets, now glistening in the sun with five or six inches of smooth glop dredged up by the flood. Who will scrape the muck off the trunks of fruit trees to give them a chance to survive. When I ask if the government would send someone to help, the men laugh so hard they have to wipe tears from the sun-worn crinkles around their eyes.

"The government's hungry, the government's thirsty," says one farmer, Kurbai Shah, after the laughter dies down. "The government will just take the money and put it in their pockets."

When was the last time the government offered any help to the people of Wuima Ut?

Kurbai Shah closes his eyes to think.

"Under Daoud." Mohammed Daoud Khan, one of Afghanistan's most successful dictators, was killed in the Saur revolution in 1978.

The ebb and flow of Afghan politics has barely registered in Wuima Ut. Villagers remember the communist regime of President Mohammed Najibullah for the crops destroyed by Soviet aerial bombardment. They remember the Taliban for punishing the men who were not pious enough. The overthrow of the Taliban meant they no longer have to pray five times a day—nothing more. Their life has not become better, or worse. It remains as difficult as it has been for centuries.

Leaving Wuima Ut in an all-wheel drive that periodically stalls in the mud, I notice four villagers dredging the irrigation canal that had steered the flood to the village. Three men in their 30s, hip-deep in water, are trying to hold off the current by pushing against it with a large sheet of reinforced plywood. A much older man, perhaps their father, stands a few paces downstream, raking the bottom with a metal shovel and tossing rocks and sediment onto the shore. The men's clothes are splattered with mud, like everything else in the village: the cows, the donkey carts, the children slipping about in the streets, the little girl carrying fresh cottage cheese on an aluminum tray balanced on her head. The only clean thing I saw in Wuima Ut was a white pigeon.

White pigeons are rare in Afghanistan, but in Balkh province they are a common sight: 10,000 of them famously flock to Mazar-e-Sharif's Blue Mosque, the reputed final resting place of Zoroaster and of Prophet

Mohammed's cousin and son-in-law, Ali. The locals say the 15th-century site is so holy that should a gray pigeon join the flock, it will become completely white in 40 days.

Day 5. **Camp Shahraqi Mawjirin**

The salt-frosted desert outside the settlement curves into the horizon, as though the refugees here needed another reminder that they live on the edge of the earth. I walk out of the camp and head northeast, toward where the world ends.

A hundred or so paces away from the last hut of crumbling mud brick, a colorful, shiny playground rises out of the barren earth, like a twisted joke played on the 145 families dumped in this forlorn wasteland.

Because who needs a playground, asks Fateh Mohammad, his mouth contorted into a warped smile, when there is no food? Who needs a playground when the houses are falling apart?

Who needs these two red and blue metal slides, four swings, two soccer goals, and a seesaw, Fateh Mohammad demands as the smile fades from this man's sun-browned face completely, when the children are dying?

The cemetery is not far from the playground; you find it easily if you follow the curve of the earth along the periphery of the camp.

There are 10 graves. They are unmarked, elongated mounds of clay. Seven belong to children. It is not difficult to tell them apart: They are half the size of the adult graves. They are decorated with rocks, cheap trinkets, rainbows of broken glass bracelets, a shard of a plastic salad bowl. The salt that cakes the desert floor percolates to the surface of the mounds above the dead children, like dry tears.

The one on the southern edge belongs to Fateh Mohammad's son, Amir. He died last winter; he was 2 years old. He had been sick, incessantly coughing the frightening, dark cough of poor children from the slums.

Next to his grave is the grave of Nurkhan, the grandson of Meher

Ahbuddin, the village elder who wears a watch on each wrist. Nurkhan died around the same time as Amir; he was 4. Meher Ahbuddin says the weather killed him. It was a cold winter, so cold that the generator-operated pump froze, and the refugees had to collect ice from frozen puddles on the road and melt it in their pots for drinking.

"We had no warm clothes," Meher Ahbuddin explains. "One morning we woke up, and he did not." Ajabkhan, the grandson of Abdul Samat, a tall man with a tribal tattoo on his right wrist that looks like Tamashek writing, is buried two graves away. Ajabkhan was a year and a half when he died, of some disease no one can explain to me.

The cemetery is marked by a tall, uneven wooden pole flying a green flag, planted there by the refugees. The playground is marked by a large billboard, planted there by U.S. government contractors.

"Title of Project: Creating Livelihood Opportunities for Refugees in North Afghanistan. Project Code: 02 AFR. Component: Play Ground and Safe Play Area." the billboard proclaims in blue letters. "Donor: Bureau of Population, Refugees and Migration (United States of America)."

What the billboard really says is that the international aid that is supposed to help rebuild Afghanistan is tragically failing.

I came here from Mazar-e-Sharif, about 15 miles to the south. Like Afghanistan's capital, Kabul, Mazar-e-Sharif has blossomed in the eight years since my first visit: Internet cafés jostle for space with fancy pizza parlors, old turbaned men sell cell phone scratch cards on street corners, scarlet and pink roses bloom in the medians, and there is electricity most of the time. Today, many Afghan cities are like this.

But much of rural Afghanistan, like Camp Shahraqi Mawjirin, has been frozen in time. Eight years after the U.S.-led invasion pushed the Taliban out of most of the country, child mortality here remains second only to Sierra Leone's. Fourteen Afghan children die every half hour, largely from preventable causes. Two-thirds of Afghans still don't have access to potable water, and slightly more than a quarter of all adults can read and write.

Is there something inevitable, then, about the return of the Taliban to Afghanistan's northern farmlands?

"When there is no work and no money, young people are pushed to theft, to robbery, to joining the Taliban," Abdul Ansari, one of the imams at the Blue Mosque in Mazare-e-Sharif, told me the other day. Partly because NATO and the international donors have focused most of their attention on Afgahnistan's troubled south, and partly because of the extraordinary corruption of the kleptocracy in Kabul, the international recovery effort has barely reached the villages—and the projects that did make it here often came in the form of twisted, absurd donations like the playground in Camp Shahraqi Mawjirin.

The camp is home to 145 Afghan families who, three years ago, heeded President Hamid Karzai's call to return from exile after living in Pakistan for more than 20 years. They were enticed by promises of housing and jobs. The government gave each family a small plot of land in this salt desert—land that will never bear anything but rocks and some sparse blades of gray weeds. The United States donated the playground, a clinic, and a school for boys.

The clinic is a neat concrete building painted pale blue, with a staircase and a ramp, thoughtfully installed for wheelchair-bound patients. (I try to explain the ramp to Meher Ahbuddin, the settlement elder. He stares at me blankly. Who here could ever afford a wheelchair?) The clinic is absolutely bare: There is no medicine, and no medicine cabinets to hold it; there are no chairs, no cots, no desks in the doctors' offices. There are no doctors—just like at the school there are no teachers. White curlicues of peeling paint flake from the ceiling and flutter onto desks and chairs. The classrooms have an eerie feel to them, as though the school were the site of a recent nuclear catastrophe.

"It's like we live in a cemetery," Abdul Samat says, crushing a bit of paint with the toe of his sandal.

The main problem is that there are no jobs, Abdul Samat tells me. The nearest village is about an hour and a half away by foot, and it is almost as poor as the camp. There are some jobs in Mazar-e-Sharif, but the trip to the city is 80 cents and 30 minutes over unpaved roads in a van so crowded that some men end up standing up in the open door, grabbing onto the roof and the windows as the dusty wind worries at the loose tails of their *shalwar kameez*. Few in Camp Shahraqi Mawjirin can afford the ride.

Because there is no work, there is also no food. People bring discarded dry bread from the village, soak it in boiling water, and eat the glop. Boiling the water is tricky, too. There is no firewood, and the women make brittle cooking fires with the dried grass their children gather in the desert.

I think of these children when the villagers offer to bring me tea. As politely as I can, I tell them that I'm not thirsty.

At the entrance to the settlement, I see some men with pushcarts shoveling rock. Meher Ahbuddin says they are trying to build a road.

But to me it looks as though they are working simply not to be idle in the motionless, dead desert. When they spot our car, from a quarter of a mile away, they stop and watch, leaning on their shovels. We are a wonder, an apparition. No one ever comes here in a car.

Day 6. **Kampirak**

O, daughters of Balkh! Your unrivaled beauty is the stuff of legends. One of your own has enchanted Alexander the Great with her pulchritude. And the violence you have suffered under the clay roofs of your Bactrian homes is unspeakable, unspoken, and unpunished.

In late 2001, after helping kick the Taliban out of Northern Afghanistan, two militias allied with the United States raped and plundered their way through your villages. One was the ethnic Uzbek militia of General Abdul Rashid Dostum; the other was made up of ethnic Hazara followers of the warlord Muhammad Mohaqiq. They killed your men, slaughtered and stole your livestock, pillaged your homes, and violated your sisters, mothers, and daughters. Some of them took the time to explain why they had picked you as their victims: because you are Pashtun, the ethnic group that made up most of the Taliban.

They were victorious; they were in the mood to avenge the rapes and massacres Taliban fighters had committed against their own wives, sisters, and daughters. In the evolution of warfare, swords replaced javelins and guns replaced swords—but rape has remained just as efficient a weapon as it was when the Achaemenid armies laid waste to this land 2,600 years ago. You, daughters of Balkh, were the latest targets of the latest revenge cycle that swept through your country. Wheat in your fields has shuddered at the anguished screams of generations of your foremothers.

Eight years ago, four Pashtun women told me of their assailants, three fighters from Dostum's militia, Junbish-e-Milli-e-Islami, who took turns raping them all night. Technically, only one of them, Nazu, was a woman; her daughters were 10, 12, and 14. The youngest, Bibi Amina, was playing with the fringe of the giant red scarf that covered her head and smiling. It seemed to me that she had not understood what had been done to her. The local police chief, an ethnic Tajik, said at the time that his men were too few, and too poorly armed, to hunt down the assailants. He was waiting for reinforcements.

Years passed; the militiamen who ravaged the Pashtun villages in Balkh remained free. Their warlords became government ministers; their lower-ranking commanders received posts in parliament; many of the rank-and-file fighters joined the police and the army. Their victims stopped talking about the crimes they had endured. Rape in Afghanistan carries a mark of unutterable disgrace.

In the same villages I visited years ago, I now find different women grieving quietly, and alone, under their breast-shaped roofs—perfect hemispheres that face the limpid clay sky and virescent fields of wheat. They knead their tragedies into the golden sundials of naan they bake in smoky tandoor ovens in their impoverished courtyards; they weave them into the oil-black braids of their young, beautiful daughters; they immure them into the crumbling house walls they mend with fistfuls of straw and mud. When they do speak of those terrible days after the Taliban fell, they equivocate.

"They touched all the women and the teenage girls," one widow, whose cheeks and forehead are dotted with deep blue marks of tribal tattoos, whispers to me in the corner of her dust-choked house.

"They dragged us out of our homes. Women and girls are ashamed to talk about what happened then," says another, modestly covering her face with a tattered scarf the color of ripe wheat.

"In my father's house they gathered all the women in one room," says the third. Her amber eyes bore through me. "We will never forgive these crimes. Until we die."

In March of 2010, the Afghan government confirmed that it had signed into force the National Stability and Reconciliation Law—and what a tragic misnomer that is. The law effectively amnesties all warlords and fighters responsible for large-scale human rights abuses in the preceding decades. "Their view," says Farid Mutaqi, a human rights worker in Mazar-e-Sharif, "is that justice should be the victim of peace."

You know what this means, daughters of Balkh: This means your rapes will never be punished. Perhaps, in some future iteration of war that has been rolling back and forth through these green wheat fields almost incessantly for millennia, they will be avenged—through some other rapes, of some other women.

Day 7. **Mazar-e-Sharif**

At sunup, a white pigeon flies through the open window of my bathroom and settles, cooing, on the edge of the sink. A good omen, says my young translator, Ramesh. An invitation, I think. I lock the door to my rental room and set out on foot down the somewhat paved sidewalk toward the Blue Mosque.

A local legend says that after Ali, Prophet Mohammed's son-in-law, was struck down by a poison sword during a Ramadan prayer south of Baghdad, his disciples tied his body to the back of a she-camel and sent it east to prevent his enemies from desecrating his remains. (Iraqi Muslims dispute this story, saying that Ali's body never left Iraq, where, they insist, it is buried in the holy Shiite city of Najaf.) After a 1,300-mile trek through modern-day Iraq and Iran, the camel—the story continues—finally collapsed of fatigue and thirst in what today is the blue heart of Mazar-e-Sharif, and Ali was interred here, giving the city its name: "*Mazar-e-sharif*" means "tomb of the saint" in Farsi. The double-domed mosque, tiled in kaleidoscopic patterns of cobalt, ocher, white, and turquoise, went up in the 15th century; 10,000 white pigeons are said to roost among its ewans and columns.

Every evening at 5:30, Karim Ahmad Qasim, the chief muezzin of this mosque, lowers his face to the microphone wired to the minarets' speakers and graces the city with the delicate arpeggios and tremolos of his singing.

Karim Ahmad Qasim is 79 years old; he has been a muezzin at the Blue Mosque forever. Abdul Ansari, an imam there, tells me the muezzin keeps strong by eating sheep fat ("We worry about cholesterol, but he just grows healthier every day") and walking three or four brisk laps around the perimeter of the mosque each day through the neatly trimmed garden perfumed by roses and wild black cherries. He hasn't seen a doctor in years. He has made the hajj twice since 2001. He spends his afternoons in a tiny L-shaped room with whitewashed walls at the base of a minaret, which he enters through a narrow lapiz-blue doorway that is less than four feet high, like a prop from *Alice in Wonderland*.

I met Muezzin Karim in November of 2001, when I came to Mazar-e-Sharif for the first time. I was staying at a hotel across the street from the mosque; each evening, the intricate syncopations and quartertones of his prayer coiled into my unheated, dark, filthy room, filling it with beauty. Think John Coltrane improvising the Koran. I asked to interview the muezzin; he agreed. We sat on damp mattresses beneath the vaulted ceiling of the mosque office and talked about music, and about blending traditional melodies and jazz with freedom unthinkable anywhere in Afghanistan but here, in the most cosmopolitan city in the nation.

"When I sing," the old man told me then, "I do whatever I want."

I asked whether his singing had ever gotten him in trouble with the puritan Taliban. The muezzin flashed a quick, mischievous smile, and winked at me.

"They couldn't tell me how to sing," he said. His small, birdlike body rested against the wall with such tranquility he seemed to glow. I could feel his contentment. "They didn't dare."

For days now I have been trying to leave Mazar-e-Sharif and head east, through Baghlan, to Kunduz and Takhar provinces, to write about the return to those provinces of the Taliban and the Islamic militia of the rebellious warlord Gulbuddin Hekmatyar, and to visit my old friends. But how to get there? German troops who patrol the north are dying almost weekly in clashes with armed gangs; the week before the pigeon alighted on my bathroom sink, someone had kidnapped five Afghan U.N. workers in Baghlan. Trying to get a sense of security on the road I hope to take, I have been hearing from drivers, travelers, journalists, and various security officials about the extent of unrest. Each story promises new dangers, each rumor contradicts the last; the confusion is torturous, exhausting, mind-numbing.

As I guide the protesting white bird from her porcelain roost and out the bathroom window, I recall the sensation I had the time I spoke to the old muezzin all those years ago. Serenity: a scarcity in war zones. I need it now.

At the outer walls of the shrine, I remove my shoes, hand them to a boy in exchange for a small ticket stub, and join hundreds of pilgrims who have come to see the mosque. Men in suits, men in long robes, men in *shalwar kameez*. Women in dresses and headscarves; women in loose-fitting suits. Women in burqas eat potato chips on the steps of the mosque; when they are finished, they lift their burqas like brides' veils to kiss each other goodbye on the cheek, three times. Children kick a pink rubber ball. Toddlers splash in the fountain for ablutions.

I pause to take a picture of a white pigeon. It takes me 10 minutes to get a shot I like. Pilgrims walk slowly around me. No one stares. No one asks why I'm here. We are all barefoot together in a place where pigeons are said to turn white in 40 days.

Then I circle the shrine, find the tiny blue door, and step inside.

The muezzin is reclining against a threadbare pillow beneath an unshaded fluorescent light bulb. The room smells of the cilantro he has brought to work in a plastic bag. An open book lies in front of him: a history of Sufi mystics. The skin on his face is so wrinkled it drapes over his eyelids; his beard is gray and white. I sit down on the mattress next to him and place my right hand, palm open, on my heart: the Afghan gesture of greeting, of thanks. I begin to introduce myself, but he waves me away with a small flick of his wrist. From beneath his droopy skin, he flashes me that boyish, bright smile.

He says:

"Why haven't you visited for nine whole years?"

And I smile back at him, and my mind finally unknots, and I understand that I am crying.

Day 8. **Mazar-e-Sharif**

At 1 a.m., my bed wobbles as though some enormous beast underneath is shifting in its sleep.

Earthquake. Afghanistan's tectonics are active and violent; the country's bellicose history echoes the tremors of its crust. How fitting, I think: This is the night before I hit the road that leads southeast to Baghlan province and then north to Kunduz—the road that has recently seen clashes between NATO and the Taliban, as well as kidnappings, extortions, and robberies by the Taliban, by the antigovernment militia of the warlord Gulbuddin Hekmatyar, and by ordinary—but just as potentially deadly—roadside thugs. Last week, five U.N. workers were kidnapped on this road; four German soldiers died in a firefight with the Taliban, along with three Afghan policemen. NATO airstrikes killed 29 insurgents and wounded 52, according to Afghan police officials.

At 5 a.m., I bid farewell to my hostess, a portly matriarch with a gold stud in her right nostril. She nods back, and as I step off her tiled porch she throws some water in my direction from a red plastic pitcher, for good luck. The fierce-looking Pashtun driver everyone calls Qaqa Satar (*qaqa* means "uncle" in Dari) is wiping the rearview mirror of a hired sedan with the sleeve of his *shalwar kameez*; Ramesh and I pile into the car. We drive off into the giant, tangerine sun quivering on the eastern edge of the pink mountain ridge.

I have been asking about the road since I arrived in Afghanistan. A security officer for a Western relief agency in Kabul told me flat-out not to take it. An Afghan colleague in Kunduz told me the road is safe from 8 a.m. until 2:30 p.m. (why 2:30 and not, say, 3 or 2:15?) and that Taliban fighters kidnap at least one person from the road each night. I spoke with a driver who travels from Mazar-e-Sharif to Kunduz every other day. He dismissed stories of kidnappings, but he told me that armed gangs pretending to be Taliban do set up checkpoints and rob travelers at gunpoint after dark.

His friend elbowed him out of the way to promise me that the road is absolutely safe, no trouble whatsoever. He drummed loudly on the hood of my car and yelled that he could guarantee my safe arrival in Kunduz "100 percent," for $100.

In the end, I stick with Qaqa Satar, who has been driving me since I arrived in Mazar-e-Sharif—but I have no idea what to expect. The sun rises and it is hot. We ride past copper mountains touched with a downy patina of tender spring grass, mostly in silence. The northern mesas of the Hindu Kush are lavender in the morning light.

Mazar-e-Sharif to Samangan

The Afghan countryside has barely changed since my first visit here in 2001. The same tired donkeys with their noses in the blood-red wild poppies. The same shepherds squatting beside outcroppings of ancient rock. The only visible change to the rural landscape are cell phone towers and the repaved two-lane tarmac, which in 2001 and 2002 was so scooped out by decades of aerial bombardment it was barely navigable. The smooth road delights Qaqa Satar, who goes 80 miles per hour, swerving in and out of traffic to pass a slow-moving convoy of heavy Afghan army trucks. Oncoming Mercedes 18-wheelers painted turquoise and fuchsia flash their lights, then honk. If we die on this road, I think, it will be in a head-on collision.

I once drove on this road during a locust invasion. It was in 2002. The uneven pavement was slick with crushed grasshoppers, and their delicate shells shattered against the windshield with a crunch, like potato chips.

Samangan to Pul-e-Khumri

At a roadside market in Samangan we buy two loaves of *nan* for a dollar.

The bread is warm, crusty in the middle where the baker has pressed it into a flower pattern and sprinkled it with thyme and salt. Fog licks at the velvet hills and the gutted hulls of old Soviet tanks. Were they abandoned by the retreating Soviet Army in 1989? Were they the tanks of Ahmad Shah Massoud, the legendary mujaheddin leader, that the Taliban had blown up during his retreat in 1997? Were they Taliban tanks, destroyed in 2001 by U.S. warplanes? Their rusting metal is silent, their tracks are gone, and grass peeks through their turrets.

Pul-e-Khumri to Baghlani Jadid

We are nearing the place where the U.N. workers were kidnapped, the German soldiers and Afghan policemen perished, and NATO planes killed and wounded scores of militants.

But Pul-e-Khumri is used to war. In December 2001, one warlord tricked U.S. forces into believing al Qaeda fighters were hiding in the city so that the Americans launched airstrikes against fighters of a rival militia. Nearly 50 people were killed. A month before my journey, Taliban forces battled with Hekmatyar's men here; 60 people died in the fighting. Pul-e-Khumri betrays no emotion, not grief or elation, as we drive through streets drowning in muck churned up by a recent rain.

Two dozen day laborers in orange vests stab at the mud on a side street with shovels, and about as many Afghan soldiers stand guard around them. The Taliban has threatened to kill anyone who works for the government. The workers are risking their lives for a stretch of paved road, and so are the soldiers.

Some German military trucks pass by, heading south. I cannot see the men inside, but I imagine that they are very young.

Baghlani Jadid to Kunduz

Near an auto body shop (RAFI'S BROTHER'S WORK SHOP, the hand-painted sign proclaims, in English), two men in plainclothes with Kalashnikov rifles are standing in the shade of a poplar tree. Taliban? I ask Qaqa Satar. No, he responds: These are local vigilantes the government has hired to fight the Taliban, to help the overwhelmed police and soldiers.

But they are worse than the Taliban, Qaqa Satar opines. During the day they work for the government; at night, they set up impromptu checkpoints and rob travelers. I make a mental note not to travel here at night.

My cell phone vibrates; it is a message from the security section of an international relief agency in Kabul.

"Ops Room security alert! There is an ANSF-AOG clash in Baghlan province, pul khumri district (150 meters south of Pul Khumri, Kunduz-Mazar junction) please avoid the area."

The German convoy, I think.

"Passed pul-e-khumri an hour ago," I type back. "In kunduz province. Road clear so far. Saw no clash."

"Thanks a lot for informing us, have a safe trip and take care."

On a hillock, a square concrete building of an Afghan army checkpoint. Four or five sentries stand on top of a sandbagged roof, facing every direction. This is a sign of an army surrounded, a fighting force trapped.

Kunduz

"In kunduz city," I text the security guys in Kabul. Ramesh and I high-five. Qaqa Satar smiles for the first time during the trip. We drive slowly through alleyways shaded with poplars and wild black cherries, the familiar busy market street, the kebab shops, and a palatial doctor's office promising WEMENS HELTH.

I am looking for someone: a former Northern Alliance fighter,

Hanon, with whom I shared many front-line cigarettes and rivers of weak, murky tea in 2001 in Takhar province, where he was fighting the Taliban.

Hanon is from Kunduz, but I don't remember the address of his father's house, which I visited more than eight years ago. Nor do I know if he is still around, or alive. I scan the faces of Kunduz men: hard, careworn faces. I have a picture of Hanon, which I whip out at the checkpoint in front of the provincial governor's headquarters; at an unnamed local dive where we stopped for a $3 lunch of fresh lamb, vegetables, and tea; at the office of a local human rights organization. I show Hanon's photo to street vendors, to policemen, to soldiers. Some shake their heads. Others vaguely say they seem to recognize the face, but they are not sure from where or when. With his bushy black beard, his soiled *shalwar kameez,* his brown *paqul* hat, he is more an ideogram than a real man. There are millions of Hanons in this country—bearded, illiterate men in *paqul* hats, thrust into war by Afghanistan's ever-moving tectonics.

Day 10. **Ai Khanum and Dasht-e-Qal'eh**

Above the dung-colored rapids of the Panj River, in the shadow of some stern sedimentary cliffs, sprawls the carefully measured grid of the city Alexander the Great built for his Afghan trophy wife, Roxanne, in 328 B.C. The recordkeepers at the time described Roxanne as the second-most beautiful woman in the world, after Stateira, the wife of the Persian king Darius III.

Little remains of Alexandria Oxiana. Nomad invaders sacked the temples and the main palace in the second century B.C. Front lines washed over the gymnasium and the living quarters during the Soviet invasion. Taliban howitzers pummeled the bathhouse and the citadel. Northern Alliance marksmen used the limestone curlicues of Corinthian columns for target practice.

But you can guess the outlines of a perfectly round theater where wild garlic now sprouts through bits of pottery in a circular field. You can clasp your fingers around a warm shard of red, glazed clay and imagine the pitcher it once completed, full of wine. You can picture, amid the patterned brickwork French archaeologists excavated in the 1960s and then abandoned, girls running down to the river—the Oxus of antiquity—to fetch water in ewers they balance on their heads, and shepherds heading to the jade hills at sunup with their flocks. You can see men and women living and dying anonymously in the city the Afghans poetically call Ai Khanum: Lady Moon.

It is easy to envision all this because on the other side of some abandoned tank berms and trenches lies the silt-rich farmland of Dasht-e-Qal'eh, where people still live this way, nameless and abandoned by everyone—even by time itself.

I haven't been to Dasht-e-Qal'eh in eight years. It could have been 800. It could have been eight days.

The road to the village is still made of mud. Jackknifed farmers still hoe the quilts of their wheat and pea fields with wooden, handheld tools. Boys no older than 10 still holler neighborhood sheep into flocks to take to pasture at dawn. Mahbuhbullah, my friend in whose house of mud and straw I roomed in 2001 and 2002, still spends his days squatting between the furrows of his pumpkin patch.

With the help of some local boys and my half-erased memory, I locate his house at the very end of a long, crooked alley barely wide enough for our sedan. I find Mahbuhbullah where I left him eight years ago: in his field, talking with a neighbor. He rises slowly from the ground on the far edge of the field. He has gained weight. The dimple in his forehead is more pronounced. He walks heavily, squinting at me against the sun: His eyesight, like mine, has gotten worse with age.

Then his face crumbles into that wonderful smile that graced many of my days in Northern Afghanistan at the beginning of this war, his pace quickens, and I am scooped up into a bear hug and rushed into the house, where his wife Nargiz is kissing me on the cheek, three, six, nine, twelve, eighteen times. Photos come out. Children, all grown up, come in. Nargiz is laughing; her voice sounds like a river. She has not aged a bit.

Some things have changed. Najiba, Mahbuhbullah's first wife, lives in a separate house now, in a different part of the village, with her five children. This seems to please Nargiz, who shares Mahbuhbullah's bed. She has borne him five more children since I saw her last. Her youngest son yawns and smiles in my arms. He has his father's smile.

Mahbuhbullah is not smiling. He worries that war will return here. In recent months, the Taliban has begun to encroach on his village. The Islamist militia has taken over three villages to the northeast—the nearest less than an hour away on a dirt road. (So time does exist here, after all—it is needed to determine the proximity of conflict.) Much of Kunduz province, which begins a dozen miles to the west, is under Taliban control. If the Taliban comes to Dasht-e-Qal'eh, Mahbuhbullah worries, NATO and Afghan troops will follow.

There will be fighting. The D30 field gun that now rusts in a highland pasture overlooking the village may once again pummel his fields with 122-millimeter shells. There may be house-to-house searches that will frighten his children and upset his wives. Maybe even air raids, which in Afghanistan have a history of discriminating poorly between civilians and combatants.

Who will protect the good people of Dasht-e-Qal'eh, who trade their vegetables, flour, and rice in the broad market street and bake their own bread each morning, the people who wrap thorn branches around aspen saplings growing near public wells, to keep goats away?

Not the government. The government has done nothing here, Mahbuhbullah spits. Did it bring electricity to the village? No. Paved roads? No. Clean water?

Garbage disposal?

Garbage disposal? Ha!

Mahbuhbullah laughs; the dimple in his fleshy forehead becomes a well.

His bathroom is still a clay cabin in the corner of the yard, with an oblong, putrid hole in the earthen floor over which to squat. He dumps his trash, biodegradable and not, into a hole a few paces away. He buys electricity for about $15 a month from a local entrepreneur named Gul Agha, who at some point realized that waiting for the government was pointless and put in a generator to serve the village of about 6,000 people.

The generator goes on for a few hours at night, on most nights. (When dusk falls, Mahbuhbullah strips two live wires hanging from the ceiling of his living room with a kitchen knife he first wraps in a soiled wash-cloth, and hard-wires a light bulb.)

This could be any of the dozen other villages I have visited in different parts of Northern Afghanistan in the last week and a half: blighted, forsaken, ageless.

We noon on rice with black-eyed peas and the enormous disks of naan Nargiz baked in the morning: a poor man's lunch. Mahbuhbullah used to augment his earnings as a farmer by looting small artifacts from Ai Khanum and fencing them to smugglers, but business has been slow in recent years because the Afghan government has clamped down on the illegal trade of relics. (This is the one way, perhaps, in which Kabul has interfered with the course of life in Dasht-e-Qal'eh.) My friend pulls out of his cupboard a few bits of ancient pottery to show Ramesh and Qaqa Satar.

He places one vessel, the size and shape of a human heart, in my palm. Its umber glaze is still intact. Twenty-three hundred years ago, it probably held perfumed oil. Some woman may have dabbed her neck and wrists with myrrh from this bottle.

"This is a hand grenade," Mahbuhbullah explains to me. "An ancient hand grenade." The explosives went inside, and the fuse, he says, came through this tiny opening, here, at the top. I do not argue. Here, everything seems to be measured in familiar terms of war.

We head to Ai Khanum after lunch: Mahbuhbullah, Ramesh, Qaqa Satar, and Mahbuhbullah's neighbor, Asad. It begins to rain. Sparrows alight from the ruins: fragments of columns whiting among overgrown rectangles of abandoned French excavations, bits of clay pottery glistening amid sheep droppings. Gusty wind carries the dirge of a shepherd's flute. The camel-wool blankets in which the men have wrapped themselves flap like wings.

Suddenly, one of the men spots a snake amid the ruins. It is a rat snake, *Ptyas mucosus,* a harmless constrictor that feeds on small rodents. The men take turns hunting it down, grabbing it by the tail, twirling it around over their heads, then slamming it against the ground, headfirst.

The snake's mouth opens; it tries to writhe out of its captors' grips. The men are grinning at first, but a minute later they no longer smile. They grab the snake, twirl it, smash, repeat, with purpose. There is something primordial about this, a basic kind of hatred.

On a lime-green hilltop, three boys watch some cattle and a dozen recently shorn sheep. They are holding long sticks. The oldest looks 8. I think they have been sitting here for more than 2,000 years.

Day 11. **Kunduz**

"The roads are safe," the police chief of Kunduz province, Gen. M. Razaq Yaqobi, declares categorically. "Day and night."

The map behind his desk suggests otherwise. It is covered in green and red dots. The green dots are police outposts; they fan out from the provincial capital, the city of Kunduz, in concentric circles, thinning out as they approach the edges of the province. The red dots are the forces of the Taliban, al Qaeda, and Gulbuddin Hekmatyar. On Yaqobi's map, red dots line every major road in Kunduz.

"Kunduz city is under government control," the provincial governor, Engineer M. Omer, who goes by his second name and an honorific, elaborates more cautiously an hour later. Shortly after our interview, I lose my cell phone reception. I assume it's a glitch in the network. Later, I learn that the Taliban switches off the local cell phone towers every night. No one can call for help until dawn. They say the Taliban owns the night in Kunduz. It's unclear who owns the day.

"Let's say this is Kunduz," says Ahmadullah Daagh, the editor of the local magazine *Afghanistan Today,* pointing to a copy of his monthly. On the cover, a woman in a blue burqa is buying gold bracelets at a jeweler. Daagh draws invisible circles with his fingers all over the magazine: "Taliban, Taliban, Taliban, Taliban, Taliban."

A tiny area, no larger than a quarter, is left in the center. Daagh points at it: "Government," he says. "What can it do?"

Somewhere inside that dot of impotent government in Kunduz is a man named Meher Ali. I like him right away. He has a nice smile under a graying mustache, kind eyes, and horizontal wrinkles on his forehead to suggest that he spends a lot of time in melancholy.

Meher Ali is the head of the local department of Afghanistan's Ministry of Refugees and Repatriation. All day long, he sits in his crepuscular office in a tired brown suit over a pale blue shirt. Three pink bouquets of plastic flowers on his desk clash with the beige window curtains, which are always drawn. Three crystal candy bowls, one next to each bouquet, stand empty.

There are, by Meher Ali's estimation, 222,000 refugees in this province of 1.2 million people. Last year, he received enough funding to hand out blankets and mattresses to about 400; he distributed those at the onset of winter.

This year, he has received no funding at all.

"They need food. Flour, rice, oil, tea. Medicine. We have nothing to help them with," Meher Ali tells me, showing me the empty palms of his small hands, as if to prove he has nothing.

Some of the refugees have returned from exile in Pakistan, Tajikistan, and Iran after the U.S.-led war began in 2001 but found the lands that once had belonged to them taken by someone else. Others were displaced from their homes by the cycle of ethnic and tribal revenge that followed the fall of the Taliban regime. They have settled in camps, in abandoned villages, in homes they have hastily slapped together with clay and straw on tiny parcels of land the government has given them. Most of the refugees are unemployed.

I imagine the indigence of these refugees easily. In Camp Shahraqi Mawjirin, I have met families whom the Afghan government had dumped in a tract of salty desert, where nothing will ever grow, where there are no jobs, no electricity, no doctors. The refugees told me their children have been dying of cold. I tell this to Meher Ali, and he nods that yes, yes, that, sadly, is quite common. In Kunduz, children of refugees have been dying of cold, too. But he can do nothing about it.

How exactly they survive at all is unclear, Meher Ali says, because no government surveyor, or relief worker, can visit the refugees where they live. Most live in areas that have fallen under Taliban control in recent months: no-go zones for government officials and security forces. Many live just east of the city of Kunduz, in Chardara, where the Taliban infamously hijacked two NATO fuel tankers the previous fall, provoking a U.S. airstrike that killed up to 142 people, mostly civilians. Another village, Gor Teppah, about 10 miles northwest from the provincial capital, is home to some 1,200 refugees—and "about 23 Chechen and Uzbek fighters, foreign fighters from al Qaeda," according to General Yaqobi.

This is no coincidence, Meher Ali says. He believes—and this is a sentiment I have heard from many quarters—that the refugees' desperation, their inconceivable poverty, and their sense of abandonment by the government are prompting them to embrace the Taliban, giving rise to the return of the Islamist militia.

"People come here and say: 'You promised to help us; where is your help?' They call us liars. They say: 'You have betrayed us,'" he says.

"Since last year, we haven't had any contact with them. For all we know, they have joined the Taliban."

Meher Ali raises his palms toward me again: still empty. Behind one of his beige curtains, a trapped fly thrashes against the window glass, drones, thrashes again.

Day 12. **Mazar-e-Sharif**

Friday in Afghanistan: a day of leisure, war and poverty permitting. The more pious families dress up for a trip to the mosque. The less pious pack lunches and drive out of the smoggy tumult of the city for roadside picnics.

I sleep in, until 5:30. Half the house is up, mostly the women, who take turns insisting that I eat: bread, tea, the delightful lamb dish the family's matriarch is already stewing outside in a giant aluminum vat over a fire in a cut-up oil drum. I nibble on the meat and take leave. A young man named Hamidullah, a good friend of Ramesh, has invited me to go hiking in Sholgara.

The last time I was in Sholgara, eight years ago, the city was a front line in the massive turf war between the private armies of two powerful

Afghan warlords, Ustad Atta Mohammed (now the Tajik governor of Balkh province) and Abdul Rashid Dostum (the Uzbek general whom human rights organizations accuse of mass murdering war prisoners, and who keeps falling in and out of favor with the Karzai government).

Combat has ebbed but never ended, and small, locally based detachments of the two militias still clash here from time to time. A few months ago, the local police chief tells me, there were some kidnappings; a Western relief agency's car was ambushed and burned; a group of road workers were shot at.

Hamidullah pouts when I bring this up.

"You are my guest," he says. "Where I am taking you, it is secure."

Mazar-e-Sharif to Sholgara

Afghanistan's blood-drenched history, ancient and recent, rolls past the car windows.

Here is the turnoff to the city of Balkh, where Alexander the Great took his first wife, Roxanne.

Here are the crenelated bulwarks of Qaleh-e-Jangi, a 19th-century castle where Dostum, in 2001, stabled his horses and kept his prisoners. Here, in November 2001, a CIA operative was killed during an uprising of Taliban inmates; the U.S. air raid called in to quash the uprising killed almost 400 prisoners. The air raid also killed Dostum's horses; their cadavers were left to decompose long after the human bodies had been removed. My memory of that smell hits me as we drive by.

Twenty minutes west of Mazar-e-Sharif the paved road ends. Our car kicks up pale dust as we drive alongside the turbid, mocha-colored Balkh River, pregnant with the snowmelt and clay it picks up as it meanders from the Hesar mountain range 100 miles to the south. The river gurgles like the names of the landmarks it scythes through: the Alborz range, the Chishmish Afa hot springs.

Past the Alborz range, the temperature drops 10 degrees and the air clears. In the far distance I see snow where the Hindu Kush tapers into the Turkestan Mountains, with peaks propping up the pale sky at 10,000 and 13,000 feet. The mountains are white, then blue, then gray, then green as they swell toward us.

"I love you, Afghanistan!" Hamidullah exclaims. He is 21.

Sholgara

We pull up to a pedestrian rope bridge sagging over the murky Balkh River, leave the car, and cross the bridge on foot. In a month, after the snowmelt that feeds it is gone, the current will slow down, disgorge the mud into the fields and pastures up north and run clear blue, and men and boys will swim in it on hot summer nights, if there is no fighting.

At a farmhouse on the other side of the river, Hamidullah's cousin and an 8-year-old nephew join us. We will return to this house for a lunch of creamed spinach, rice, fresh vegetables, lamb, and wheaty *nan* served on a *dastarkhan* spread over the carpeted floor, and Qaqa Satar, as he always does when we eat together, will make little lifting motions with his hands, ordering me to eat, eat, take more, because I am too thin, because I eat too little—but, really, because I am his guest and because he wants to show me a good time. So what if his homeland is a war zone?

For now, we begin our hike.

Up a road strewn with chert, then across a few acres of flat farmland. Sparrows skim cotton fields drowned in stagnant water, to soak the hard soil. Most of the fields are empty: The farmers are taking a day off. A snake slips into a ditch in the shadow of some rowan trees drooping with saccharine blossoms.

We hike up a goat path that bisects a hill into a sloping wheat field and an almost vertical lea of cerulean wildflowers I don't recognize. Tortoises—there are scores of them here—shy away into their brown panzers at my footsteps. Below, a dazzling crimson and turquoise cloud moves along the unpaved road: a band of Kuchis, Afghanistan's nomadic herders. The tiny mirrors sewn into the men's skullcaps and the women's enormous, homespun silk scarves sparkle in the sun.

We pass a few houses, where farmers sitting in the sun squint at us without moving their heads and raise their hands only halfway to their faces in the frugal greeting of men who work hard and are rewarded poorly for it: fingers together, the palm facing sideways. Not waving. Waving means more work.

Another hilltop reveals a panorama of Sholgara. To our west, rectangles of jade and olive and pea-green roll over knolls and buttes into a valley. I spot a square patch of red: a poppy field. Qaqa Satar wants to have his photo taken with me and insists that I wear his *paqul* hat for the occasion. Then he points to a clearing between two hills:

"Do you know this place? This is where, after the Soviets left, there was fighting between Jamiat"—the Tajik militia of Burhanuddin Rabbani, Ahmad Shah Massoud, and Ustad Atta Mohammed—and "Gulbuddin Hekmatyar's party, Hezb-e-Islami."

"Hekmatyar," he elaborates, pointing to a low hill to the northwest.

"Rabbani," he points to another hill, to the southwest.

And this one, the one we are standing on now, the one cascading toward a zigzagging, pale ocher road in neat furrows of green wheat?

This one, smiles Qaqa Satar, was anyone's for the taking.

Look at this land from far away.

You will see a country blighted by wars that have swept over these hills like the smooth waves of wind that now roll the unripe wheat ears.

Now look closely.

You will see a turtle peering out from its nest between the stalks of blue wildflowers.

You will see an ant dragging a husk of last year's grain, several times its size, to a crevice between lumps of the dry clay soil.

You will see an old, one-humped she-camel at pasture. (Two-humped Bactrian camels came from here, but they are very rare.) It is Friday for her, too: She is at leisure. Her lips tremble slightly and she pulls a chamomile flower from the ground and chews. She chews slowly, tucking the plant into her mouth with unhurried motions of her tongue, flower by tiny white-and-yellow flower, until the last blossom disappears inside her cleft lips.

Her hide is shedding. She is unsaddled but still weighed down by years of road dust, of carrying who knows what, from who knows where to who knows where. Her cushioned feet shift little: Like the farmers who barely acknowledge our presence—not out of unfriendliness but out of economy—she has learned through a lifetime of labor to move parsimoniously.

Her eyelashes are sparse and hard, like the brush hairs of a wheat ear. The veined bridge of her long nose is velvet-soft and surprisingly hot to the touch, and if you whisper to her for a few minutes in any language, she will allow you to put your nose to hers, and her slanted nostrils will breathe back at you a grassy history of the land she has traveled.

This land—ravaged by never-ending wars; enervated by interminable, grueling labor; but, at this very moment, on this Friday afternoon in April, unwinding—will reflect in her dark, moist, globular eyes.

Day 13. **Sholgara**

There have been so many police chiefs in the district of Sholgara in recent years that the people who live in this granitoid bowl of smooth mountains tapering toward the Balkh River in a mellow polychrome of fields have forgotten to count them. All that anyone can tell you is that Captain Ghawsuddin Tufal has been chief of Sholgara police for five months.

Who knows how long he will last?

The Taliban is not known to operate in Sholgara, but someone claiming to be a member of the Islamist militia has already called Captain Tufal's cell phone twice to threaten to kill him if he doesn't quit. To protect a population of 100,000 he has a police force of 45 men. And three cars. And a sole police station on the edge of downtown Sholgara: a gravel-strewn compound suffocating in the sun where the men, wrapped in impressive bandoliers of 7.62 rounds, stand and squat along low walls all day, swatting at flies, while the chief chain-smokes in his tiny office.

The couches that clutter the room exhale puffs of dust every now and then, as though the captain's lungs and the furniture's upholstery are somehow connected.

Has he mentioned—he inquires between drags—that he receives absolutely no money to pay for gas for the police cars? When someone calls the cops, he pays out of his own pocket. Some villages are 30 miles away from the police station. Captain Tufal's monthly paycheck is $400; a gallon of gas costs about $3.60.

The 120 villages in his charge are a dizzying kaleidoscope of ethnicities, political alliances, family and village feuds so old that the sides cannot quite remember how they started. There is a lot of bad blood here; there is a lot of spilled blood. In the last three decades, everyone has fought everyone in Sholgara: The mujaheddin fought the Soviets; the Tajiks fought the Uzbeks; the Hazaras fought the Pashtuns; the Taliban fought the Northern Alliance; various Northern Alliance warlords fought each other.

The fighting continues today: A few months before my visit, in the riverside village of Siaub, one former anti-Taliban warlord killed another. Provincial police drove down from Mazar-e-Sharif to arrest him; five days later, the prosecutors set him free.

"Let's put it this way: He has powerful supporters," Captain Tufal says, tweezing another cheap Korean cigarette out of the pack. "If I were to arrest him, I wouldn't last a day. This is Afghanistan, not America."

The people of Sholgara don't call the cops very often. Once they called Captain Tufal when they found a cache of rocket-propelled grenades hidden under some crumbs of dry clay by an old T-54 tank that sits upside-down on the unpaved main road, the words "People of Sholgara, Vote for Abdullah!" scrawled in black spray paint, in Dari, across its corroded hull.

Another time, some men called when they stumbled upon four 122-millimeter rounds wired together to form a powerful, remote-controlled roadside bomb, farther south on the same road. The captain doesn't know who put the explosives there: maybe a warlord trying to kill a rival, or a villager seeking revenge for some century-old offense.

Generally, though, people here don't look to police for security. Anyone here will tell you: They don't trust the police. And why should they? En route from Sholgara to Mazar-e-Sharif today I watch a policeman at a checkpoint demand a bribe from a pickup truck. A camel and some burlap sacks are tied to the truck bed with rope.

"Too little," the officer tells the Uzbek driver offering, through a rolled-down cab window, a soiled, sweatdrenched green bank note: 10 afghanis, or about 22 cents. A line forms. Men stuck behind the camel truck relax the grip of their steering wheels and rummage in their pockets for bills.

At this checkpoint, in the middle of a road that could at any moment be besieged by bandits, by Taliban fighters, by kidnapping gangs, Afghanistan's centralized government doesn't offer protection to these men. Instead, the men require protection from it. No wonder they cling to the traditional feudal semi-anarchy of fortified villages, and erect the thick mud and straw walls of their family compounds patiently, by hand. They know: in the end, these will be the only walls that will matter.

Less than a mile away from the Sholgara police station, a small, 60-year-old castle presides over 15 acres of farmland that belong to two brothers. The outer walls are recently painted ocher; at first, I think the two towers and the primitive battlements are a stylization.

No, no, the owners assure me, and show me the four-foot-thick walls and the castellations that provide a 360-degree view of the valley. "Our grandfather built this, for fighting. For defending ourselves so that our houses are not looted and our women are not raped. This is real, it can be used very efficiently, you see?"

"From whom are you defending yourselves?" I ask.

The farmers study me for a moment, trying to discern whether I am being deliberately obtuse.

Then, one of the men shrugs, and they say, in unison:

"Everyone."

Day 15. **Mazar-e-Sharif**

Before it dead-ends in a crowded burst of kiosks, pilgrims, and taxicabs at the northern gate of the Blue Mosque, Dasht-e-Shor Street is a motley procession of businesses that constellate by type.

First come the auto body shops, with gauges and hoses and pipes protruding from dark, sooty metal shipping containers. Then the welders, displaying heavy iron gates painted blue and green to ward off evil spirits. Then the bicycle dealers, decked out with rows of well-worn bikes and wheelbarrows (here the street is interrupted by a soccer field behind the wrecked wall of a bombed-out building); then a few small rice pilau and kebab stalls; and finally, a long white-and-blue stretch of pharmacies.

Somewhere between the welders and the bike dealers, I buy a small box of pomegranate juice from Mahdi.

Mahdi is 11 years old. He has been running the soft drinks stall on Dasht-e-Shor for his uncle since he was 7. At first, the work was part-time, but after he graduated 4th grade he quit school to become a full-time street vendor.

Mahdi rolls up the metal blinds of the shop at 6:30 in the morning; he closes at 7 or 8 p.m. The uncle is usually there to help open and lock up the store, but generally, Mahdi is on his own. How much does he earn for his work? I ask. Mahdi counts my change and juts out his chin in proud indignation.

"He is my uncle!" the boy says. "It would be totally embarrassing to take money from him."

The child mortality rate in Afghanistan is the second highest in the world. More than 2 million Afghan children are orphans. Children are also the casualties of the war over Afghanistan's modernization: The weekend before I met Mahdi, someone had pumped poison gas into two schools for girls in Kunduz, poisoning scores of students.

Despite the billions of international aid dollars funneled into Afghanistan since 2001, the country is weighed down by crushing poverty—a burden that falls heavily on children. The United Nations estimates that one-third of Afghanistan's children under 14 work. Drive out of any city in any direction, and you will see children as young as 7 herding livestock, tilling fields, leveling dirt roads. Peek inside the shops of Dasht-e-Shor Street: Half of the workforce on this grimy boulevard appears to be children. There are child welders, child carpenters, child auto mechanics, child haulers of bags of cement, child shredders of carrots for someone else's pilau.

There are no child pharmacists. A child cannot be trusted with something so delicate as medicine. Especially if he hasn't finished elementary school.

Walk south on Dasht-e-Shor, toward the cyanic mosque. Several blocks before the mosque, take a right on Mandawi Street, toward the main bazaar, and if you are in the mood, pick up some cottage cheese from Hasan. He is the kid in the canary yellow T-shirt emblazoned with the words TOM AND JERRY and AIR HERO COME. He buys his cottage cheese from a wholesaler down the street and sells it at a very slight markup that will set you back a penny or two.

Hasan says he is 10; from the distance of a few feet, he looks about 6. But look at his face. Those worry wrinkles across his forehead. That skeptical down-curve of his mouth. Those eyes, suspicious of life. It is the face of an old man, a man who has already seen everything and knows that no more is coming.

While Hasan and I chat, a crowd of boys surrounds us. One sells tomatoes, another wild garlic; a third sells toys for children whose parents can afford to buy toys—children who don't have to work in the street all day. Although these children work, too, in the homes of their parents: doing the dishes and the laundry, preparing and serving breakfast and dinner, serving innumerable cups of tea to their parents' guests and cleaning up afterward, even if it means they have to stay awake up till midnight on a school night. They eat leftovers of their fathers' dinners. Few eat meat.

Amin, his broad face discolored in blotches by malnutrition, comes pushing his beat-up wheelbarrow: For 20 cents he will follow you around the market and trundle your purchases to your car. If the car is far away, he will charge 40 cents.

I ask Amin how old he is. He doesn't know.

The boys don't chatter the way kids usually do, don't push each other out of the way. They listen to each other talk, then offer their reserved, monosyllabic opinions about street work.

"Porter work pays better than selling plastic bags," one opines.

"You'd better move your wheelbarrow closer to the cheese row: You'll get more customers," another advises Hasan.

Businesslike. Adult-like. In the evening, when purple and red rhombi of boys' kites cut through the smog colored orange by the sunset, none of the kites will be theirs. Theirs will be the kiosks to push through the streets and lock up, the wheelbarrows to put away, the juice stalls to shutter, the money to bring home.

I bid the boys farewell, and they nod. They don't like to waste words.

I am 20 paces away, and someone calls: "Bye, auntie."

A block down Mandawi Street, across the black gutter from where men and boys sell little hot suns of fresh bread, two boys who look like brothers squat at the edge of an oblong heap of rotting trash. They don't seem to notice anyone else. The older picks out of the fetid mess two strings of green onions and brushes off the more decomposed parts with his fingers. He hands one of the onion shoots to the younger boy, and they eat.

Day 16. Oqa

The wooden loom takes up the whole room, clay wall to clay wall, south to north. In the southern end of the room, two women sit crosslegged on top of the first few inches of the carpet they started weaving this month.

Fine clay dust dances in the light that seeps into the room through the entryway, a woozy approximation of a rectangle. There is no door. There is no roof, just some dry desert scrub brush over unfinished wooden rafters. There is no glass in the windows the size and the shape of a sheep's head. There are only the coarse, undyed wefts stretched tautly over the loom; the maroon, beige, and black warp threads; the women's fingers that knot the warps over the wefts; and the small, black scythes the women use to cut the warp thread after each tiny knot has been fastened.

Then they fasten the next knot.

The scythes go: Thk. Thk. Thk.

It takes six months to weave a carpet because the women can only weave from 8 until 11 in the morning, and then from 1 until 5 in the afternoon. Before 8, they have to bake bread in the clay ovens that stand outside and boil eggs laid by the emaciated chickens that wander into the room to balance on loom beams. From 11 to 1, they must cook rice for lunch. After 5, they must cook rice for dinner. The diet has not changed for years, maybe centuries. In the fall, the women's husbands will kill some chickens and hunt hare and gray fox in the infertile desert, and the women will cook some poultry and meat.

Thk. Thk. Thk.

This carpet will be six feet by 18 feet, and in the West, it will sell for $5,000 or more. The two weavers have never seen this kind of money. When they are finished, their husbands will take the carpet to a dealer in Mazar-e-Sharif—first, a three-hour trek by donkey to the nearest town; after that two hours by taxi—who will buy it for $150, plus wool for the next rug.

"The shopkeeper keeps half the money," complains Chareh, the husband of one of the weavers. The shopkeeper keeps much more than that, I think to myself. But what's the point of saying this to Chareh? I say nothing.

Under the fingers of the women—and one day, under the faraway feet of some unknown patron who will pick out this carpet to grace a distant living room floor—small octagonal flowers with ogival petals bloom in frames of brown and beige rhombi over a field of deep maroon. Each flower is a thousand knots.

Thk. Thk. Thk.

Each knot traps the omnipresent dust, the hot sun that heats up the room like one of the clay tandoors the women use to bake bread in the morning.

It traps the dreadful cough of the small children who sometimes sleep in the two cloth cradles mounted to the walls above the loom. The small, perpetually sick children who sometimes die in these two cradles: because winters here are cold and there are no doors and no glass in the window, and the roof sponges and seeps cold rainwater onto the cribs, and the nearest doctor is three hours away by donkey (but even that only in the summer, because there is no road out of Oqa, only clay desert, and in the winter, when it is so cold that children die from sickness, rain and snow make the clay impassable, even by donkey).

Last winter, little Siaqol died like that. He was 3 months old.

Thk.

Forty families live in Oqa, a village on a hilltop that protrudes slightly from the gray desert. There is no farmland, and no livestock. Most of the women weave carpets. Most of the men collect dry desert brush, burn it into coal, and sell that in Mazar-e-Sharif for $4 a bag. A four-day trip to the desert will yield four or five bags of coal. The men mount the bags on camels and take them to the town where there are taxis. The taxis charge $1 per bag.

Qaqa Satar brought me to Oqa; in the fall, he often comes here to hunt fox. He said it was a place I needed to see. To find Oqa, you drive through the desert. At first a dirt road weaves through minefields, which some international demining agency has thoughtfully marked with clusters of rocks painted red. Then the road ends, and there is just silvery scrub tufting a clay expanse. There is no road to Oqa because no one in Oqa has a car. From a distance, because of diffraction, the village looks like a city of skyscrapers. The villagers' dozen camels look like dragons floating on air.

Qaqa Satar has heard that a thousand years ago, or maybe more, Oqa men ruled the desert on stealthy camels that flew like the wind, conquering and sacking castles all over northern Balkh. He thinks it might be true. People from Oqa had told him this, and their ancestors before them had told them.

Sometimes the women weave camels and dragons into their carpets.

Thk. Thk. Thk.

The women don't want to talk to me. One is hiding behind a soiled white burqa. The other interrupts her weaving to assess me, an alien presence over her loom. The room is dim; the woman's pupils are very small. I have seen these pupils before, in the eyes of narcotics addicts. With no doctor around, the villagers use the traditional remedy for every kind of ache, the local panacea: opium. Opium eases pain, stupefies hunger. At night, the villagers give it to their children to chew, to ease them into sleep.

Opium helps the women focus on the ogival petals and the acute angles of the rhombi.

Thk, thk, thk.

What has changed in Oqa in recent years, I ask Baba Nazar, the local elder who says he is 70 years old.

Nothing, he says.

He thinks about it.

At first we had to travel to Mazar-e-Sharif by donkey or camel, and then cars appeared in the nearest town.

How long ago was that?

Thirty years? he guesses.

Chareh interjects: Three years ago the government came here in trucks and brought a generator. The generator is easy to find. It is inside the only building with sharp corners and straight walls.

It is a 23-horsepower generator, made in China by Shandong Laidong Engine Co., Ltd. It is not connected to the short power line the government has stretched the length of the village on poles. Nor is the power line connected to any of the houses, or street lamps, or any electric outputs anywhere.

When the generator first arrived, the villagers ran it at night to see how much it would cost to operate it. After two nights, the fuel ran out. The men figured that each family would need to pay 20 cents per night for gas. Chareh laughs. No one here has this kind of money. At $75 a carpet every six months, the weavers earn 40 cents a day. The villagers have not turned on the generator since.

But there is hope from foreign aid. One time, last year, two Britons came every day for 20 days by car and filmed something. Then they left; no one can quite tell me who they were. And last month, a group of doctors showed up in Oqa and asked if there were any opium addicts who needed treatment. Three villagers went with the doctors: two women and one man.

They took them to a hospital in Mazar-e-Sharif, to make them healthy, Chareh says. They will come back in a month or so, Baba Nazar adds. The doctors will bring them back, corrects another villager. The doctors came in big shining trucks: Of course they will bring them back, and pay them money, says another.

The men tell the stories of these foreign visitors as though they have already appropriated these accounts into the oral library of village yarns, full of legends of weavers who wove sun into the sky, and of thousand-strong armies of Oqa men who conquered distant castles on the backs of winged camels.

As though the foreigners and the hope they bring will fade into the woolen warp thread and become, just like the other sagas of the past, something the Oqa women might one day weave into their knotted carpets.

Thk, thk, thk, go the scythes over the loom.

Day 18. Mazar-e-Sharif

At dusk, the woman of the house kneels on the edge of the tandoor built into the cement floor in the corner of her yard, slips her hand into a sleeve ripped off years ago from some old jacket, reaches in, and pulls.

Nothing. The loaf of *nan* is stuck; the clay oven refuses to release it. She straightens up, pulling her hand away, and hollers for one of the handful of grandchildren in her twilit yard to fetch a long knife from the kitchen. The heat from the coals has colored her full face the shade of a ripe orange. She throws back her head, takes a swig from a tall plastic bottle in which a chunk of ice has begun to melt, wipes her mouth with the back of her hand, spots me watching her, and laughs.

My hostess has 13 children. Since I came to Mazar-e-Sharif, I have been the 14th.

Every morning, after I pull on my shoes outside her front door, she throws water in my direction from a red plastic pitcher. A protective charm. The woman knows: This war has no front lines. Any highway or dirt road or city street or courtyard can become a battle zone at the clang of a bullet slipping into the breech of a Kalashnikov. The Taliban is nowhere and everywhere. One day, insurgents wearing police uniforms set up a roadblock near a rotary I often take and searched passing cars for government employees and Afghan civilians working for NATO. A foreign journalist would have been a prize.

Who knows whether, one morning, the Taliban won't set up a check-point down the street?

If the Islamist militia finds out my hostess has been sheltering an American, the punishment will be severe. Unutterable. (That's why I will not publish the woman's name.) But she is a risk-taker. In 1997, when Hazaras and Uzbeks launched an ethnic cleansing campaign against Pashtuns in Mazar-e-Sharif, she provided sanctuary to a Pashtun family. In 1998, when the Taliban slaughtered and maimed Hazaras, she took in Hazara neighbors.

I know how these people felt inside the mortared walls of my hostess's compound.

Safe.

At home.

Mothered.

During the day, I keep the door to my room open because I know people will be filing in and out anyway, usually without knocking. That's how life happens in this family of 24 (or 27, the matriarch is not sure). Someone will come by to bring me a thermos of fresh green tea. A china saucer of green raisins, sometimes with tiny brown teardrops of almonds mixed in. A pewter tray with some apples, and a paring knife.

One of the woman's nine sons will stop by to see if I need anything else, and if I am feeling well. Another will borrow some stationery. The 8-year-old granddaughter will run in to give me a quick, firm hug, and then run off to the kitchen, where the women are always cooking something good in giant pressure cookers. The 2-year-old granddaughter, the baby of the family who calls me auntie, will stop by to raid the pistachios I keep on the magazine table.

One morning the grandchildren ambush me as I am headed out the door and spray me with men's deodorant, all over my clothes and heads-carf. They want me to smell extra nice out there, in the hostile and un-predictable world beyond their grandmother's protective walls.

Sometimes the matron herself comes in and sits on the couch her sons thoughtfully brought up to my room the day I arrived. She fans herself with the free end of her gauze scarf and complains about the heat. About the housework that has consumed her 50-something years. (She does not know exactly how many. Few Afghans keep track of their age—who wants to count the seasons of privation?)

She complains about the war that has plundered her country during most of these years.

She talks in Dari, a language I do not speak. But I know what she is saying. An Afghan woman's lot, like war, requires no translation.

Each afternoon, I stumble into the house distraught after another day of reporting. Villagers abandoned by the world to survive or perish in the violence that has been wracking Afghanistan since time immemorial. The slow caving in of the mud-brick compounds whose owners were either fortunate enough to have run away from war—or unfortunate enough to have been killed in it. Refugees who survive on stale bread soaked in boiling water. Opiated women handweaving priceless carpets for 40 cents a day. Children as young as 7 forced into hard labor by their indigent parents.

If she could, my hostess would take in all these children, too.

She would let them fly kites on the flat cement roof of her house. She would mix up their names the way she mixes up the names of her children and grandchildren. (She'll go through five or six names before getting to the one she is looking for. Mothers do that.) They would sleep in the room where I am staying now, with its second-floor view of the labyrinthine sprawl of mud-brick and poured concrete rooftops and courtyards that recede toward the gunmetal knuckles of the northern Hindu Kush. Round loaves of cow manure, for cooking fuel, dry on the rooftops.

She would feed these children fresh disks of whole wheat *nan* from her hot clay oven.

The *nan* tastes like love.

I will never forget its taste.

A granddaughter—the one who likes to run into my room for a quick hug and a kiss—arrives at the tandoor with a kitchen knife. The woman draws a sharp breath, as though before a deep dive, and leans back into the oven. At knifepoint, the oven surrenders; the bread loaf emerges crusty underneath and soft and ocher on the top. The color of the land that produced it.

She dabs the hot *nan* with some water from an aluminum basin, to keep it moist, tosses it onto a cut of folded, clean cotton cloth, and reaches into the tandoor again. More loaves come out. Night has sprinkled stars into the high Afghan sky, the rice pilau is seething in the pressure cooker in the kitchen, and it is almost time for dinner.

Day 19. **Naubad and Umakoi**

On moonless nights, after the agony of a fuchsia and orange desert sunset fades to complete blackness, U.S. helicopters airlift Taliban fighters from Kandahar and Helmand to highly secretive drop areas on the sedimentary planes of Northern Afghanistan.

Qaqa Satar, my opinionated driver from Mazar-e-Sharif, believes this. My host in Kabul, a shoe salesman, believes this. His daughter's fiancé, a freelance radio journalist, believes this, as does my old friend Mahbuhbullah in Dasht-e-Qaleh, and the head of the Afghanistan Independent Human Rights Commission in Kunduz, and the turbaned elder of Naubad and Umakoi, two farming villages just outside the ancient, limestone walls of Balkh, their porous dry clay pale through the fields of unripe wheat like the bones of some prehistoric dragon.

Do not rush to dismiss this far-fetched conspiracy theory as the unenlightened jabber of uneducated men. Consider it, instead, a byproduct of the grotesque failure by international donors and NATO to improve life here, despite the billions of dollars and tens of thousands of troops pumped into this country since the war began on Oct. 7, 2001.

Think of it this way: The notion of an unholy, clandestine partnership between the United States and the Islamist militia it has been trying, unsuccessfully, to defeat for eight and a half years is the only plausible explanation of a reality these Afghans find all but unbelievable—that the Taliban is getting stronger. That for most people here, life is not changing for the better.

Eighty percent of Afghans today live in the same exact landscape Alexander the Great must have beheld when he sacked Balkh in 327 B.C., and Genghis Khan when he sacked it again in 1221: walls of straw and mud, half gnawed away by weather and age; hand-sown fields tilled by doubled-over farmers in unbleached robes with knobbly, wooden tools. Most have no electricity. No clean water. No paved roads. No doctors nearby.

Naubad and Umakoi are like that. There, Ajab Khan, a turbaned elder in once-tasseled slip-ons that now are more mud than leather, demands that I explain to him why, despite the alphabet soup of relief agencies that operate in Afghanistan, despite the cutting-edge military technology that allows U.S. planes soaring invisibly high to precision-bomb tiny targets on the ground, despite cell phone towers that have sprung up all over the country, his people still live in the 11th century (if the 11th century had limited access to cell phones).

"The Taliban levied taxes on everyone," Ajab Khan says, "but"—he holds up a gnarled finger for effect—"there was order, there was security. There was no corruption. No theft."

I hear the same refrain from Sayed Karim Talash, the head of the Kunduz office of the Afghanistan Independent Human Rights Commission. I ask him what precipitated the return of the Taliban to parts of Northern Afghanistan that, in 2001 and 2002, seemed relieved to be rid of the Islamist movement's unforgiving rule.

He replies, "The Taliban had a fair, unbiased justice system. People's problems were solved in less time. The Taliban helped the needy. They didn't allow crime."

I hear it, also, from Qaqa Satar—except the driver is reminiscing about life under the Soviet-backed rule of President Mohammed Najibullah instead of the Taliban.

"The Russians cared for the people," he tells me. We are driving to Mazar-e-Sharif after slogging through a camp called Mawjir Kishlak, a constellation of dugouts, tents, and clay huts some 1,000 former refugees slapped together by hand after returning from exile in Pakistan two years ago. From each tent, each dugout, hands thrust at me wads of prescriptions the refugees cannot afford to fill. Doctors' orders they cannot afford to follow. Filthy infants they cannot afford to clothe.

This never would have happened when the communists were in charge, Qaqa Satar assures me, shaking his head.

"People were happy," he says.

Never mind that the Taliban publicly maimed and executed people for misdemeanors and officially excluded women from public life.

Or that Soviet troops killed upward of a million Afghans, deliberately bombing hospitals, razing entire villages, and scattering bomblets disguised as children's toys.

The men I speak to profess no recollection of any such crimes.

"Sure, the Taliban didn't allow women to go out—but the security was good," says Talash.

"The Soviets punished very few people, and only those who deserved it," Qaqa Satar retorts.

It occurs to me that perhaps they need this selective memory loss, this nostalgia that erases and smoothes out the impressions of past iniquities. In a land where history is a progression of savageries inflicted by men with everevolving weapons upon the same mud-brick landscape, a sanguine recollection of the past allows for the belief that life has been better.

It allows for the chance that one day, life will be good again.

Day 20. **Mawjir Kishlak**

Homesickness.

Dictionaries define it as the longing for home during a period of absence. There must be, then, a separate term for the pining of the 1,300 people who have settled in Mawjir Kishlak. Their homesickness is without a specific object or duration; it is metaphysical and infinite. Their period of absence began before most of them were born.

Who knows when it will end?

The two wind-beaten knolls of Mawjir Kishlak—"Immigrant Village" in Dari—rise out of the clay road like the twin humps of a Bactrian camel. Children in bright dresses eddy around the dwellings that saddle the hillocks. Most of the children are barefoot. Their hair and voices are thick with dust. None of them seem to know their exact age. But their parents can tell you in which refugee camp they were born.

Most were born in Jalozai Refugee Camp, near Peshawar, Pakistan, where the 225 families that now squat in Mawjir Kishlak lived after fleeing the Soviet invasion of Afghanistan 28 years ago.

Some were born in Sholgara, in a field designated for buzkashi, the Afghan national sport that involves several horsemen and a beheaded goat. The buzkashi field was where the Afghan Ministry for Refugees and Repatriation first dumped the families when they returned to their homeland two years ago.

The littlest ones were born here, in Mawjir Kishlak, where the ministry's officials moved the families when the buzkashi season started. The ministry promised the refugees that Mawjir Kishlak was their final destination. That this land was in government possession and the government was allocating it to them. That finally, they were home.

When word of this reached Malim Salam in his large family house in Kishlak Qadim, two miles away, he was surprised.

Malim Salam spreads a piece of paper on the carpet of his large living room. The paper shows a map and some official-looking stamps. It is a deed to the hills of Mawjir Kishlak. His father owned the land before him, and his father's father owned it before that. It is the pasturage of his sheep and goats. The government has never asked Malim Salam for permission to put any refugees on this land.

"I respect these people; I have nothing against them," Malim Salam tells me. "I respect their human rights and I respect the government, so I have not kicked them out by force. But they have usurped my land."

Misallocation of land has plagued the return of refugees to Afghanistan. Many refugees end up on land like the stretch of infertile, salt desert in Camp Shahraqi Mawjirin, with no access to jobs or health care or schools for the children. Many others, like the families in Mawjir Kishlak, are placed on contested or private land. People in Mawjir Kishlak, incidentally, have no access to health care or schools, either. The nearest water source is the Balkh River, a muddy mountain runoff that gurgles through a valley past Malim Salam's house.

The conflict over Mawjir Kishlak is all the more contentious be-cause the landowner is an ethnic Uzbek, and the returnees are Baluch, a Pashto-speaking people. Northern Afghanistan is steeped in the blood Uzbek and Pashtun militias have spilled over more than a century of fighting with each other.

April is ending; it is time to take livestock to pasture. Malim Salam wants his grazing land back. He filed a petition to the government, ask-ing that the refugees be removed. He says he has heard nothing back.

"I'm not a powerful man. I am not against the government. I am not a warlord. I want to solve my problem legally," he says, pushing the deed toward me again across the black-and-red crystal pattern of his carpet.

But the squatters' elder, Mullah Ghulam Rasul, says that the fami-lies are not leaving. That the government has put them on this land and therefore it is rightfully theirs. That vagrancy has exhausted his small flock. He is a beautiful, tall man with an aquiline nose and ember-like eyes. He looks three decades older than his 54 years. A homesick year counts for two.

I don't know the age of Bibi Rangina, who lets her wild gray hair hang unbraided under a large black scarf. She looks to be 100.

"They should either give us land, or bury us all in it," she croaks, and spits.

Last year, the settlers began to fortify their encampment. Among the weathered donated tents bearing sky blue UNHCR stamps, they built single-room huts out of clay. They clawed caves out of the face of the hill and roofed them with straw and sticks. They spread colorful, threadbare kilims inside and nailed wooden hooks into walls to hang handwoven cradles for their infants. Their dwellings began to take on the appear-ance of home.

Like the Little Prince, who started each day by pulling baobab sprouts out of his tiny planet, the women of Mawjir Kishlak begin each day by sweeping out snakes and frogs that have crawled into their huts and caves overnight.

And then, they keep sweeping. All day. Until their arms go numb. Until the kilims are impeccably, painfully, surreally clean. Until they can almost forget that clumps of dry earth shake loose out of the walls each time someone walks by. Until they can almost believe that they are home.

Until night seeps into the unlit camp in streaks of dusty ultramarine and umber, and white flashes of dry lightning flare over the twin humps of Mawjir Kishlak, and it is time to put another homeless, homesick day to bed.

Day 21. **Mazar-e-Sharif**

By the time the government-run Mazar Civil Hospital finally accepted Nadia four days ago, the 22-month-old girl had been unable to hold down any food for eight months. She couldn't walk. She couldn't stand.

Now she lies motionless, sweating on top of a cruddy synthetic blanket in 90-degree heat, with an IV catheter sticking out of her limp right foot. The catheter is hooked up to nothing.

The diagnosis on the handwritten chart Nadia's grandmother has tucked behind some clothes tied into a filthy checkered scarf reads: Diarrhea. Dehydration. Malnutrition. Pneumonia.

The same diagnosis is scribbled on the chart of the 22-day-old Khurzadeh, who passes in and out of consciousness next to a plastic bag holding two cucumbers, his mother's beggarly dinner.

And on the chart of the 3-month-old Naqibullah, he of the thumb-thin legs and the horrid, scratching cough; he whose moonfaced mother spends her days rocking him in her arms—because what else can she do? Her breasts are barren from too many children and too little food.

She cannot afford to buy most of the medicine the doctors here have prescribed. Love and oscillation is all she can offer.

The hospital is foul-smelling and grimy. The floor has not been washed for days. A piece of old gauze hard with black dried blood lies in the hallway. But the children who are here are the lucky ones. In most of rural Afghanistan, sick children just die. Oxfam, the British relief agency, reports that the mortality rate for Afghan children under 5 is 257 out of 1,000.

In a country where policemen adorn their stations with rams' horns to block jinxes, taking a sick child to the hospital is usually the last resort. Government hospitals and clinics are free, but travel is too expensive, or too distant. Few parents recognize the symptoms of disease. The mothers who squat over their children at the pediatric ward had waited for weeks, even months, before they decided to come here. Abdul Rauf Furukh, the chief doctor of the pediatric ward, says two out of every 100 children arrive in his care too late to be saved. That number seems low, given the circumstances.

With a piece of coal, Sharifa has drawn a black vertical line on the forehead of her 5-month-old son, Hasan, to ward off the evil eye. She also has stitched a special prayer—written for her on a piece of paper by a mullah at her mosque—into a square of brown cloth, pinned that cloth and some beads to a white cotton sheet, and wound the sheet tightly around Hasan. Hasan was born prematurely; his twin brother died at birth, before Sharifa had a chance to name him.

Sharifa says Hasan has always been sick.

"Even with the doctors and the mullah, he is not well," Sharifa sighs.

The same four words—diarrhea, pneumonia, dehydration, and malnutrition—are written in Hasan's chart. But who is to say for sure that the diagnosis is correct?

"Our diagnostic system is antiquated," says Dr. Furukh. "It has not been updated in 50 years."

Across the aisle from Hasan, two emaciated toddlers share a rusty metal cot by the window, next to the cardboard box inscribed, in English, with the word BIOHAZARD; three used syringes stick out of the top of the box. There are not enough cots in the 120-bed pediatric ward for each patient to have one to himself. The boys' mothers sleep in this cot, too: The ward has only 15 nurses, and relatives have to stay by their children at all times.

I ask the women how the four of them fit on the same bed at night. They don't seem to understand the question. Their children got admitted to the hospital. Maybe they will get better. Who are these mothers to complain?

At one point during the winter, when the annual pneumonia epi-

318 / WAITING FOR THE TALIBAN

demic spread through Northern Afghanistan, the ward had three, even four children—and their mothers—to a cot.

As the desert air outside the hospital windows pulsates in the heat, Dr. Furukh prepares for another annual epidemic: dysentery. Children will ingest infection with river water (only a third of Afghans has access to clean drinking water) and lick it off their fingers at family meals; they will pass bacteria to each other at night, on the sweaty mattresses they share with their siblings.

Sick children at the hospital will have to double and triple up on beds again. Doctors will have to stop admitting new patients.

It was winter, pneumonia time, when the hospital turned Nadia away.

"They said there was no room, no medicine," says Nadia's grand-mother, Safia. "Eight days ago, they finally accepted us."

Flies land on Nadia's face. Her eyes are open, unfocused, unseeing. Her treatment at the hospital consists of some IV fluid and milk formula, which she still does not hold down. The doctors also have prescribed Nadia antibiotics and antidiarrheal drugs. But the prescriptions add up to almost $150 worth of medicine to fill at the bazaar. Nadia's mother is recovering from giving birth to another baby, her fifth. Nadia's father, a day laborer in a western suburb of Mazar-e-Sharif, earns enough for the family to eat dinners of stale bread soaked in hot water. Where to get the $150?

Safia has wrapped the prescriptions into the same filthy checkered kerchief in which she keeps a change of clothes.

She will not buy the medicine.

Day 22. **Shingilabad and Karaghuzhlah**

An Afghan grave is rarely more than an ovoid mound of dry clay. Some-times there are a few rocks, arranged in no particular pattern, or a few shards of chipped pottery. Occasionally, some strips of colorful cloth whiffle from an uneven wooden pole that cants over the dead.

But don't be fooled by this lack of mnemonics. The living remember their dead very well here. Especially if the deaths were violent.

Especially if the killers crossed one of the many ethnic divides that carve the Afghan countryside into a volatile jigsaw puzzle.

Beneath the vaulted ceiling of his living room in the village of Shingilabad, Hajji Sultan, a Pashtun elder with henna-painted toenails, recounts murders that took place 15 years ago as though they happened yesterday.

"Hazara people from Karaghuzhlah village killed my brother and my nephew," Hajji Sultan says. His long gray beard fades to ivory where it reaches his chest. "In broad daylight. At four o'clock, on a Thursday. They ambushed them on the road, walked them off to the desert, broke their arms, and shot them in the head, several times."

Hajji Sultan bends his fingers to count the 22 people Hazaras killed in Shingilabad that year: "Khan, Ghazi, Qamalladin, Sakhedad, Matai, Abdul Rauf . . ." Half of the old man's right thumb is missing. "Shrapnel," he explains, but refuses to tell me which battle the shrapnel had come from, and whom he was fighting.

I ask Qaqa Satar to drive me over to Karaghuzhlah, a mile or so to the southeast. Hot spring air along the gravel road quivers with bad blood and recriminations. In the shadow of a white mulberry tree, Hajji Nizam, the Hazara leader in Karaghuzhlah, offers a tally of his own.

"Mohammad, Alivar, Haidar, Ghulam Sakhi, Nawruz." Hajji Nizam touches the outstretched fingers of his right hand with the index finger of his left. His grandchildren, squatting around him, listen carefully, so that they, too, can remember the names of their ancestors murdered by the Pashtuns. So that they can one day repeat them to their children.

"We also found two dead bodies of our people near Shingilabad," Hajji Nizam says. The old man cannot recall the exact year the Karaghuzhlah Hazara were murdered. Was it 1998, the year the Taliban, which is made up mostly of ethnic Pashtuns, mutilated, shot, and slit the throats of some 6,000 Hazaras in Mazar-e-Sharif?

Or was it 1997, the year members of the Hazara Hezb-e-Wahdat party joined the Uzbek Junbish-e-Melli militia in the massacre of 3,000 Pashtun Taliban soldiers in the Balkh capital?

In a country racked by ethnic bloodshed for centuries, what's a year or two—and who is to say that the decade-old crimes will not repeat tomorrow? The presence of Pashtuns in Northern Afghanistan is itself the product of a 120-year-old state-sanctioned ethnic cleansing of Hazaras, the Shia Muslim minority who are believed to have descended from the armies of Genghis Khan, and who are traditionally shunned by other Afghans. As part of an anti-Shia campaign, the Afghan king Abdur Rahman—the "Iron Amir," the history books here call him—forcibly settled 10,000 Pashtun families north of the Hindu Kush in the 1890s.

Today, the resurgent Taliban is finding a foothold in the pockets of Pashtun settlements across Northern Afghanistan that date back to that forced migration. Fear of ethnic violence is one of the reasons some Pashtuns in the north embrace the return of the Islamic militia. Hajji Sultan says that only during the Taliban regime did he feel protected from his Hazara neighbors.

"Maybe there are good men among them," the Pashtun elder concedes. "But how can we trust them? They want to rape our women and kill us, kill all the Pashtuns."

"Maybe there are good Pashtuns in Shingilabad," responds a young Hazara man named Sayed Aref. His village, Nawaqel, is a small oasis about three miles southeast of the Pashtun settlement. Sayed Aref's cousin, Azghar, was one of the 14 villagers Pashtun Taliban soldiers killed in 1998. The soldiers put him in a ditch and emptied a Kalashnikov magazine into his body. Azghar was 13 years old.

"I think these villagers are Taliban, or helped the Taliban," Sayed Aref says. "We see them as a threat."

On the way back to Mazar-e-Sharif, the gravel road takes me past a smattering of settlements: Pashtun, Uzbek, Tajik, Hazara. Each village sits apart from the rest, isolated within its thick clay walls like a small fortress. A few minutes outside the district center, Dawlatabad, the road cuts through what is left of the village of Desham.

Ethnic Pashtuns lived here once, until the U.S.-led offensive drove out the Taliban regime in 2001. Fearing reprisals by Uzbek and Hazara militias, the villagers fled. Some say they went to Pakistan; others say they moved to Chardara, the Taliban stronghold in Kunduz province. Stray blades of wheat and pale blue wildflowers have sprouted beneath the caved-in domes of derelict rooftops.

But beyond the ruined houses, the fallow fields are still furrowed. As though eight years count for nothing. As though the abandoned village still remembers the men who once tilled its blood-soaked earth.

Day 23. **Mazar-e-Sharif**

The world was new each day for God so made it daily. Yet it contained within it all the evils as before, no more, no less.

—Cormac McCarthy, *The Crossing*

Southwest of the airport, where the Northern Plains slope up into the dramatic massif of the Hindu Kush, a clay road meanders through some farmland until it meets a dried-out freshet. Park here and turn off the engine. Step outside and sit among the earthy tang of the grazing goats. Turn your back on the mountains and watch gusts of wind drive herds of green wheat horses across the emerald valley; the coffee-colored billow of dust undulate above the low sprawl of Mazar-e-Sharif; and beyond it, the dun, barely irrigated desert shimmer with diffraction.

If you sit here long enough, you will hear a low rumble at the airport: a B-52 Stratofortress bomber taking wing. It can carry eighteen 2,000-pound "smart" bombs, fifty-one 500-pound bombs, 29,250 cluster bomblets, 12 nuclear cruise missiles. It could pulverize the Hindu Kush into beach sand.

A B-52 cruises at almost 50,000 feet. You can't build a clinic or a well from that high up.

In 2001, I watched this plane's sisters drive the Taliban out of power. I watched Mahbuhbullah's children dance atop the mud-brick fence of his farm and sing, "Airplane, airplane!"

Northern Afghanistan was brimming with hope then.

Almost nine years later, I traveled across the region to visit Mahbuhbullah and his children. The two-day road trip from Mazar-e-Sharif took me in and out of Taliban territory a dozen times. This time around, there were no checkpoints to mark my entries and exits, no friendly gunmen to direct my route. The Afghan government may control a town by day, and the Taliban, by night. There is no front line.

There is also no electricity, no clean water, no health care, and no education for most Afghans. The land seems suspended in time. I notice two big changes. One: Islamist insurgents are gaining new ground in the north—a region largely hostile to the Taliban the first time I came here—almost daily. Towns that never saw Taliban rule before the war are now little fiefdoms of the militia. Taliban strongholds pincer my friend's village.

Two: the proliferation of cell phone towers. In 2001, there were no cell phones.

Afghans have little hope for the future. But they have good cell phone reception almost everywhere.

Mazar-e-Sharif to Kabul

Through the window of my Boeing 737, I see the pale veins of ancient clay paths over which the Achaemenid invading armies marched, then the Greeks, then the British. A handful of craters in no particular pattern: a Soviet air raid. A neat row of 12 craters: a B-52 dropped its payload of 1,000-pound bombs here.

Among these scars, people eke out a living the way they have forever: with primitive wooden tools, nursing centuries-old grudges, alone. They

bake delicious *nan* and cook giant vats of rice pilau and grow pomegran-
ates with seeds the color of the fratricidal blood that soaks their tree roots.
They live in fear that their closest neighbors will kill their men and rape
their women. They don't trust a government that has done nothing for
them. They have no faith in the international donors whose aid has yet,
nine years later, to reach them.

They do not invite the Taliban. They do not resist its advance, either.
They are just trying to get through whatever misfortune rolls their way
across these wracked plains next. These people are experienced at the art
of war survival. They have been practicing it, almost incessantly, for millennia.

I had traveled to the north to see what had happened to the people
I saw celebrate the Taliban's downfall in 2001. Of all the friends I had
made then, I could find only Mahbuhbullah. The only effect the post-
Taliban government has had on his life has been a negative one: Kabul
has clamped down on the illegal trade of artifacts, and my friend can no
longer augment his earnings by fencing small relics looted from Ai Khanum, the town Alexander the Great built 2,300 years ago on the banks of
the ancient Oxus River.

I could not find Hanon, a former Northern Alliance fighter who,
in 2001, taught me how to cross a minefield and how to recognize the
proximity of a bullet by the sound it makes. I could not find Ghulam
Sahib, who drove me around Northern Afghanistan in a Soviet-
made military jeep with no suspension. The last time I saw them,
they lived in Kunduz. Today, the province is mostly under Taliban
control.

I imagine that they are not doing too well. Few people in Afghanistan
are these days. But I like to think that they, like Mahbuhbullah, are surviving.

A few days before I left Northern Afghanistan, I met an old man in
a soiled turban sitting on his haunches on the sidewalk of Dasht-e-Shor
Street in Mazar-e-Sharif, cupping a white pigeon.

"Take her," the man said, thrusting the bird at me. The pigeon fluttered her hollow-boned wings whitely, then settled in his palm again.
"Take her."

Men tending nearby juice stalls strolled over to watch. A young boy pushing a wheelbarrow loaded with cement slowed down. Women craned inside the stifling blue nylon of their burqas. I touched the pigeon's neck with my fingertips. Soft, weightless.

She unfolded her wings again, and I could see the marble of her underbelly.

Something seemed amiss. I looked again.

Her legs were broken.

Recipe Index

Index

About the Author

Anna Badkhen was born in the Soviet Union. She has been covering conflicts since 2001, first for the *San Francisco Chronicle,* and later, for other publications in the United States and abroad. Her wartime journalism won the 2007 Joel R. Seldin Award for reporting on civilians in war zones from Psychologists for Social Responsibility.

PEACE MEALS

*Candy-Wrapped Kalashnikovs
and Other War Stories*

Anna Badkhen

Reading Group Guide

Author Q&A

ABOUT THIS GUIDE

The following reading group guide is intended to help you find interesting and rewarding approaches to your reading of *Peace Meals*. We hope this enhances your enjoyment and appreciation of the book. For a complete listing of reading group guides from Simon and Schuster, visit www.community.simonandschuster.com/.

INTRODUCTION:

Peace Meals is a moving, first-hand account of one woman's travels through some of the world's harshest war zones. In her stirring memoir, Anna Badkhen takes the reader from the mountain passes of Afghanistan to the drought-stricken plains of Kenya. Badkhen, a war correspondent, seeks out the personal stories behind the headlines. She finds that often the best way to meet people and learn about their culture is to share a meal with them. As Badkhen travels from one battle-scarred village to the next, it is the people she meets, and the meals she shares with them that remain with her.

TOPICS AND QUESTIONS FOR DISCUSSION

1. One of the most memorable people Badkhen meets in her travels is Ahmad Shawkat, a writer and journalist in Iraq who is repeatedly punished for criticizing the Iraqi government. In the chapter, "Dolmas with Ahmad," how does Ahmad's life give us a unique view of life in Iraq? Why are Ahmad and his story so important to Badkhen?

2. In the chapter "Dreaming of Lettuce," Badkhen writes about the limited diet she had while covering the conflict in Afghanistan. How does food play a part in Badkhen's experiences as a war reporter? How does her appreciation of good food help her in these remote areas?

3. In "The Kebab Diaries," Badkhen describes a chaotic scene in which Americans attempt to air-drop humanitarian care packages of food and clothing into a remote area in Afghanistan. How does Badkhen reveal the unexpected realities and the tragic irony of some humanitarian programs in the aftermath of this scene?

4. One of the many people who help Badkhen is Mahbuhbullah, who runs an "inn" for journalists in the mountains of Afghanistan. Badkhen is particularly moved when Mahbuhbullah offers his preteen son, Abdullah, as a nighttime guard. Discuss the risks and rewards for people like Mahbuhbullah who offer help to foreigners, and what it means to Badkhen to have a young boy risk his life for her.

5. Another person who helps Badkhen is Najibullah, who once

fought with the Taliban. On page 69, Badkhen asks, "How do we tell freedom fighters . . . from terrorists?" In which ways do the decisions Najibullah makes in his life help answer this question?

6. In "Candy-Wrapped Kalashnikovs," Badkhen's faith in those she trusts to protect her is shaken when she is held up by her own guards. How does this incident alter Badkhen's perception of Afghan hospitality and the nature of loyalty in a war zone?

7. In the chapter "Dumplings at Cafe Titanic," we meet Nazu and her three daughters. How do their experiences illustrate Badkhen's point that women are often the "hidden front line" of war? (p. 90)

8. In the chapter "Vodka at Gunpoint," Badkhen discusses the difficulties various governments, from Ivan the Terrible to the Communist regime, have had in trying to staunch the flow of alcohol to the Russian people. Which basic truths do these anecdotes reveal about government intervention in people's daily lives?

9. In a chilling scene in the chapter "Borsch During Wartime," Badkhen compares the action of the Russian government during a hostage crisis with the governments of Afghanistan, Somalia, and Kenya. What is the point she is trying to make here? What are the different displays of power that are demonstrated during the Chechen hostage crisis?

10. Badkhen covers the Arab-Israeli conflict in the chapter, "Mezze in Jerusalem, Mansaf in Al Quds." How do the events she writes about, such as Ahmat's funeral, or meeting the aspiring *shahid*, help the reader move beyond the headlines of this conflict?

11. What does the incident with Badkhen's Camelbak water bottle (p. 168) reveal about the limitations a journalist faces when working intimately with the people who live in abject poverty?

12. On page 177, Badkhen remarks, "Just because someone is hungry does not mean they are not going to feed their donkeys peanut butter." What is she referring to here? What do Badkhen's

experiences in Kenya teach her about the surprising realities of hunger and poverty?

13. Badkhen recounts her experience embedding with various US troops in Iraq in the chapter "Lobster in Tikrit." What kind of perspective of the war does embedding give her? Does she succeed in gaining a multifaceted view of the conflict?

14. In the chapter "Shopping for Bread in a Bradley," Badkhen witnesses a disturbing scene as US soldiers search a local house filled with women and children. How does this scene encapsulate some of the central problems of US soldiers in Iraq? Do you think the soldiers could have handled things differently?

15. After reading the chapter "Spice Girls," what can you infer about the sacrifices women make to stay safe in Iraq? Why is strict Islamic teaching often the most popular choice for many Iraqi citizens after the regime change?

ENHANCE YOUR BOOK CLUB

1. *Peace Meals* is filled with recipes for some of the delicious food Badkhen ate during her travels. Have everyone in your book club pick a different recipe and prepare it for a pot-luck meeting.

2. Read some of Anna Badkhen's published articles online. Compare her writing in the book with the articles. Which differences do you see?

3. Badkhen finds importance not only in the food that is prepared for her, but in the stories that accompany each dish. Take turns talking about a significant food or dish in your life, and the story behind it.

A CONVERSATION WITH ANNA BADKHEN

In writing *Peace Meals,* what proved to be the most challenging part of writing about your experiences?

Putting down the manuscript and saying: "It's done."

You've covered some of the most desperate war zones in the past ten years. Have your attitudes about the world, or these conflicts, changed over time since you wrote these chapters?

The main thing I have learned was this: the war zones where I work are never "desperate." Many of the people I meet on the road live in abject poverty, in near-constant danger, with no access to health care, often no access to clean drinking water. Sometimes with no easy access to any water at all. But they are never desperate. No: My fellow travelers and hosts in Afghanistan, in the Middle East, in Africa are full of life—because today, yet again, they have conquered death. They have survived another grueling trek through the desert. Another firefight. They have walked across another minefield not only with their limbs intact, but also still in love, still able to sing a lullaby to their children, still able to look at a roadside flower and see beauty. That is why that communal meal at the end of the day—when there is food—is always such a celebration.

You pay particular attention in the book to your unique position as a female journalist in these male-dominated societies. Looking back, do you think being a woman ever helped you in writing a story, or gaining insight into the people and issues you were covering?

Some societies consider it an insult, a dishonor for women to speak to strange men. So, yes, on a number of occasions I may have had access to women that my male colleagues would not have had. But when it comes to writing, or insight, I don't believe gender matters. Insight is a matter of paying attention, and listening, and empathy.

In "Candy-Wrapped Kalashnikovs" you learn about the death of a Swedish journalist, Ulf Strömbeg, who is killed by Afghan gunmen. After events like that, what do you have to tell yourself in order to continue working? What do you have to believe, as a foreign journalist, to weather the dangers of the job?

The Polish poet Zbigniew Herbert wrote a poem called "The Envoy of Mr Cogito" that seems, to me, the war reporter's precept. It has these lines: "you were saved not in order to live/you have little time you must give testimony." I am a storyteller, and my job is to amplify the voices of people who live on the edges of the world. People who, unlike me, cannot hop on a plane to safety at the end of their assignment. For whom the choice to stay or to leave after a colleague, or a friend, or a loved one is killed in a town next door—or in the room next door—does not exist. It is an honor to be able to tell their stories.

You have a memorable fight about Swiss chard with one of your children. Have your feelings about the way they eat, or what they eat, changed since writing this book?

No. I am still an intolerable pedant at the dining table.

In *Peace Meals* you talk about growing up in the Soviet Union under Communist rule. Did your background give you a different perspective on the war zones you covered than your American colleagues?

I have no idea. I can't know what is in the minds and hearts of my American colleagues.

Do you see any hopes for new opportunities becoming available to the women of Afghanistan and Iraq?

Not until the fighting stops.

You share some delicious recipes in this book, and in many scenes food becomes a means of providing comfort. What is your idea of comfort food?

Nuts and berries. Hot tea. And baklava.

Do you have any favorite or most memorable meal from these travels?
The best meal I have ever had was a handful of gnarled, dusty raisins an old man poured into the palm of my hand in the Afghan village called Ortinjilar. The village was preparing for a cold, hungry winter. The raisins were all the man had left. He shared them with me, a complete stranger, because I was passing through his village: his sense of honor told him he had to take care of me. So he did. I will never forget it.

Is there any location that you cover in the book that you wish you could return to?
Yes. All of them.

Can you tell us about what you're currently working on?
I am writing a book about beauty and timelessness.

Acknowledgments

Thank you: To all my hosts and fellow travelers, for your generosity and compassion on the road, and to the editors of all the publications that have enabled and supported my wanderings.

To Amber Qureshi, Alessandra Bastagli, and my agent, Felicia Eth, for making this book possible. To Britt Peterson, for your absolute pitch and indefatigable devotion to word.

To David, for your support and comfort during so many journeys.

To my parents and grandmother, for passing on the joy of cooking.

To Sonya Badkhen, Kael Alford, Lori Waselchuk, Thorne Anderson, Shenid Bhayroo, Mimi Chakarova, Pasha Ross, and Christy Roman, for your stories, advice, and attention along the way.

To Paul, for the compass bearings, and to Charles, for standing by me, unconditionally, always.

One out of six people in the world does not have enough to eat. Every six seconds, a child dies of hunger.